LAST STAND OF THE LUBICON CREE

LAST
STAND
of the
LUBICON
CREE

JOHN GODDARD

Douglas & McIntyre
Vancouver/Toronto

For Wilfred and Lucy Jackson, F.G.H.

Douglas & McIntyre Ltd.
1615 Venables Street
Vancouver, British Columbia V5L 2H1

Canadian Cataloguing in Publication Data
Goddard, John, 1950-
   Last stand of the Lubicon Cree

Includes bibliographical references and index.
ISBN 0-88894-716-X (bound)
ISBN 1-55054-039-4 (pbk.)

   1. Lubicon Lake Indian Band. 2. Indians,
Treatment of—Alberta—Lubicon Lake Region.
3. Indians of North America—Alberta—Lubicon Lake Region—
Claims. 4. Indians of North America—Alberta—Lubicon Lake
Region—Land tenure. 5. Indians of North America—Alberta—
Lubicon Lake Region—Land transfer. 6. Indians of North
America—Canada—Government relations—1951- * I. Title
E78.A34G63 1991   323.1'1973   C91-091491-5

Editing by Barbara Pulling
Design by Barbara Hodgson
Cover photograph by Tom Walker, *Calgary Herald*
Photographs courtesy of Tom Walker, *Calgary Herald*; National Archives of
Canada; Detselig Enterprises; Yvonnette Comeau; Angus MacDonald;
Rolland Smith; Canapress Photo Service—Ray Giguere; Jeff Jacobsen;
John Goddard.
Typeset by Vancouver Desktop Publishing Centre
Printed and bound in Canada by D.W. Friesen & Sons Ltd.
Printed on acid-free paper ∞

THE PAST IS NEVER DEAD.
IT'S NOT EVEN PAST.

—William Faulkner, *Requiem for a Nun*

CONTENTS

PREFACE

I LIVE A WRITERLY, apartment life in downtown Montreal. I enjoy the city; but in the early 1980s I spent two years as a kind of roving correspondent in the Far North. From Yellowknife, I flew regularly to remote native settlements along the Mackenzie River and across the Arctic archipelago, reporting for the Canadian Press news agency. Much of my work had to do with resource issues, mostly mining and oil-and-gas, and with questions commonly referred to as "land claims." What I liked most about the job was the chance to head off on snowmobiles with local families. They took me hunting for caribou and seal, and once I spent a week trapping with a Dene couple and nine of their children west of the Mackenzie River near the Arctic Circle. On such excursions I was always a guest, dependent on others for survival, and I was always impressed by how skilled my hosts could be on the land, how adaptable to changing weather and circumstances. What surprised me was how often these same competent people turned out to have lives troubled by drinking and family violence. Constantly I came up against one of the great riddles of modern Canadian life: how is it that native people throughout the country are sunk in a deep social malaise?

I first came across the Lubicon band while on a freelance assignment in 1984. I attended a meeting in Edmonton where Chief Bernard Ominayak spoke about how oil development was driving native hunters and trappers from the northern Alberta bush, and about how provincial authorities appeared to be deliberately sabotaging the band's efforts to assert aboriginal land rights. When the meeting ended, a consultant to the band, Fred Lennarson, handed me what he called a "press kit"—three red binders weighing a total of seven kilograms. Nobody, including oil-company publicists, had ever handed me so much material so readily, and the binders proved to be only a fraction of a vast archive on the band's history to which I was later given full access.

Long after my original assignment ended, I continued to follow Lubicon events. I added my name to a mailing list that Lennarson was compiling and began to travel to meetings in Europe, the United States and various Canadian cities to chronicle the band's land-rights campaign.

Among the satisfactions of the job was getting to know Ominayak. We discovered that we are the same age, born exactly four months apart in 1950, and as we continued to meet in various places and situations a companionship developed. I came to enjoy his sometimes playful humour and to admire his profound sense of himself. So congenial was his company that I would often be lulled for long periods into thinking of us as similar, with the same values and aspirations. Then some chance occurrence would break the spell.

Mirror incidents once drove home to me how different we really are. The first came during a stopover in Munich in 1987. Lennarson went to make phone calls, leaving Ominayak and me on the railway platform with the suitcases. We stood together not saying much. Over our heads, an immense canopy of glass and steel filtered sunlight into a uniform, milky pool through which hundreds of people moved in different directions. There were schoolchildren and businesspeople and a young backpacking couple licking ice cream. I ached to join the crowd. I told Ominayak that I was leaving to buy a postcard and an *International Herald Tribune*; and when he didn't answer, I turned to see a downcast, shrunken man unhappy at being abandoned at the centre of Europe to guard a heap of bags. Reluctantly, I stayed with him.

Two months later, Ominayak and I were riding through Lubicon territory in his pickup truck, searching for a stand of timber. Ominayak wanted to replace a cabin occupied by two elderly trappers, Albert and Summer Joe Laboucan. We stopped and Ominayak unloaded the chain saw, noticing that we had left other equipment half an hour away at our camp. He showed me how to select trees, judging them for straightness and diameter. "I'll go back for the stuff," he said. And when I didn't answer, he turned to what must have looked to him like a downcast, shrunken man afraid of being left alone in the middle of the northern bush.

"Are there bears?" I said.

"I'll give you a gun," he replied, then reconsidered. "We'll both go back."

Over time, I began to make a connection between the assertion of Lubicon land rights and the differing ways in which Ominayak and I relate to the world. Gradually, I went from thinking of aboriginal rights as historical baggage—a trick native people were using to get more than they deserve—to appreciating how essential the recognition of such rights is to the well-being of Canadian native peoples, and to the general prosperity of the country.

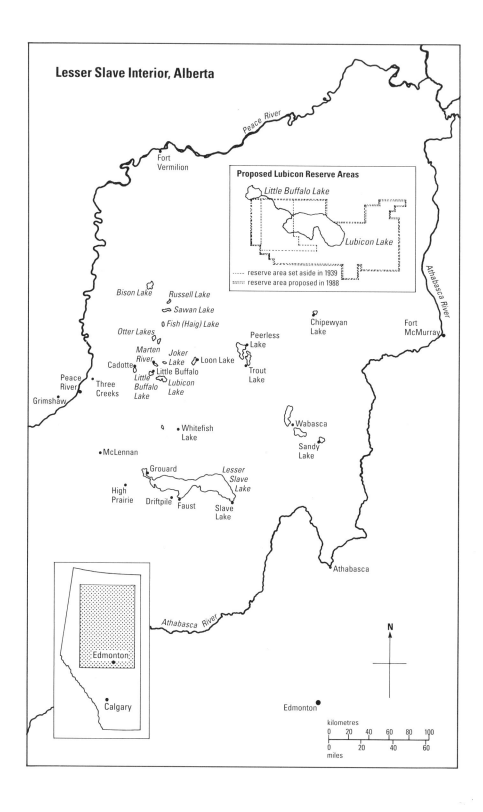

Lesser Slave Interior, Alberta

Peace River

Fort
Vermilion

Proposed Lubicon Reserve Areas

Little Buffalo Lake

Lubicon Lake

- - - - reserve area set aside in 1939
- - - - reserve area proposed in 1988

Athabasca River

Bison Lake

Russell Lake

Sawan Lake

Fish (Haig) Lake

Chipewyan
Lake

Fort
McMurray

Otter Lakes

Marten
River

Joker
Lake

Loon Lake

Peerless
Lake

Cadotte

Little Buffalo

Trout
Lake

Little
Buffalo
Lake

Lubicon
Lake

Peace
River

Three
Creeks

Grimshaw

Whitefish
Lake

Wabasca

Sandy
Lake

McLennan

Grouard

Lesser
Slave
Lake

High
Prairie

Driftpile

Faust

Slave
Lake

Athabasca

Athabasca River

N

Edmonton

Calgary

Edmonton

kilometres
0   20   40   60   80   100

0   20   40   60
miles

1 TO LIVE
AND
DO WELL

ONE OF THE QUALITIES people tend to notice first about Bernard Ominayak is his inner calm. Sometimes he looks out of place in his blue jeans, chiselled cowboy boots and white, cowboy-style shirts, but people invariably respond to his obvious self-possession. He is also handsome, with broad shoulders, slim hips and observant, well-spaced eyes, which he often obscures by lowering the brim of his black cap with gold lettering that once read "Lubicon Lake Band" and now reads "Lubicon Lake Nation." He can be winsomely candid. "I understand people looking at us as real bush people because we were," he once said. "We were just not exposed to modern technology or people in great numbers at all."

Ominayak (pronounced OM-nee-yak) began making a name for himself in 1984, through appearances as chief of the five hundred Lubicon Lake Cree people living in a remote area of northern Alberta. "The young chief," newspapers called him then; he was thirty-four years old but looked younger. He would speak to small, serious-minded groups in living rooms and church halls, and at one typical noon-hour gathering late that November, he faced seventeen pastors and laypeople in the basement of Christ Anglican Church in Edmonton, all eating sandwiches from their laps and posing grim-faced questions.

"We were out there and we were okay," Ominayak told them evenly. "We never had anything fancy but we never went hungry. Then all of a sudden they found oil and we were caught in a situation where we were in the way."

Next to him sat Fred Lennarson, a consultant to the band, who spoke rapidly in a Chicago accent about broken promises, unrecognized rights and recent attempts by the Alberta government at what he called "bulldozing the Lubicon Lake Indians off the face of the earth." He was nine years older than Ominayak, but boyish in the way that he rubbed his short, sandy hair flat with his fingers and pitched himself energetically forward in his chair.

They made an odd combination: one bush-oriented and shy, the other articulate and savvy. Responding to questions, Ominayak would give a short answer and stop. Lennarson would elaborate, filling in dates and precise, harrowing details.

The story they told was this: In 1899, federal commissioners travelled through northern Alberta to sign a treaty with every Indian group they met. They stuck to the main rivers, however—the Peace and the Athabasca—missing the Lubicon people and several other bands living between the rivers and north of Lesser Slave Lake. For years, members of the overlooked bands sought to be included in the treaty, venturing out of the bush almost annually to make contact with the government. Finally, in 1939, two federal officials penetrated the region as far as Lubicon Lake to discover a kind of model native community. "I was very much interested in this band," one of them wrote with surprise, "and found them clean, well dressed, healthy, bright and intelligent; in other words, people who want to live and do well." The officials recognized the band formally and promised a reserve.

Then the long nightmare began. In the 1940s, a federal accountant travelled through northern Alberta telling people that they were no longer Indians. He expelled members from reserves, divided families, took orphans from their adoptive parents and forced children out of mission schools in places where no other schools existed. At Lubicon Lake, he cut band membership from 154 to 82, and eventually to 30: too few people, he said, to warrant a reserve.

Beginning in 1950, oil-exploration crews passed through Lubicon territory almost every winter. A village with close ties to the Lubicon band was later burned and bulldozed in an area where exploration was most intense; and in the mid-1970s, the Alberta government passed a law retroactively to stop the Lubicon people and several other bands from declaring an aboriginal interest in the region. In 1979, oil development exploded. Without a single environmental or social-impact study, more than a hundred resource companies entered the territory looking for a piece of the action. Work permits hit the highest prices in the province, and the region became the most active exploration and drilling field in the country. Over the next five years, crews drilled more than four hundred wells within a fifteen-mile radius of the Lubicon community. Seismic crews cut a spider-web pattern through the bush. Wagon routes became roads busy with tractor-trailer units. "No Trespassing" signs went up. Bulldozers buried traps and blocked animal trails, sometimes deliberately; other traps were looted. Fires raged out of control: in 1980 alone, fire destroyed as much of the Lubicon hunting area as in the previous twenty years. Animal numbers plummeted. The oil companies were soon producing revenues of $1.2 million a day, while the Lubicon hunting and trapping economy was for all practical purposes destroyed. In 1983, international human-rights organizations began to take notice. Anwar Barkat, director of the program to combat racism for the World Council of Churches in Geneva, studied the Lubicon case and concluded: "In the last couple of years, the Alberta Provincial Government and dozens of multi-national oil companies have taken actions which could have genocidal consequences."

"Our situation is desperate," Ominayak told the church meeting in his elemental way. "If we give up now, we're lost for good. The provincial government keeps coming at us from all directions. The federal government is waiting, hoping we disappear. There's lots of stress in the community and a lot of times we feel alone fighting these powerful people."

That evening and twice the next day, Ominayak and Lennarson repeated the story at other Edmonton churches, each time causing a stir. "What can I do to help?" some would ask, and Lennarson would almost always answer, "Write your MP." Letters to Ottawa from across the country, he said, "are all that stand between the Lubicon people and extinction."

Such audiences were accustomed to stories of injustice, but in quiet talks around the province, a laconic trapper and a social activist were developing a constituency far beyond that normally associated with a small northern Indian band. They were building a movement. After every meeting, Lennarson took names and addresses of people who showed special interest, adding them as subscribers to a kind of private news service made possible by the photocopy machine. Two or three times a month, sometimes more frequently, he mailed copies of letters, memos, news clippings and government reports. Editors of church and labour newsletters summarized the material for their own members, so that by late 1984 the mailings were reaching thousands of readers.

Underpinning the mailings were extensive archives: countless pages of genealogy studies, Indian agent records, missionary diaries, treaty-commission reports and interdepartmental correspondence. Researchers from the Indian Association of Alberta had amassed a core of material from Indian Affairs records in the mid-1970s, and Lennarson had built on it. He had dug deeper and more extensively, tracing church documents to the mid-1800s, until every possible historical mention of the Lubicon people appeared to be included. He had also indexed and summarized the records, making them unprecedented in native-rights circles for their thoroughness and organization. "The best-documented aboriginal rights case in the world," one member of the United Nations Human Rights Committee was to say.

Clear goals added to the campaign's appeal. The Lubicon people sought to maintain themselves as a distinct aboriginal society by establishing a reserve at Lubicon Lake for all members of the band, including those cut from the official band list over the years. To develop the reserve, they were drafting a comprehensive socioeconomic development plan. It included a wildlife-management regime that would allow some hunting and trapping to continue alongside the oil work, and a proposal to develop a new local economy based on farming, small businesses and wage jobs in the oil industry. The band was also insisting on compensation for past neglect and the loss of the Lubicon bush economy, destroyed for billions of dollars' worth of oil.

After the Edmonton meetings, Ominayak drove north to Peace River, then east along the oil roads for another hour or so to the Lubicon settlement of Little Buffalo, arriving under a perfect half-moon. Horses were silhouetted against the snow, and beyond them spread the settlement itself: houses and cabins standing well back from the road, widely separated from each other by woods and corrals. There were no shops and no businesses; no main street and no street activity. Behind every house stood a privy. Electricity had only recently been introduced, and a few people were still getting around in horse-drawn wagons.

In some native communities, unhappy experiences have instilled a bitterness against white people that can surface in subtle and overt ways. In Little Buffalo, no such tension existed. People were shy, and most adults spoke little English, but everybody proved pleasant and accommodating. Visitors were few, but those expressing interest would readily be shown through the surrounding muskeg-and-bush country. They would be taken to traplines and oil installations, and be included in meetings and events—experiences that helped a visitor appreciate the rich texture of Lubicon life. Band members would quickly reveal themselves not merely as neighbours to each other but as kinfolk tied by blood, marriage, language, cultural traditions, a shared hunting area and a web of interdependencies that at least until recently had ensured their collective survival. A sense of anxiety also pervaded the community, however, a sense that if Lubicon land rights were not recognized soon, the society could fall apart.

As the Lubicon campaign grew in national prominence, Ominayak grew with it, gradually gaining confidence in front of crowds. He began to speak up more, relying less on Lennarson for dates and numbers. Standing on a stage with the peak of his cap shading his eyes, he grew into a kind of folk hero, projecting integrity and conviction. "That guy makes me proud to be an Indian," native people would often say after seeing him. Something in him reminded people that "Indianness," however difficult to define, still exists.

But experience also honed in Ominayak a harder edge. Delays to a land settlement accumulated; so did bodies at Little Buffalo. During one sixteen-month period, Ominayak counted twenty-two deaths in the community from road accidents, fires, premature births, suicide and murder—many of them alcohol-related. "Our people are dying left and right and the government seems to like it," he said.

More and more in his public appearances he spoke of the need for Indian people to unite. "As long as we're fighting individually we're not going to get anywhere," he told one Toronto rally. "The fight that we're in is a fight for all native people. Maybe we don't have the resources financially, but it's always encouraging to see other native people and non-native supporters standing behind us. As long as people are coming out in numbers, we're going to have the power that is going to crack some of these blocks that are ahead of us and that have been there for a long, long time."

With every block Ominayak cracked, another seemed abruptly to appear. Throughout the campaign a pattern continually recurred: the band would assert itself, a well-placed figure would be won over and begin to champion the cause, then powerful interests would destroy all progress. On the surface, many explanations would appear possible. A particular minister would seem to be to blame, or a set of immediate political circumstances, or a terrible misunderstanding. Sometimes the band's troubles would be perceived as part of a sad but inevitable consequence of a bush technology coming into contact with an industrial one. Gradually, however, a suspicion grew that the root source of the problem was that no government in Canada, federal or provincial, wanted the Lubicon people to remain a viable, self-sufficient, aboriginal society. A kind of raw colonialism still seemed to operate: massive resource development hits an Indian territory, the bush economy is destroyed, and hunters and trappers are displaced from the bush to live as landless squatters dependent on welfare.

The story of the Lubicon Cree shows what can happen in Canada when a native community tries to assert rights to a territory rich in oil. It demonstrates that many people in Canada care deeply about the well-being of native peoples; but it also reveals to what extremes of deceit and cruelty federal and provincial governments are prepared to go to crush native rights.

2 GOOD
BIG
CHIEF

MISUNDERSTANDINGS ABOUT the Lubicon Cree date from May 29, 1899, at around noon, when a delegation of civil servants, Mounties and clergymen left Edmonton to sign an Indian treaty covering all of northern Alberta and beyond. Leading the group was David Laird, a well-intentioned man who knew much about government administration but almost nothing about the northern woodlands.

David Laird's mark on history has faded now, but he was distinguished in his day for his role in some of the formative events of the Canadian Dominion. Laird grew up in Prince Edward Island, and in 1873 became a Father of Confederation by helping to negotiate the colony's entry into Canada. Within months, he was elected to Parliament and made minister of the interior. Part of his job was to help open the prairies to railway construction and settlement, which meant that he first had to extinguish aboriginal title to a broad swath of territory between Lake Superior and the Rocky Mountains.

"Aboriginal title," he later wrote in a historical booklet, "is simply an admission that the Indians should not be deprived of their occupation rights without compensation and their formal consent." He was summing up a large body of British law which insisted that aboriginal rights had to be addressed before colonists settled on Indian lands. King George III had laid out a procedure. In what came to be called the Royal Proclamation of 1763, the king decreed that the surrender of Indian land title was to be made to a representative of the British Crown at a tribal gathering, and compensation paid. "If at any Time any of the said Indians should be inclined to dispose of the said Lands," he proclaimed, "the same shall be Purchased only for Us, in our Name, at some public Meeting or Assembly of the said Indians."

By Laird's time, Indian land surrender involved signing a treaty, seven of which were negotiated on the prairies between 1871 and 1877. It was a tense process. Native leaders had to insist on being dealt with in the first place, and at talks leading to the first two treaties, the government offered only small reserves and token cash annuities. The chiefs, sensing that life based on the buffalo was about to be destroyed, insisted that farm animals, horses, wagons and tools be included in a settlement to help lay the basis for a new life based on agriculture. Federal negotiators agreed to the terms orally, then failed to deliver. Only after a public inquiry ruled in the Indians' favour did the government honour the commitments.

Laird first witnessed treaty-making in 1874. He attached himself to the Treaty Four commission in southern Saskatchewan, making it known afterwards that native leaders had dubbed him "Meywasin Kitche Ogemow," or "Good Big Chief," for his patience and steadying influence during negotiations. In 1877, he led his own delegation to Blackfoot Crossing in southern Alberta for the largest treaty ceremony ever. He pitched white tents on the narrow south bank of the Bow River, while on the broad flats opposite more than four thousand members of the Blackfoot, Blood, Peigan, Sarcee and Stoney nations pitched their buffalo-skin tepees. Again there were objections and delays, and again Laird kept the process moving. "In a very few years the buffalo will probably be all destroyed," he told the assembly in his booming voice, "and for this reason the Queen wishes to help you to live in the future in some other way. She wishes you to allow her white children to come and live on your land and raise cattle, and should you agree to this, she will assist you to raise cattle and grain, and thus give you the means of living when the buffalo are no more." Reluctantly, the Indians signed Treaty Seven, completing the extinguishment of aboriginal title over the prairies.

More than twenty years later, Laird became a treaty commissioner again. To open the North to gold seekers rushing to the Klondike, he was asked to negotiate Treaty Eight with the Cree, Beaver and Chipewyan peoples living in what is now the northern half of Alberta and adjacent corners of British Columbia, Saskatchewan and the Northwest Territories—an area larger than that covered by the seven previous western treaties combined. Sixty-six years old but still vigorous, he left Edmonton on May 29, 1899, in a convoy of team-drawn wagons.

Travel was excruciatingly slow. For three days, the delegation rode to Athabasca Landing, then piled into two scows and a York boat for the trip up the Athabasca and Slave rivers to Lesser Slave Lake. The boats had to be pulled by harnessed men called "trackers." They made eight miles in the first two days.

"Nothing indeed can be imagined more arduous than this tracking up a swift river, against constant head winds in bad weather," wrote one of the passengers, Charles Mair. "Much of it is in the water, wading up 'snies,' or tortuous shallow channels, plunging into numberless creeks, clambering up slimy banks, creeping under or passing the line over fallen trees, wading out in the stream to round long spits of sand or boulders, floundering in gumbo slides, tripping, crawling, plunging, and, finally, tottering to the camping-place sweating like horses, and mud to the eyes."

On June 19, eleven days behind schedule, the party arrived at the west end of Lesser Slave Lake where scores of Indian and Metis people were waiting. The site is overgrown now, but the hamlet of Willow Point occupied it at the time, and the hamlet of Lesser Slave Post could be seen two miles away on a rise where the village of Grouard now stands. Diplomatically, Laird pitched his tent between the two communities, not wishing to favour one over the other. The various groups selected their "chiefs" and "headmen"—a novel idea in the northern bush where decision-making had always been by consensus. The following day Laird called an assembly.

"Red Brothers!" he boomed, as recorded again by Charles Mair. "We understand stories have been told you, that if you made a treaty with us you would become servants and slaves; but we wish you to understand that such is not the case, but that you will be just as free after signing a treaty as you are now."

Laird outlined his offer, similar to the terms of the prairie treaties. On signing, chiefs would be paid $25, headmen $15 and everybody else $12 each. In addition, chiefs would collect $25 annually, headmen $15 and everybody else $5. A silver medal, a Union Jack and an axe would go to each chief, and every three years each chief and headman would get a suit of clothes, the suit of a chief to be superior in quality to that of a headman. Reserves would be allotted, their size calculated at 128 acres per person, or one square mile for every five people. People wishing to grow crops on reserves would get farm implements. Others wishing to raise cattle would receive livestock. Still others wishing to do neither could collect ammunition and twine for hunting and fishing. Schools were also promised "where there is a sufficient number of children."

Metis people, those of mixed white and native ancestry, could choose either to join a band as Indians or to take scrip, a one-time certificate with a face value of $240, or 240 acres of land. Laird's party counselled against taking scrip. Corrupt scrip buyers had cheated people elsewhere, paying far less than face value. (Two Winnipeg bankers named Alloway and Champion would arrive at Lesser Slave Lake three weeks later to buy scrips at $75 cash.) "Half-breeds living like Indians have the chance to take treaty instead, if they wish to do so," Laird emphasized. "They have their choice." He made clear that the criterion for treaty eligibility was not how much Indian blood ran in a person's veins, but whether the person lived an Indian way of life—a point that was to be debated years later. "It was said that as long as a man was a man and not a dog he could be taken into treaty," an Oblate missionary in the area, Jean Baptiste Giroux, was to recall.

As on the prairies, the native groups were uneasy. Speaker after speaker denounced the terms.

"You say we are brothers," Chief Kinosayoo told Laird. "I cannot understand how we are so. I live differently from you. I can only understand that the Indians will benefit in a very small degree from your offer."

"You have called us brothers," said one of the headmen, Moostoos. "Truly I am the younger, you the elder brother."

Almost everyone feared being overrun by prospectors and settlers, and being confined to reserves. Such restrictions might make sense on the prairies, some said, but in the northern bush Indians must be guaranteed the freedom to hunt and trap. Laird tried to allay fears. Twine and ammunition were being offered to foster hunting and fishing, he said, not to curtail them. Any laws regarding wildlife would be made only in the best interests of Indians, he also said, and everyone "would be as free to hunt and fish after the treaty as they would be if they never entered into it." There would be no interference with the Indian way of life, and nobody would be forced onto reserves. Land selection could be postponed until required for a band's protection. Reassured, the Indian leaders signed, and Laird broke open a supply of T&B tobacco to celebrate.

The next task was to find all the other bands. Once word of the agreement at Lesser Slave Lake spread, Laird expected the assent of others to follow easily, but he had to meet them. Almost two weeks behind schedule, he divided his delegation, sending two assistant commissioners in different directions and himself in another. Racing to finish by summer's end, the parties travelled the region's two major waterways—the Peace River on the west and the Athabasca River on the east. "Our journey from point to point was so hurried that we are not in a position to give any description of the country ceded which would be of value," Laird later wrote.

Considering the circumstances, the commissioners did well; they hit all the main posts. They did not, however, penetrate the wilderness interior north of Lesser Slave Lake where the Lubicon Lake people and several other Cree groups lived. The following year a new commissioner, James Macrae, tried to reach everybody who had been missed and pay annuities to bands that had already signed. He was rushed, too. Macrae met 3,323 Indians—1,106 more than Laird's delegations—bringing six new bands into treaty, two of which were not previously known in Ottawa to exist. But like his predecessors, Macrae made no attempt to penetrate the Lesser Slave interior.

He was at least candid about his shortcoming. He reported to Ottawa that he had heard of Indians living in the interior and living well, but that he had not been able to visit them and had not brought them into treaty. "There yet remains a number of persons leading an Indian life in the country north of Lesser Slave Lake," he wrote, "who have not accepted treaty as Indians, or scrip as half-breeds, but this is not so much through indisposition to do so as because they live at points distant from those visited, and are not pressed by want." Macrae went on to estimate the number missed at "about 500," giving no indication how he arrived at the figure. He also speculated that those missed belonged to river bands already brought into treaty, a piece of wishful thinking offered to support the conclusion that his job was more or less complete. "Indian title to the tract [covered by Treaty Eight] may be fairly regarded as being extinguished," he reported.

Thus began misunderstandings that were to frustrate the overlooked groups for decades. Genealogical studies conducted jointly by the federal government and the Lubicon band in the early 1980s now indicate that the treaty parties missed several thousand people in the interior north of Lesser Slave Lake (although the population was to fall sharply during the Spanish influenza epidemic of 1918). The studies also show that the interior Indians were separate from the river bands brought into treaty.

Distinct regional groups inhabited the interior. Each occupied a wide area, and each had its own variations on Cree customs, rituals and language. The Lubicon group included the people of Loon and Cadotte lakes, now seen as separate communities, and numbered in Laird's day at about 2,500 people. "We were all one," recalls Edward Laboucan, a Lubicon member born in 1913. He continues to regard the original Loon and Cadotte groups as kin, and considers people at the more easterly communities of Trout, Peerless, Chipewyan and Sandy lakes to be unrelated to the Lubicon band.

Life followed a cyclical pattern set by the changing seasons. In the fall, the band dispersed into hunting parties of two or three families each. Moose was the staple food. Hides of fur- bearing animals provided barter for ammunition, tea, flour and other goods. In late spring, people would congregate into local bands at lakes, forming small communities named after the lakes themselves. Lubicon and Loon lakes were the most popular gathering points in the early twentieth century, but elders have identified a total of thirty-nine other camps and semipermanent settlements in the region that were also in use until recently.

Social organization within a regional group was fluid. A hunting party might be affiliated with one local band in winter and a different one in summer. A party might spend the summer at one lake year after year, then suddenly switch. If a hunter stopped getting along with the rest of his party, he could arrange to join another; if a marriage broke down, one spouse could go elsewhere. The make-up of hunting parties and local bands was in constant flux, forever adjusting to everything from personal relations to natural catastrophes.

One of the rare written accounts of Lubicon life in the early twentieth century comes from C. D. White, the principal of an Anglican Church school at Whitefish Lake, about a week's journey south of Lubicon Lake by horse and wagon. White travelled the region in the late summer of 1909, before hunting parties dispersed for the winter, visiting Little Buffalo Lake, Lubicon Lake, Otter Lakes, Fish Lake, Trout Lake and Loon Lake. He referred to Lubicon Lake as Prairie Lake, a common name for it at the time.

"All the Indians in this district are engaged in trapping during the Winter, some occupy all their time, others a part of their time," he wrote, generally impressed by what he had seen. "Those who own horses and sleighs, have the opportunity of doing some freighting, or other work with their teams, while they are not engaged in looking after their traps. In the spring most of them put in a small garden of potatoes and vegetables . . . . The haying season is quite a busy time . . . they put up hay for their own stock and have the opportunity of making money by putting up hay for sale . . . .

"The Indians as a whole are fairly industrious, they build their own houses, make their own tents, canoes, dog sleighs, snow shoes, etc."

White made special mention of Lubicon Lake and nearby Buffalo Lake as a kind of oasis of good spruce, rich black soil and open fields of hay where people were living marginally better than Indians elsewhere. "At Prairie and Buffalo Lakes," he wrote, "the soil is the best in this district, here some of the Indians have ploughed up small patches and put in potatoes, and garden seeds, the produce of which I have seen, considering the time they were put in, they were a very good sample."

White's account is corroborated by that of Yves Marie Floc'h, an Oblate priest at Grouard, on Lesser Slave Lake, who first visited Lubicon Lake in 1910. "The territory is bushy and muskeg, except for a few cultivated spots at Lubicon and Buffalo lakes," he was to testify formally in 1944. "In winter time a few [families] make wooden teepees and small houses. At Fish Lake and Lubicon Lake they have little houses in the winter time."

Another priest travelling in the eastern part of the interior beginning in the 1920s described people as extremely isolated and sometimes desperately shy of strangers. "I know Okema at Trout Lake," Jean Baptiste Giroux also recalled in formal testimony. "He did not want to see anyone. I visited him. I was sitting on the bed and drew my feet in suddenly and there was a scramble and here were four big girls under the bed scared to death."

≈

In 1909, the year of White's travels, an event took place that was to have long-term repercussions for the people of the district: David Laird secured a posting in the Lesser Slave region for his youngest son, Harold. "With hard work I got him the position," Laird senior wrote with undisguised relief. Harold had failed law studies and remained mostly unemployed for several years, but he swam well and could paddle a canoe, qualifying him to some extent. Part of his job was to help pay annuities to all treaty members of the Lesser Slave Lake Agency, which at the time included most of northern Alberta. A single circuit took up to six months; travel was variously by packhorse, sailboat, mission steamer and Peterborough canoe, often in appalling weather. The responsibility officially fell to the Indian agent, Laird's superior, but the job was too big for one person.

In the summer of 1911, looking for a short cut, Laird penetrated the interior north of Lesser Slave Lake—the first federal employee known to do so. He headed cross-country from Wabasca, at the southeast part of the agency, to Fort Vermilion in the northwest, encountering previously unrecorded bands at Trout, Peerless and Equisetum lakes. The following year he journeyed straight north from Grouard, encountering bands at Loon, Otter, Fish and Lubicon lakes.

Laird mentioned the bands in his sketchy reports, but received no instructions about how to deal with them, and such were priorities in Ottawa that when the Indian agent quit at Grouard in 1916, nobody was sent to replace him. Laird was named acting Indian agent and left on his own.

Underpaid and overworked, he developed a drinking problem. "I remember him staggering out of bed in the morning," says Rose L'Hirondelle, whose mother was Laird's housekeeper. One account tells of him fording the Peace River on horseback at Fort Vermilion, barely making it across, then dropping his moneybags, which burst open and released hundreds of dollar bills to the wind.

Laird also developed an accounting problem. Treaty paylists would constantly have to be updated as people died, or gave birth, or changed marriage partners, or switched bands. To complicate matters further, members of some of the overlooked groups, including the Lubicon, were beginning to show up at reserves at treaty time asking to be paid like everybody else. Laird wrote to Ottawa asking what to do. The head of Indian Affairs, Duncan Campbell Scott, suggested that people from the interior be paid a five-dollar annuity, plus the seven dollars that others were paid on first signing the treaty, plus arrears to 1899. The chief accountant, Frederick Paget, objected. "As for paying these Indians north of Grouard arrears of annuity right back to the date of the original Treaty, I am afraid this would cause complications and would involve the Department in a large amount of extra expenditure," he wrote to Scott. "I would, therefore, recommend that the Indians in question be paid both the gratuity and annuity at the time of admission, and that no arrears be allowed them." The accountant's view prevailed over principle. Laird was instructed to pay twelve dollars to each person he added to his treaty paylists, and five dollars thereafter; he was to pay no arrears. He received no instructions to bring the bands formally into treaty and no orders to set aside new reserves.

When word reached the interior that Laird would pay an annuity to anybody travelling to a reserve on treaty day, more people began to make the trip. Rather than begin separate lists for the new bands, however, Laird added names to his existing paylists. Sometimes he indicated where a person was from, sometimes not. The first Lubicon member known to be added was at Whitefish Lake, about a one-week trip from Lubicon Lake by horse-drawn wagon, in 1915. Laird entered nine more Lubicon names to the Whitefish list in 1923, three more in 1926 and eight more in 1927. He listed a few Lubicon members with the Bigstone band at Wabasca and others with the Tall Cree Band at Fort Vermilion.

Over time, Laird's paylists became hopelessly muddled. Overworked and still drinking, he added new names to existing lists and let routine updates fall desperately behind. His records showed Spanish flu victims being paid years after their deaths, and at some point he went from pocketing the money out of incompetence to actively fiddling the accounts. In 1931, he was fired and convicted of forgery and fraud.

≈

Laird's successor was Napoleon L'Heureux, a man of diligence and stamina. "The Flying Frenchman," people called him. He spoke fluent Cree and was originally hired as a farming instructor, but with Laird's departure the job description changed. L'Heureux quickly established a new headquarters in Driftpile, just east of Grouard on

Lesser Slave Lake, then set about putting the paylists in order.

"On my first tour throughout the District paying the Annuities, all the Indians were total strangers to me," he later wrote of the mess he faced. "I possessed no positive means of identifying them as very few possessed Treaty Tickets and many did not know their name as shown in the rolls. My predecessor, through manipulation of the Agency records and carelessness had left a deplorable situation as far as the lists of the Members of the various Bands were concerned and in the first two years that I paid the Annuity it is possible that I paid the Annuity to Indians who were not entitled to receive it and some who actually did not exist as far as the records were concerned at the time. To explain how this occurred I will set out a situation which frequently arose in the first two years. An Indian would present himself or herself for Treaty money and on consulting the existing records I could not find such a person listed; however, I could find an Indian family or individual under another name who would fit the marital or family status in the case and there being no other means of identification I paid the Indian his or her Annuity. It is a well known fact that many of the Indians have one or more names and some actually did not know their names at all. Others gave one name the first year I paid the Annuity and the subsequent year gave another name. Despite all precautions taken to properly identify the Indians certain ones were paid and the payment recorded against the name of an Indian who was absent. I cannot state with accuracy in how many instances this happened but I am certain that no person was paid Treaty whom I knew was not entitled to the Annuity."

Conscientious and wishing to make sure that he was proceeding correctly, L'Heureux asked the inspector of Alberta Indian agencies to travel with him on his circuit of 1933. Together, they again checked and revised the treaty paylists. But they did not venture into the interior, and they did nothing to clarify the make-up of the interior bands. Like Harold Laird, they continued to add names of interior residents to existing lists at Whitefish Lake, Wabasca and other reserves.

By then, the interior groups were pressing to be taken formally into treaty. In 1932, a man from Loon Lake approached L'Heureux at the Whitefish Lake reserve. "He told me that they have 125 men, women and children who have never been taken into Treaty, and would like to join," L'Heureux reported to Ottawa.

The following year, the people of Lubicon Lake appealed for recognition. On August 25, 1933, with help from perhaps a clergyman or trader, they sent a petition to Ottawa bearing fourteen names and signed with Xs. The petitioners referred to themselves as "treaty Indians," meaning their names were on the treaty lists at Whitefish Lake and elsewhere.

"Enclosed herewith please find a Petition, asking for a Reserve here at Prairie Lake, signed by the heads of all the families living in this district," their covering letter began.

"These Treaty Indians with few exceptions were born, and have lived in this district all their lives, making a living by hunting and trapping. We are over 40 miles from Whitefish Lake by the present trail, which is also a very bad one, and we find it hard to attend the yearly Treaty payments there, in fact some have not been present at Treaty for several years.

"None of the parties who signed this Petition, have homes or have lived on the reserve at Whitefish Lake, and none of us wish to do so.

"The rations that are issued at Treaty time go to the Indians on the reserve, and we are neglected, I have personally spoken to the Chief about this ration, but never got any satisfaction.

"I would be glad to know as to whether this Petition will be considered or not, so that I can report to those who have appointed me their spokesman." The letter was signed with an X by Alex Adams, one of the fourteen.

All fourteen signatures appeared on a separate page with a paragraph at the top saying: "We, the undersigned . . . having resided at or near Prairie Lake all our lives, and being the heads of our respective families, do respectfully ask that we be granted a land reserve here at Prairie Lake, and that our treaty payments be made on the said reserve."

L'Heureux received a copy of the petition via Ottawa, and in his response revealed that he still misunderstood the make-up of the interior groups. "I beg to say that, formerly, Prairie Lake was the refuge of all the drunkers and lazy Indians of Whitefish Lake and other bands who did not like to be under close supervision," he replied.

The interior bands continued to press for their rights. In 1935, Loon Lake representatives issued a formal petition to L'Heureux at Whitefish Lake. The same year, a man named Joseph Cardinal approached L'Heureux at Wabasca saying the people of Chipewyan and Trout lakes wished to be granted the reserves, annuities and allotments of twine and ammunition to which they were entitled. In correspondence with Ottawa, L'Heureux supported the demands. "They . . . are not asking for any help that they would not be entitled to" under Treaty Eight, he wrote. "I would pray the Department to grant their application as the first step to bring about a gradual rectification of their standing." In 1938, he travelled to Trout Lake for the first time, confirmed the validity of that band's position and requested that a reserve at Trout Lake be established.

In 1939, L'Heureux made his first trip to Lubicon Lake. He and the federal inspector for Alberta agencies, Pant Schmidt, chartered a float plane to meet the Lubicon people on their home ground—the first government delegation to do so. More than a hundred band members gathered at the western shore to greet them. L'Heureux paid annuities, then he and Schmidt heard the band's case for recognition and reserve status.

"As it was the first time that a treaty party was afforded the opportunity to visit these Indians in their own district, particular pain was taken to scrutinize their claim," L'Heureux later reported to Ottawa. He wrote glowingly of the band, reversing his earlier reference to "drunkers and lazy Indians" by describing the people he met as healthy, with a positive outlook.

"It was well noticeable from the outset that these Indians are far different from those of Whitefish Lake," L'Heureux said. "They are gay, look bright and seem active, qualities that are conspicuously absent in the others. Their leader, Alexis Laboucan, #81, made a short speech well to the point and concisely stated their claim: their band as a unit has existed forever as far as they can remember, their residence at Lubicon Lake began well before Treaty was ever mentioned; commented on their ability and hunt following the game where it goes but stating their willingness to learn agriculture for the time soon to come when fur will be too scarce for them all to make a living at hunting. They wish their children educated but are reluctant, they admit it, to send them to such distant schools as at Grouard and Whitefish Lake, the nearest 55 miles away by trail and the other another 40 miles beyond. At last he said that the Department sends provisions to the Whitefish Lake Indians but they receive none of it. The able-bodied men of his band do not need it but he wishes their

aged and infirm to be assisted to the full of their rights; they wish
their share of ammunitions because they are entitled to it by Treaty
stipulation; for the years past the [Whitefish Lake] Indians have got
away with their share."

When band members suggested that land at the west end of the
lake would make a good reserve, L'Heureux agreed. "An area of good
open land, well suited for an Indian Reserve," he called it. "The land
rises away from the creek; bordering the creek is good hay meadow;
the next higher level is suitable for plowing and the high land is forest
of poplar and spruce."

Schmidt was equally enthusiastic about what he saw, describing in
detail a tour he took with a Metis settler, Josie L'Hirondelle. "Mr.
L'Hirondelle has some 60 head of cattle, 50 head of horses, farms 25
acres of oats each year for green feed, one acre of garnet wheat for
chicken feed, which ripens nicely," Schmidt wrote. "He said he
always has a good crop of potatoes and a good garden. I saw his
potatoes and two bags of rhubarb, which he had with him and was
giving away to the Indians. He claims that the Lubicon Lake district
is much less subject to frosts than are the Enilda, Grouard and Salt
Prairie districts where he has lived. I am mentioning this to show what
can be grown in this district."

Schmidt went on to make other observations. "At the present time
these Indians live on the banks of the lake, near the old Hudson's Bay
Co. trading post site, which is now abandoned," he wrote. "They
have log shanties for winter use. At time of my visit they were living
in tents and tepees. I saw a number of small gardens and potato
patches all fenced in with rails. I noticed also that they had very good
horses. I was very much interested in this band, and found them clean,
well dressed, healthy, bright and intelligent; in other words, people
who want to live and do well."

Schmidt and L'Heureux recommended that the Lubicon Lake
people be recognized as a separate band and that a reserve be established for them at the west end of Lubicon Lake. In a separate
document, Schmidt reported counting 127 people, which at 128 acres
per person, as provided in Treaty Eight, would mean a reserve of 25.4
square miles.

Ottawa approved the recommendation. No treaty was signed, but
in early 1940 the surveyor general ordered that a reserve be staked
out at Lubicon Lake. L'Heureux was also authorized to hold an

election, and on June 4, 1940, the Lubicon Lake band chose Joseph Laboucan as its first chief.

That fall, a survey team flew north. Under terms of the Alberta Natural Resources Act of 1930, federal authorities were required to complete an official ground survey, evidence of which would go to provincial authorities, who then had to transfer the land to the federal Crown in trust for the band. Leading the team was Cecil Donnelly, a federal surveyor. Carl Ranche represented Alberta forestry and L'Heureux went along for Indian Affairs. Their orders were to define reserve boundaries for three bands in the Lesser Slave interior—at Lubicon, Peerless and Chipewyan lakes—and for six groups in the extreme northwest of the province. At the last minute the orders changed, however. Surveys at Peerless and Chipewyan were cancelled for budget reasons. The group flew directly north to survey sites in the remote Hay Lakes district, then headed to the west end of Lubicon Lake. There they ran smack into a forest fire.

"Owing to smoke and shallow water it was impossible to land," Donnelly later wrote. "The area was covered from the low altitude of 100 feet, from which it could readily be seen that it was ideal for mixed farming, with sufficient timber at the northerly end to supply the Indians' needs. The soil is a rich black loam." Happy with the site, he sketched boundaries enclosing "25 square miles, more or less" on a map.

The creation of a Lubicon reserve was almost complete. The band was formally recognized, a chief elected, a reserve site marked on a map. But before somebody could return to drive stakes into the ground, the first obstacle arose in what was to be a long, bureaucratic ordeal for the inhabitants of the Lesser Slave interior. Over the next several months, Ottawa officials exchanged contradictory memos on whether any surveys would go ahead. The surveyor general was in favour. The Indian Affairs director was pushing hard to have them finished "in order to definitely secure the reserves to which the Indians in this district are entitled." Ministerial approval for $6,000 even came through to cover costs. But people at Reserves and Trusts were stalling. There was a war on, they said. The money might be needed elsewhere. Surveyors, they said, were in short supply.

3 BRUTALLY REDUCED TO SILENCE

THE REAL REASON for delay can be traced to Malcolm McCrimmon, a senior accountant who for the next twenty years was to exercise enormous influence at Indian Affairs. He grew up in southeastern Ontario near Alexandria, the oldest Scottish Presbyterian settlement in Canada. His first language was Gaelic, and his first job was as a bank clerk at the local branch of the Bank of Ottawa. Later, he moved to Indian Affairs. He reorganized chaotic Indian Land Sales accounts by introducing a new loose-leaf ledger system and a uniform method of calculating interest. From there, he went to the Reserves and Trusts section to straighten treaty annuity records.

They were a mess. McCrimmon dug out hundreds of paylists that had never been checked, and as he worked his way through them his attention was drawn to the records of the Lesser Slave agency. He scrutinized Harold Laird's work, noting that Laird had been jailed after adding fictitious names to the paylists long after Treaty Eight was signed. He also noticed that L'Heureux was still adding names. Not realizing, perhaps, that these people were interior inhabitants who had previously been overlooked, McCrimmon concluded that L'Heureux might be a crook as well.

In the fall of 1940, McCrimmon asked L'Heureux to send copies of his current paylists to Ottawa. With the ground survey at Lubicon Lake still pending, McCrimmon studied the lists and challenged some of the figures. L'Heureux admitted minor errors: the Bigstone band had been overpaid by five dollars; a baby's birth date was missing; two boys had earlier been listed as girls. On one list, a typing error had transposed the figures for the total numbers of boys and girls, although the overall total was correct. "I must explain that being alone to write up this paylist from the beginning to the end, the lot of figures and names make me weary and some figures are bound to escape notice," L'Heureux wrote apologetically. "Most of this work was done in the light of a gasolene lamp and this did not help either."

McCrimmon persisted, apparently determined that some names on the lists should come off. He challenged dozens of individual cases, forcing L'Heureux to prove people's treaty entitlements with pages of detail on marital affiliations and blood ties. In response to a query about Norman Noskiye of Lubicon Lake, L'Heureux defended the family's Indian status by saying: "I classified his wife as a half-breed somewhat inconsiderately. The Loon Lake district [where the wife was born] is the habitat of a large number of non-treaty Indians and if there are any halfbreeds in that district, they are of the most primitive type, the actual admixture of white blood being so little as to be inconsequential. I wish you would reconsider your decision and retain the wife's child on this man's ticket with his mother."

McCrimmon struck the Noskiye wife and child from the treaty list anyway, along with sixteen other people from Lubicon Lake, giving no reason other than, "it would appear that they are not eligible for membership." He also removed fifty-two names from the Wabasca list, most of them members of other interior bands.

At some point, he may have satisfied himself that L'Heureux was an honest man, but McCrimmon was becoming obsessed with the idea of somehow trimming the treaty paylists. One motivating factor might have been the Second World War; all departments were under pressure to cut costs. Another might have been his upbringing, in which frugality had been as much a virtue as a necessity. In any case, McCrimmon clearly resented the annuity payments to northern Alberta. "We were spending money like cold water up there," he once said. With the blessing of his minister, Thomas Crerar, McCrimmon soon left for northern Alberta to handle annuity payments himself. He made it his mission to lighten the government's Indian burden by reducing the number of Indians.

He arrived by train in Driftpile on May 29, 1942, and moved into L'Heureux's house for several days, because there was no hotel. It was a tense time for the agent, his wife, Beatrice, and their five children. The two men pleasantly compared war stories, but the eldest daughter, Yvonnette, remembers McCrimmon mostly for his meanness. She says her mother was the agency's unpaid office clerk, keeping the records and writing out L'Heureux's diary from notes after he returned from a circuit. When McCrimmon stayed with them, the family had to hire a girl to help with the extra cooking and washing, an expense McCrimmon later refused to cover.

On the morning of June 3, McCrimmon, L'Heureux and several assistants left by chartered plane from nearby Faust. They stopped at Whitefish Lake to pay annuities, then continued north to Lubicon Lake, touching down at 5:30 P.M.—the moment in history that ends the era of benign neglect towards the Lubicon Lake Cree and begins the modern period of officially sanctioned sabotage. "No speeches, we are pressed to leave," McCrimmon announced briskly to those gathering around, as recorded by a visiting priest, Nicolas Roué. McCrimmon paid annuities to only twelve of the thirty-seven families listed with the band, telling the rest that they were no longer Indians, including everybody who had registered with L'Heureux. Altogether, McCrimmon deleted 75 names from a list of 154.

"I saw one of the principal Indians of Lubicon Lake brutally reduced to silence when he started to speak in order to defend his rights," Roué wrote. At 7:30 P.M., the delegation took off again. "We have been treated like dogs," Roué overheard one of the band members say.

For the rest of the summer, McCrimmon went from settlement to settlement paying some people and striking others from paylists without explanation. He seemed to invent rules as he went along. In his report to Ottawa, he listed six categories under which he deemed a person to be ineligible for treaty status—rules having to do with scrip-taking, late registration and low percentages of native blood. But the rules didn't cover most of the cases he submitted; he seemed to operate more by rule of thumb. He once said that he could tell an Indian from a non-Indian by the way a person lived and dressed. And he told some groups that anyone added to the paylists after 1912 must prove pure Indian blood on the father's side. While he was still in Alberta, the department issued a statement from Ottawa saying that "to lead the Indian life is not the determining factor in deciding if a person may be regarded as an Indian"— a reversal of the criterion under which people were accepted into Treaty Eight in the first place.

Not a flicker of compassion seems to have informed McCrimmon's judgment as he made the rounds. He expelled the old and the lame, and split families. He expelled Thomas Bone, an eighty-year-old Whitefish Lake man with severe rheumatism, because Bone couldn't prove pure Indian blood on his father's side. Half the Henry Prince family was forced from the Sucker Creek reserve near Grouard; although the father proved Indian status, four of his children from his wife's first marriage could not. A young woman and her children had to leave the Brownvale reserve west of Peace River because her husband could not prove treaty status; he was overseas fighting in the war.

People doing particularly well for themselves were especially vulnerable to losing Indian status. McCrimmon figured that a successful person couldn't be a true Indian, and he took measures against them that destroyed their lives. One victim was Robert Walker of the Driftpile reserve, McCrimmon's last stop before returning to Ottawa. Walker, twenty- eight years old at the time, was one of the band's leading members. He owned twelve milk cows, sold butter and cream, grew grain and raised hens, calves and pigs. From a Polish neighbour he had learned to make bacon. He also cut and hauled logs for a mill every winter in return for half the lumber, some of which he used to build a house with finished hardwood floors. "I was born there and I was farming," he says. "Even the army wouldn't take me because I was farming too much and raising a lot of pigs, I was helping others. They said, 'We have to hold you here because we need you.' "

On treaty day in 1942, Walker remembers going to the chief's house and filing past a table where McCrimmon and L'Heureux were sitting. He collected five dollars each for himself and his wife, but stayed when he saw McCrimmon refusing other people money. McCrimmon grew annoyed at Walker's presence in the corner, and at some point in the proceedings a man named Pierre Giroux declared that Walker's father was a white man.

"Give me that money," McCrimmon told Walker, as Walker remembers the exchange.

"I am a treaty Indian," Walker replied. His father was Weechewasis, or Ben Walker—a registered treaty Indian.

McCrimmon asked Walker twice more for the money and told him he would also have to leave the reserve. Walker gave back the ten dollars and said, "Anyway, you can't put me out."

A local priest took up Walker's case, writing the bishop that "Pierre Giroux is known to every one here as a public liar. He is a man who has done time on several occasions. Nevertheless, Mr. McCrimmon did not hesitate to take the word of such a man without taking the trouble to check up on his statement. This fashion of administering justice on behalf of the Department gives an idea of the kind of investigation that has been carried out by Mr. McCrimmon throughout the Lesser Slave Lake Agency."

In the end, Walker was forced off the reserve. McCrimmon gave him until May 1, 1943—time enough, McCrimmon said, to harvest crops and remove belongings. The deadline also applied to everybody else removed from the lists, unless they lived in the interior and had no reserve in the first place. For his assets Walker received $2,200, a fraction of their value, and for the next twenty-five years he worked for logging, fishing and oil companies as a labourer.

Altogether, McCrimmon struck 640 people from band lists in northern Alberta in 1942, driving large numbers of people off reserves. He forced 124 children from Indian mission schools, although most of them had no other school to go to. He also got L'Heureux fired, saying the agent had paid $1,265 more than he should have in 1931–32, the confused period following Laird's departure.

The following summer, in 1943, McCrimmon returned to the Lesser Slave agency to travel the circuit again, increasing his tally to more than 700 names. At Lubicon Lake, he increased the total to 90, leaving 64 members. Among those cut was Alexis Laboucan, the man L'Heureux and Schmidt had identified as leader of the band on their pioneering visit of 1939. Laboucan's father was Pepawakiew of Fish Lake and his mother was Chagag, both pure-blooded Indians. "Alexis Laboucan, a half-breed, was admitted to membership in 1930," McCrimmon reported tersely. "He stated that he had no desire to be in Treaty."

Alexis Laboucan might have expressed indifference to McCrimmon, but other evidence shows band members going to unusual lengths to secure their rights to both treaty status and a reserve. McCrimmon reported that he had trouble finding the band that summer. The year before, he had encountered the group at the east end of Lubicon Lake, where many of the members had summer cabins. But this time Chief Joseph Laboucan had pointedly assembled everyone at the west end, on the site of the promised reserve. The chief had built two log houses there himself, one a substantial two-storey structure, and on the delegation's eventual arrival, he invited McCrimmon to examine the area.

McCrimmon was unmoved. "I advised the Chief it was my opinion that they had been provided with all the land to which they were entitled at Whitefish Lake," he reported. "This matter will have to be further investigated." Back in Ottawa he wrote to the head of Reserves and Trusts: "This request should be held in abeyance until the membership problem is settled. If my recommendation is approved by the Minister, the number of Indians remaining on the membership list at Lubicon Lake would hardly warrant the establishment of a Reserve."

The removals provoked outrage in northern Alberta among local leaders, priests and members of Parliament. The Liberal member for Peace River, Jack Sissons (later the famous flying judge of the Far North), declared himself "incensed," and summarized numerous complaints for the minister, Crerar, a fellow Liberal in Mackenzie King's government. Sissons said people were complaining "that striking these persons off the lists was arbitrary, discreditable and indefensible; that these were Hitler tactics; that the Government has broken faith with the Indians; that the Action indicates that there is in the Department lack of proper knowledge of the Indians and the territory; that the Indians are being treated like dogs; that this is oppression of the weak by the strong; that these people have no one to fight for them; that the Department is indifferent and unsympathetic to the welfare of the Indians, and generally that the action is contrary to both the spirit and the letter of the Indian Act."

Chief Joseph Bigstone of Wabasca, a Treaty Eight signatory, wrote to Crerar with the help of a priest, reminding the minister of the government's commitments.

"We were told again and again," Bigstone's letter said, "that the treaty in the name of the great Queen Victoria, with the chiefs and councillors will be sacred and respected as long as the sun will walk in the sky, the rivers will flow in their beds: there are only 42 years it has been signed and yet you have broken your word; we have made together a furrow with a plow, with the mutual promise it will stay there forever, and yet you have covered it without any respect for your word, without any regard for our poor Indians.

"We were told that any man living in the country then and all their children living or to come, on the condition they will not have received a sheet of paper [scrip], as Halfbreeds, will be a member of the Indian Treaty. We were promised to have the time to think about it, the same advantages as the other members. Naturally it should be so. We were all without any exception, the true owners of this large country, each of us has the same right to be paid in the same way for abandoning in favour of the white people the privilege to come and settle in our land . . . .

"Because you are strong, have you the right to abuse of your powers to deprive the poor and the weak of what is due to him. But there is a God, you know, and he may find one day those who fail to be just towards us . . . .

"I hate to talk to you in such a manner, you may be a good hearted man, but we also are men and we do not like to be whipped just like dogs, who, we were told, were the only ones excluded from the treaty."

Two inquiries were held into the removals, the first in 1943. Mr. Justice C. M. McKeen from Westlock, near Edmonton, accompanied McCrimmon on the agency circuit to hear appeals. Not only was McCrimmon present and still expelling people, but he had also written the judge's mandate, restricting him to asking two questions: "Are you or your father Half-breed?" and "Did you or he take Scrip?" If a person replied "yes" to either question, McKeen was obliged to refuse the appeal. (In northern Alberta, the term "half-breed" was so loosely defined it could mean anybody without official Indian status—including a pure-blooded Indian too isolated ever to have been recognized and anybody who had been struck by McCrimmon. "Are you or your father Half-breed?" was a trick question designed to prompt a "yes" reply.)

McKeen quickly realized that he was being used. In his spare time, he read a history of the prairie treaties, the text of Treaty Eight, the Indian Act and David Laird's reports. Politely, he advised the minister that posing two simple questions fell short of addressing the appellants' complaints. He argued that because anybody living an Indian way of life was eligible for treaty in 1899, their descendants should likewise be eligible. He referred to scrip as "the worst racket in this Province," explaining that "many an Indian or Half-Breed received anywhere from two bottles of whisky to $50.00 for this scrip and [there were] many hearsay cases where the recipient's name was forged and he received nothing." McKeen also lamented the "great injustice" of men, women and children being expelled from reserves where they were born and raised. The case of orphans he found particularly sad. Not being able to prove pure Indian status on the father's side, many orphans were wrenched from their adoptive families.

Crerar ignored the report entirely. The expulsions stood, provoking Jack Sissons and another Alberta MP to take the case to Louis St. Laurent, then justice minister and later prime minister. St. Laurent called a formal judicial inquiry.

In the summer of 1944, Mr. Justice W. A. Macdonald of the Supreme Court of Alberta held public hearings into the removals, taking evidence at twelve communities, including Lubicon Lake. Like McKeen, he studied the history of the treaties, with particular attention to Treaty Eight, and concluded unequivocally that "persons of mixed blood who became identified with the Indians, lived with them, spoke their language and followed the Indian way of life were recognized as Indians." Scrip records could not be trusted, he said, and should not be used to bar a person from treaty. As for late registrations, he wrote, "I can find no justification for the view that delay in applying for treaty is or ever was an effective bar to admission to treaty." He also opposed the practice of expelling orphans, saying that "every instinct of natural justice" proclaimed that the children should be reunited with their adoptive families and restored to the band rolls.

Among the more than 700 people removed, Macdonald examined nearly 500 cases. He had had to skip three far northern communities because of transportation problems, and many people elsewhere simply hadn't come forward, possibly having grown skeptical about the process. But of the cases studied, Macdonald euphemistically listed most of them—284—as "removed in error" and ruled they should be restored. He recommended reinstatement of a further 58 illegitimate children, 2 legally adopted children, 36 naturally adopted children and 80 scrip-takers. Altogether, he recommended reinstatement of almost eight of every nine cases he heard; the rest he grouped as miscellaneous to be investigated further.

At Lubicon Lake, Macdonald was able to examine 57 of the 90 names removed. He found 51 of them to have been "removed in error." The other 6, he said, were scrip-takers who should also be restored to the list.

Although Justice Minister St. Laurent had called the inquiry, the report went directly to Crerar, who assigned McCrimmon to implement its findings. McCrimmon reinstated only 120 people, meaning that in the end he stripped nearly 600 people in northern Alberta of Indian status.

At Lubicon Lake he reinstated 18, meaning that he cut 72 members of 154, splitting the band nearly in half. One of them was John Felix Laboucan, a son of Alexis Laboucan and now a key Lubicon elder. His case tells the history of the period. He was born at Little Buffalo Lake in 1913 as a member of the Lubicon Lake people, was officially recognized as an Indian by L'Heureux in 1930, was cut from the list by McCrimmon in 1943, was recommended reinstated by Mr. Justice Macdonald in 1944, and was kept off by McCrimmon in the final tally.

≈

After the Second World War, McCrimmon found himself in particularly congenial company at Indian Affairs, enabling him to expand his influence and to reduce the Lubicon Lake band officially to almost nothing. A new minister, Allison Glen, was taking an aggressively assimilationist line. "The ultimate goal of our Indian policy is the integration of the Indians into the general life and economy of the country," he told the House of Commons in 1946—an acceptable-sounding way of undermining native rights. And when Bishop Henri Routhier of Grouard tried to launch one last protest against the McCrimmon expulsions, Glen replied: "Our policy should be to do everything possible to encourage Indians to become full citizens of the Province in which they live." Prime Minister Louis St. Laurent likewise said that he wanted "to make Canadian citizens . . . of the original inhabitants of the territory."

In 1951, the St. Laurent government also passed a new Indian Act. It featured a new legal definition of "Indian" that closely resembled McCrimmon's eligibility rules for the Lesser Slave agency. Under the legislation, a child could be registered as an Indian only if he or she was the direct descendant in the male line of a person with Indian status. An exception was a child born out of wedlock: if the mother qualified as an Indian under the first rule, so did her offspring, unless the father was known to be non-Indian. The definition had less to do with Indian blood and way of life than with entrenching a philosophy that held Indians as inferior to white people and Indian women as inferior to men of either race. If an Indian man married a white woman, she became an Indian; it was assumed an Indian man was not a capable provider and his wife would need treaty benefits. If an Indian woman married a white man, she legally became white; it was assumed a white man could look after her. (Only in 1985 were the rules changed to allow a woman to retain her Indian status no matter whom she married, a change that came as a result of pressure from the United Nations Human Rights Committee in Geneva.)

The 1951 Indian Act also created the post of Indian Registrar, which carried the exclusive power to administer Indian status and band membership. The job went to Malcolm McCrimmon. "I was a power unto myself," he later remarked, referring to a clause in the act saying that the decision of the Registrar was "final and conclusive" unless a person went to court. Although he never repeated the wholesale purges of his northern Alberta days, McCrimmon's individual rulings on band membership drew more than a thousand written protests.

McCrimmon also used his new power to all but wipe out the Lubicon band on paper. Two major oil strikes in the Edmonton area launched an Alberta oil-and-gas industry in 1947, and almost immediately interest was aroused in oil potential farther north. Attention was again drawn to the promised Lubicon reserve, and Alberta authorities asked federal officials to clarify the status of the land. If a reserve was needed, Alberta was ready to transfer the 25.4 square miles. If not, the province wished to open the area to oil exploration. A Quaker pastor who wanted to build a mission at Lubicon Lake was also asking about the reserve. "Due to the fact that there are considerable enquiries regarding the minerals in this area and also the fact that there has been a request to establish a mission at this point we are naturally anxious to clear our records of this provisional reserve if the land is not required by this Band of Indians," an Alberta official wrote to Ottawa.

Suddenly, internal reports at Indian Affairs began describing Lubicon Lake not as a prairie oasis ideal for a reserve, but as an undesirable location. The area is "semi-waste land," said one report. The Lubicon people don't spend much time there, said another. The proposed reserve site, said a third, was isolated, unsuitable for trapping and farming, and "rather barren."

Alternative sites far from prospective oil areas were proposed. Federal officials began a conscious effort to sabotage the reserve proposal, sometimes advising each other to proceed cleverly. "In approaching the subject with the Indians I think it would be well to keep in mind that the mineral rights that go with the land may be very much more valuable than anything else and if the Indians were deprived of these rights they could make it very unpleasant for Branch officials," wrote the federal supervisor of Indian agencies in Alberta, G. H. Gooderham. The Lubicon band must not be granted oil rights—despite the universal practice of granting all subsurface rights—no matter where a reserve might eventually be established, he said, and wished his field staff success "in coming to some definite solution this year" on the question.

McCrimmon found the definite solution. He travelled to northern Alberta to "investigate" the reserve proposal, concluding that "no official action was ever taken to establish the Lubicon Lake Indians as a Band." The finding was a fabrication but it pleased his superior, who replied: "If the group was never established as an official band it will serve our purpose very well at the present time."

McCrimmon was not so bold as to advance the same line with Alberta, but as it turned out he didn't have to. In late 1953, after waiting years for the ground surveys to be completed, provincial authorities demanded that Ottawa confirm its intention of creating reserves in the interior. "If no reply is received within 30 days it would be assumed that the reservations have been struck from the records," Alberta authorities advised. Intentionally, Ottawa did not reply, prompting Alberta to delete the provisional reserves from the books. McCrimmon, as membership registrar, then transferred most of the names of Lubicon band members—without their knowledge, the members say—to the Whitefish Lake band list.

For the people of the Lesser Slave interior, McCrimmon's work meant that twenty years of trying to achieve recognition had come to nothing. Most of the people living at Lubicon, Loon, Trout, Peerless, Sandy and Chipewyan lakes had been stripped of Indian status. As communities they also remained without band status, except for the Lubicon band, with only 30 recognized members. All six groups were living reasonably well by hunting and trapping, but without Indian status and band recognition they had almost no way of pursuing their land rights; and without protected land title they were poorly equipped, in the face of advancing oil exploration, to survive as distinct aboriginal peoples.

4 MARTEN RIVER

CHIEF JOSEPH LABOUCAN was slightly built and short even by Lubicon standards, but people who knew him say that he was unrelenting in his efforts to secure his people's land rights. One of his ideas was to create a de facto reserve. Prior to McCrimmon's second visit in 1943, Laboucan built two new houses on the promised site, one of them a two-storey structure with glass windows and a large yard fenced off with cedar rails. He encouraged other band members to build at the west end of the lake as well, in an effort to occupy the site and create a reserve-like community.

Then he tried to get a school. For years, Lubicon parents had wanted their children to learn arithmetic and English so they could deal more confidently with traders and the rest of the outside world. "They wish their children educated," L'Heureux reported in 1939, "but are reluctant, they admit it, to send them to such distant schools as at Grouard and Whitefish Lake." L'Heureux suggested having a wagon pick up children at the start of the school year, returning them ten months later, but most Lubicon parents never took the idea seriously. They were not prepared to part with their children, half of whom were barred from Indian schools anyway after McCrimmon stripped them of Indian status. McCrimmon's removals had another effect. The established clergy in the Lesser Slave area—the Anglicans and the Roman Catholic Oblates—refused to build missions at Lubicon Lake because only children with Indian status qualified for the government subsidy on which the church missions were run. Undaunted, the chief continued to make the band's desire known, and one day Raymond L'Hirondelle, son of the trader Josie, came across a new mission office in Peace River. The missionary, Rolland Smith, was looking for a group of Indians to serve, and L'Hirondelle invited him to Lubicon Lake.

"I felt God's call," Smith wrote at the time. He had wanted to be a missionary to Indians of the northern woodlands from the age of nine, when he first read about them in a book called *Human Geography* and discovered that they had no Sunday school. Although frail with a congenital heart murmur, he had stuck to his goal. He became a Quaker pastor near Cleveland, Ohio; then in 1948, at the age of thirty-one, he moved to Peace River with his wife, Thelma, and their two infant sons, incrementally establishing himself as the Northland Indian Mission in an old frame building on Main Street. He explored the area north of Peace River, thinking of taking the mission there, then considered the Lesser Slave Lake area. Not long after meeting L'Hirondelle, Smith made his first trip into Lubicon territory.

For eleven days in late November 1950, he travelled nearly four hundred miles by truck, sleigh, foot and Bombardier tractor with help from the L'Hirondelles. He visited tiny settlements at Marten River, Sawan Lake, Little Buffalo, Lubicon Lake, Weasel Lake, Bear Trap, Otter Lakes, Fish Lake and Big Buffalo (Bison) Lake. "Everyone interested in prospects of a school," Smith wrote enthusiastically in his diary. "Children want to come and adults would like to learn to read and write, too. Everyone seems bright enough, they only need a chance."

As he travelled, Smith conjured up a school of log buildings with gardens all around. There would be boys' and girls' dormitories, and one large building to serve the first year as a laundry, kitchen and storage room combined. Desks would be built so that they could be joined as tables at dinner time, and wooden bunks with straw mattresses would serve as beds. There would be a community hall for games and a workshop "so men and boys could build their own furniture and toys for the children." He would need at least $1,000 for concrete foundations, doors, windows, tables and benches. For raising money, he imagined an eight-page folder—with a map as the centre spread—which he would send to likely contributors on a mailing list of church people in eight provinces and more than thirty states.

"A school is wanted bad enough the men have agreed to get together and put up log buildings," Smith wrote. "They are willing to do all they can."

The following year, in 1951, Smith returned to Lubicon Lake on treaty day to meet Chief Joseph Laboucan, whom he had missed the first time. Smith took pictures of the occasion. They are faded now and a bit wobbly, but they show an Indian agent sitting with a Mountie in dress uniform outside Laboucan's impressive house. The chief is shown hovering at the Mountie's shoulder dressed in a black suit and hat that L'Heureux must have given him on being elected eleven years earlier. After the ceremony, Laboucan talked to Smith about a school. "I've wanted one here for twenty years," the missionary remembers the chief saying, and by the end of the afternoon Smith agreed to build a mission school on the proposed reserve site near where they were standing. The meeting was one of Laboucan's last official acts. A few weeks later, on July 19, 1951, he died of an undiagnosed illness while out cutting his winter's supply of hay.

Determined to keep his word, Smith applied to the province for a building permit at Lubicon Lake. But there was a problem, a maddening bit of bureaucracy. In 1951, Alberta records still showed a provisional reserve at Lubicon Lake. If Smith built his school there and the land became a reserve, the children struck from the band list by McCrimmon would be officially barred from attending. For the school to serve all the children, Smith would have to build outside the promised 25.4 square miles, authorities said—one of the few times in history that a government tried to honour the reserve commitment, causing the Lubicon people only hardship. For months, Smith waited for Ottawa to clarify the land's status, and when no decision came he decided to build immediately outside the proposed reserve boundary at Little Buffalo Lake, six miles west of the site agreed to with Chief Laboucan. Soon construction began. From the chief's widow, Smith bought two cabins, which Lubicon men reassembled as a staff quarters and girls' bunkhouse. The men also hauled in other buildings and built some from scratch. Volunteer teachers were recruited from outside, and after a couple of false starts twenty Lubicon children started school in September 1954.

A few details of those early mission days survive in Smith's mimeographed newsletters to contributors. Some letters are straight-out appeals for funds, but most are in the form of short stories about life in the northern woodlands, usually highlighting harsh aspects that might encourage readers to send money. "The Covered Wagon," one is called; it tells about Smith's trips into Peace River for supplies, a three-day journey mostly over what he called a "bulldozer road," a trail the width of one bulldozer blade made by the first oil-company exploration crews heading into the territory. Another, entitled "The White Plague," emphasizes the importance of testing for tuberculosis and the need to hire a full-time registered nurse for the mission. Yet another tells about a mouse called Oscar who helped raise an unexpected donation for the mission at Christmas, 1955. Listeners to a Peace River radio station donated $735 in Oscar's name, allowing Smith to buy a power washing machine, cotton mattresses and eyeglasses for some of the pupils.

Over the next several years, Lubicon families moved their summer cabins from the shores of Lubicon Lake to Little Buffalo, forming a semipermanent community grouped around the school. The annual cycle changed slightly for many families. In the fall, fathers with young children would leave for their traplines alone, while wives stayed home and children attended classes. Everyone would reunite at the Christmas and Easter holidays, and the whole community would gather as always for the summer. People were adapting, but without reserve status the settlement had no official standing, causing band members to continue to feel vulnerable. Many feared that until the land they were living on was officially recognized as a reserve, the school and houses were subject to removal, which is exactly what happened at neighbouring Marten River.

The community of Marten River stood at a crossing of wagon trails a few kilometres north of Little Buffalo, where Marten River flows into Marten Lake. Hand-cut trails once ran all through Lubicon territory and the settlement stood at a main junction, where a trail leading east to Loon Lake intersected with the route between Lubicon and Bison lakes. Goose hunting there was excellent in spring and fall. In the 1920s, three or four families built cabins at the junction, and soon Marten River became a stop-off point, with a trading post, for people of the regional band.

The actual village site is overgrown now, but partings in the long grass indicate where homes and sheds once stood. In some of the hollows, charred logs and rusty pieces of stoves can be seen, and the cement floor of what was once a store is clearly visible near the riverbank. At the east end of town near the lake, three homes still stand, used seasonally by hunters now living at Little Buffalo.

The earliest written accounts of Marten River come from Muriel Oslie, who lived there for five years and kept a diary. She and her husband, Oliver, came north in 1936 from Saskatchewan and bought the trading post at Marten River. She described their first cabin as "not any too clean." All the early cabins at Marten River had walls made of logs and mud plaster, with a layered roof of poles, birchbark and sod from which grass and flowers grew. The roofs leaked in a heavy rain or when the snow melted. There were no floors. Muriel scrubbed the walls and learned from other women how to collect sacks of white marl from a nearby creek for whitewash. Two years later, she and Oliver built a new house. It was also made of logs and mud plaster, but the Oslies hauled lumber from Peace River for a floor and a roof, and installed real glass in the windows instead of gauze.

Despite discomforts, Muriel Oslie wrote of Marten River with fondness. She wrote of the taste of Oliver's hotcakes on the trail, the feel of her favourite pony named Babe, the smell of milk and butter from the three cows she kept, and the uproar that would greet Little Joe Cardinal, the settlement's best hunter, when he arrived home with a moose. He shared it with everyone, Oslie said: "A real treat for us."

Afterwards, she and Oliver moved to Three Creeks at the western limit of Lubicon territory, but she continued to keep an eye on Marten River. In the winter of 1949–50, oil-exploration crews began to enter the region for what they called "shoot and test." Workers would bulldoze a straight line through the bush, explode dynamite in the ground at regular intervals and map the substrata on bulky seismographic equipment mounted in a truck. They were looking for signs of pinnacle reefs—subsurface rock ridges one mile or less across that indicate the presence of oil. When signs looked positive, a test well would sometimes be drilled. Oslie kept track of the crews. On a map tacked to the inside of her front door showing where each farmer lived, she marked where every exploration team was heading. "By the midfifties, they'd made it to Marten River," says Oslie, now retired and living in Peace River. "From there they spread north and east, off the map, and past the door jamb." Government records confirm early exploration of the Marten River area, and show that in 1954 a test well was drilled and capped two miles northwest of Marten River proper.

By the 1950s, Marten River had also begun to attract priority attention from the Oblate order of Roman Catholic priests. For nearly a hundred years, priests had travelled intermittently through Lubicon territory seeking converts. They would baptize people and perform wedding ceremonies, but Chief Laboucan had never been able to persuade them to establish a permanent mission. When Rolland Smith arrived for the Quakers, the Oblates reacted competitively. Two members of the Oblate mission at Whitefish Lake, a week south of Little Buffalo by wagon, began to take greater interest in the Lubicon area. Soon they committed themselves to making Roman Catholics out of people in the region before Smith could expand his influence.

"I'm a fanatic Catholic," one of the priests, Camillo Prosdocimo, still says without apology. In the late 1950s, he and Father Virgil Baratto began to travel regularly to the Marten River area, encouraging families to group their cabins together. "We offered them to make up a village and put up a school and have a little bit of organization," Baratto recalls.

In 1961, Prosdocimo and two Sisters of Wisdom moved to Marten River. They converted an old store into a school for twenty-five pupils, and more than a hundred people settled around it. The forestry department stationed two rangers nearby. A settlement formed and all seemed to be going well until Prosdocimo began to feel that he had made a mistake.

"The community was an island in a sea of muskeg," he says now at his current mission in Joussard, on Lesser Slave Lake. "In the summer there were a million mosquitoes, and the horses would be up to their chests in mud." Another irritant to him was the local trader, Harry Lambert, who by some accounts was the village's main conduit for liquor.

By early 1965, Prosdocimo had added salvation from both mosquitoes and Harry Lambert to the mission's objectives and proposed to move the community. A social services officer suggested amalgamating Marten River with Little Buffalo, but Prosdocimo said no: the Marten River people were separate from the Lubicon band. The people at Little Buffalo were Protestant, he said. Those at Marten River were Roman Catholic. The priest later announced that the Marten River people had decided to move eight miles southwest to Cadotte Lake—a decision, he said, taken at a community meeting.

"We didn't even know what's a meeting," says Joe P. Whitehead, one of many witnesses who disputes the priest's version of events. "We had meetings, but Indian meetings—how you're going to live, where you're going to trap, where you're going to hunt, where you're going when. Not white people's meetings. That's how he was able to corner us, that priest."

Prosdocimo forged ahead. He wrote his bishop about the proposed move, talked to authorities in Peace River and Edmonton, and held further community meetings at Marten River. "Some do not yet see the necessity to go out from this place, but they trust that what we suggest is for the best," he wrote to the district forestry superintendent in early 1965. "I do not see opposition nor enthusiasm, but I think they will accept the change if they will be helped."

Support for the move began to grow as the priest suggested to residents that help would indeed be forthcoming. Talk circulated in the community about windows, doors and roofing materials being supplied free of charge at Cadotte Lake. There were suggestions of free plywood and wages for building new homes. In June 1966, the provincial coordinator of community development warned Prosdocimo that "firm plans" must be approved before any move, but by then Prosdocimo was in Cadotte Lake felling trees with everybody except three holdout families and Harry Lambert, who had died in a shoot-out with a white trapper.

"The priest got everybody excited to move," recalls John Halcrow, who packed his wife, four daughters, two other relatives and a neighbour with an infant son onto a wagon and hauled them to Cadotte with a few belongings. Once his tents were up, he started looking for trees to cut. The men worked in groups, helping each other to haul wood and put up walls. Together they built fifteen cabins. Finishing materials eventually did arrive at government largesse, but in smaller quantities than residents had expected, and some materials went to build what the priests described as a "community hall." The priests used it as a school until they could haul the old one from Marten River, and it later became a store run by an Oblate brother.

The first winter proved difficult. Most men left for their traplines without having recovered the furniture from their other homes. Wives and children who stayed behind for school had nothing to sit on, and most slept on the floor at night around the stove. Prosdocimo fell ill with a kidney ailment and left Cadotte permanently. Disillusioned, a few people began to trickle back to Marten River, joining the three families who had never left.

Government authorities rushed to intervene. They said there would be one community, not two, and Cadotte would be the one community. On October 10, 1967, a forest ranger named Murray Doherty gathered the people of Cadotte together, with the priest and brother translating. More promises were made. Halcrow remembers talk about a road to Cadotte, linking the new settlement to medical services in Peace River, and promises of more materials to finish the houses. At the end of the meeting, each householder was given a paper to sign.

"I couldn't read or write," says Joe P. Whitehead. "I just put an X because the priest says everybody has to sign."

The documents turned out to be quitclaims. "I hereby authorize the Department of Lands & Forests of Edmonton, Alberta, to dispose of my trapper's cabin (No. 10 attached map) located on the NW1/2-33-86-14-W5th—Marten River Settlement," a typical one read. "I have no further use for the cabin as I am now established and residing in the Cadotte Lake Settlement."

Doherty, the ranger, says he forgets what happened next, but others recall him arriving at Marten River by helicopter to order everybody out. George Seeseequon remembers running outside to calm Peter Cardinal's horses, and Cardinal remembers shouting at the ranger to leave.

A few days later, word went around Cadotte Lake that anybody with belongings still at Marten River had better fetch them. Four men left immediately: John Halcrow, James and Leo Thunder, and Ernest Scotty, on Scotty's team-drawn wagon. When they reached Marten River they saw Roy Alm, a catskinner from Three Creeks near Peace River, preparing to knock over cabins. Doherty, the ranger, was supervising.

"One building was down already," says John Halcrow. "We told the ranger we have to try to get the stuff out of there, and he said, 'You have to make it snappy because the Cat is going to go at it.' So the first building we went to, I think it was Leonard Whitehead's house, we took some stuff out of there, and after that we went to Minnie Whitehead's. There was all kinds of stuff there. Then we went back to Leonard's to get the stove out, a big cookstove, and after we got it out we went back to Minnie's house and it's gone. Scotty turns around and says, 'That darned son of a gun he didn't give us a chance.' He was taking those buildings down in a few minutes, five buildings in not even half an hour. We tried to stop him. We tried waving at him because I know him pretty good, but he wouldn't stop knocking those buildings down, so we tried to take stuff out of the other buildings as fast as we could, and cover it up so it wouldn't get wet. It was raining. We were trying to cover mattresses and things so they wouldn't get destroyed but we didn't have a chance. We couldn't take much with just one wagon."

"The way I remember it," says Alm, the catskinner, "I skipped some houses so they could clean them out first, then I took them down." But while he disputes some of Halcrow's details, he admits the job left him with a bad feeling.

"Whether it's for the best or not, well, nobody knows, but I never liked them kind of jobs," he says. "I still don't. You can just sort of visualize the amount of hardship and work that's gone into something like that at one time or another. They built those cabins strictly by hand. A lot of those people probably never even had horses when they built those cabins. I'm sure they skidded by hand. You'd clear off the site and utilize the timber to build a cabin. That's the way they operated back then and it was a tough job."

Alm says he bulldozed forty buildings, including sheds and barns. Holdouts George and Elise Seeseequon guarded the three homes of families who had never moved, but the rest of the settlement soon "looked like beaver houses all over," George Seeseequon says. That was on October 16, 1967—six days after the ranger had people sign quitclaims on their homes. Three days later, on October 19, the forestry department hired a former ranger to burn the rubble.

Joe P. Whitehead lost two houses and a small warehouse. One of the houses had good windows and a floor of planed lumber, he says. John Halcrow lost beds, mattresses, cupboards, tables and chairs. John Ed Laboucan says he was about to renovate his house with three new windows, a door, wallpaper and floorboards bought in Peace River, all of which he lost along with a shotgun and a .22 rifle. Ernest Scotty, who had refused to sign a release, lost his house anyway. Harry Lambert's widow, a native woman, lost the store. The only people who didn't lose anything valuable were the three holdout families and the priests, who by then had cleaned out their own cabins and hauled away the school.

"I was furious," says Muriel Oslie, who followed events closely. "The government had no right. I think they knew there was oil there."

"It had something to do with oil," says John Ed Laboucan.

In 1969, two years after Marten River was razed and burned, the land next to the site became the first producing oil field in Lubicon territory. The Golden Field, it is called. No oil has been found at Cadotte.

People speaking for the Alberta government say that finding a rich oil field beside the ruins of Marten River was a coincidence. Their explanations of why the village was razed and burned are inconsistent, however. The empty cabins posed a fire hazard, forestry officials say, although they don't explain why abandoned cabins have not been destroyed elsewhere in the territory, or why three homes were allowed to remain, or why their own ranger station near Marten River still stands abandoned more than twenty years later. "It's easier to provide services in one place," says Barb Deters, speaking for the Alberta attorney general. But the only service provided at Cadotte Lake in its first fifteen years was a pay telephone outside the Oblate store. On the other hand, no solid proof has surfaced connecting the destruction of Marten River with oil discoveries. Church correspondence doesn't mention oil, and Alberta's files are closed to the public on orders from the attorney general.

All that is known for sure is that the people of Marten River attended meetings that they didn't understand, signed papers that they couldn't read, heard promises that were never kept, and had their homes and possessions bulldozed and burned virtually without warning on what soon afterwards became part of a productive oil field.

5 THE
ONLY
GOOD
INDIAN...

THE REMOVAL OF Marten River produced a kind of "never again" mentality among Little Buffalo residents. Seeing their kinfolk manipulated and a village destroyed stiffened their resolve to stand their ground, a factor that might partly explain why the Lubicon people were to persist in the land-rights struggle long after the other interior bands had given up.

"If the people weren't pushed out of Marten River, we might not have reacted," says Joe T. Laboucan, a Lubicon elder, "but we didn't want to get pushed out of here."

Almost immediately, band members had to react to threats against Little Buffalo itself. Josie L'Hirondelle, the trader who had helped L'Heureux and Schmidt assess the reserve site and encouraged Rolland Smith with the school, died in 1966. A son, Fleuri L'Hirondelle, succeeded him as family patriarch, and Fleuri's main interest was farming. He proposed that some of the land in the promised reserve area be cultivated, inviting band members to help establish a farming cooperative. Band members went along with the idea, and when Fleuri applied for an agriculture lease, the status of the entire community came under scrutiny from provincial authorities.

A new agency called the Human Resources Development Authority assigned a field worker named Clarence Longmore to assess not only the farming proposal but also the area's economic potential generally. If prospects were found wanting, the agency was prepared to move everybody in Little Buffalo far to the northwest—out of the interior—to Paddle Prairie. No mention was made of native land rights.

The threat of removal was averted only when Longmore wrote glowingly of the area. In a report dated February 11, 1969, he said that conditions for duck and grouse hunting were "good to excellent," and that "the moose population in a 50 mile radius of Little Buffalo is rated as fairly numerous with an estimated potential harvest of around 1,600 animals per year." Good timber stands existed in parts of the region, making forestry a potential industry, and jobs in the oil-and-gas industries were certain to become available, he said. At present, roads were terrible. There were no health services, no waterworks, no telephones, no post office—no government services at all except the Quaker mission school, which had become part of the Alberta Northlands School Division. But people seemed happy, Longmore said. There were few problem drinkers. With proper adult-education and job-training programs, he said, the community had reason to prosper. On Longmore's recommendation, the farming lease was approved.

In early 1970, the Little Buffalo Farming Co-op was established, but soon it became a new source of Lubicon insecurity. Once the rocks were cleared, the fields broken for seeding, the fencing put up and the roads built, band members were fired one by one for reasons each of them protested as unjustified, while Fleuri L'Hirondelle gradually acquired control. All the board positions came to be filled by the L'Hirondelle family, and eventually no band members were left in the cooperative at all. Between band members and the L'Hirondelles a permanent rift developed, as the Metis family assumed control of the promised reserve. In 1971, compounding the band's unease, an oil-company crew drilled a test well at Little Buffalo's northern fringe.

At first, nobody in the band knew how to respond. People felt an acute need to secure a reserve, but nobody had replaced Joseph Laboucan as chief, leaving the community adrift at the broad political level. Finally, in 1973, Joe T. Laboucan and several others invited a vice-president of the Indian Association of Alberta to Little Buffalo to hear the band's concerns. "We got somebody to come up here from the Indian Association to tell us how to start working on a claim," Joe T. recalls. A community meeting was convened at the mission school, and afterwards the vice-president strolled with seven or eight of the leading hunters across a field as far as Joe T. Laboucan's cabin. Standing together in the front yard, the hunters elected Walter Whitehead as the new chief. They also elected Summer Joe Laboucan and his nephew John Stewart Laboucan as the band's first councillors. Shortly afterwards, the new chief and council rode to Three Creeks on horseback, catching a truck from there to Assumption, far to the north, to attend the annual general assembly of the Indian Association of Alberta. Whitehead addressed the gathering. Small, wiry and trembling with nervousness, he asked the association to help the Lubicon people secure their land rights, a plea that thrust the band into broader events shaping the country.

≈

Essentially, Whitehead's plea was to Harold Cardinal, president of the Indian Association of Alberta, and at the time one of the most significant native leaders in Canada. He was an unusual figure. Precocious, educated and personally ambitious, he was also deeply attached to his Indian traditions and identity. People recognized him both for his distinctive black-rimmed eyeglasses and for his beaded buckskin jacket, which he wore because it labelled him as a Canadian Indian and, he said, "because it's comfortable."

Cardinal grew up at the Sucker Creek reserve near Grouard, one of eighteen children, eight of whom died in childhood. He knew northern Alberta. His father, Frank, was an exceptional hunter and community leader, active in the pioneer days of the Indian Association and chief for many years at Sucker Creek. He often asked young Harold to translate at meetings when the boy was home from the mission school located ten miles away at Joussard. Cardinal hated the school for its bleak regimen and supercilious priests, and at sixteen he quit, arousing family concern. "If you come home as a dropout," his father warned, "you must settle for the life we have." Cardinal resumed classes the next year at a white high school in Edmonton, a characteristically audacious move: it was his first time in a city. In his final year, he served as student council president, and he went on to study sociology at St. Patrick's College in Ottawa, joining campus organizations that led to jobs with the Canadian Union of Students and the Canadian Indian Youth Council. Soon he was crisscrossing the country meeting other activists, and in the summer of 1968, at the age of twenty-three, he was elected president of the Indian Association of Alberta.

Within days, another fresh political figure, whose views on Indians were much different from Cardinal's, won a resounding election victory as Liberal prime minister. Pierre Trudeau spoke of creating a Just Society in which both French and English would be official languages, enabling six million French-Canadians to deal with the federal government in their mother tongue. Partly, his aim was to deflate Quebec nationalism, which had created demands of "special status" for Quebec within confederation. Trudeau opposed special treatment of any cultural group. "I am against any policy based on race or nationalism," he said, including the idea of Indian status as guaranteed in the treaties.

Indians "should be treated more and more like Canadians," Trudeau said, as he instructed his Indian Affairs minister, Jean Chrétien, to revise Indian policy. Chrétien funded regional Indian groups to conduct research and express their views, and a year later, in 1969, he released his White Paper on Indian Policy. "White paper" is the name commonly given to a report on a government's final policy proposals, but this time the term acquired unintended irony. Chrétien had ignored Indian views, opting for an assimilation program—virtually advocating, critics said, that Indians turn white.

Special Indian rights were the source of Indian problems, not the solution, the paper argued. The solution was "equality," sometimes referred to as "non- discrimination." Equality would be achieved by dismantling the Indian Affairs department within five years and scrapping the Indian Act. Responsibilities for Indians would devolve to the provinces, and a transitional Indian Lands Act would transfer federal trusteeship of reserves to something called "Indian control," a step towards individual ownership.

The proposals shocked native leaders. At Chrétien's forums they had recommended changes to the Indian Act, not its abolition, and they had talked of safeguarding Indian land, not putting it into private hands. They had also insisted that aboriginal hunting, fishing and trapping rights be entrenched in the constitution, not laid open to the whims of provincial legislatures.

"The only good Indian is a non-Indian," said Harold Cardinal, summing up the paper in a witty paraphrase. Cardinal had a gift for satire. His response to the Chrétien doctrine was a book called *The Unjust Society*, in which he called Indians coopted by the government "Uncle Tomahawks" and dubbed barriers to Indian well-being "the buckskin curtain." Canada, he wrote, cares more about preserving rare whooping cranes than about Indians, "and Canada . . . does not ask its cranes to become Canada geese."

Early newspaper stories glibly branded Cardinal an angry young man; but as efforts increased among Indians to stop the White Paper, he emerged as the most prominent native figure in the country—travelling, making speeches, giving interviews and whipping up Indian pride. He coaxed white people to revise their image of Indians as helpless, incompetent and apathetic, and he challenged Indians to fully accept their Indianness as a way of building self-respect. "As long as Indian people are expected to become what they are not— white men—there is no basis on which they can meaningfully participate in Canadian society," he said. "Before I can be a usefully participating and contributing citizen I must be allowed to further develop a sense of pride and confidence in myself as an Indian. I must be allowed to be a red tile in the Canadian mosaic, not forced to become an unseen and misplaced white tile."

Cardinal helped make Indians a force to be reckoned with. He was a founder of the National Indian Brotherhood and, along with his book, helped write a 100-page rebuttal to the White Paper, a document put forward by the Alberta chiefs and around which all major Indian organizations coalesced. *Citizens Plus*, it was titled, but everybody called it "the Red Paper."

"Recognition of Indian status is essential for justice," it said unequivocally. "Justice requires that the special history, rights and circumstances of Indian People be recognized." Point for point, it knocked Chrétien's proposals, emphasizing instead the importance of land and treaty rights, and suggesting ways to improve the well-being of native people through education, economic development and better living conditions on reserves. In June 1970, Cardinal submitted the Red Paper directly to the prime minister at a tense meeting between the full federal cabinet and national native leaders in the cavernous Railway Committee Room on Parliament Hill. Trudeau's response took virtually everyone by surprise.

"I'm sure that we were very naive in some of the statements we made in the [white] paper," the prime minister said. "We had perhaps the prejudices of small 'l' liberals, and white men at that, who thought that equality meant the same law for everybody."

≈

With those words, the White Paper was officially withdrawn, leaving Cardinal free for a while to focus on northern Alberta. Being from Sucker Creek, he knew that the interior bands had been overlooked, and after Whitehead's presentation to the assembly Cardinal made the land-entitlement question a priority. The issue also became urgent for other reasons. In October 1973, OPEC, the Organization of Petroleum Exporting Countries, declared an embargo against the United States and Europe, quadrupling world oil prices and prompting the Alberta government to build roads into the Lesser Slave interior. An all-weather road was begun east from Peace River towards Little Buffalo.

By then, it was clear that northern Alberta contained the biggest oil supply on earth. The substrata of the Athabasca River valley and a large portion of the Lesser Slave interior were found to be soaked in a thick, tar-like oil. The "oil sands," they were called, or "tar sands." Estimates of total quantities ran to 800 billion barrels—greater than the entire world's conventional oil reserves, judged to be less than 600 billion barrels. The problem was how to extract the oil, an expensive and technologically complex proposition, but the hike in oil prices appeared to favour development. Conventional pool-like deposits also appeared prevalent in the region, judging by the Golden Field discovery at Marten River and promising signs farther east near Loon, Trout and Peerless lakes.

Cardinal welcomed development. He spoke of oil development as "an obvious and exciting opportunity" to improve the Indian's lot in places like Sucker Creek. As long as treaty rights were respected, native land rights upheld, and special training and hiring programs implemented, Cardinal was confident that native people would benefit from the new jobs and services that industrial activity promised.

Almost as soon as he started talking about rights and opportunities for Indians, however, Cardinal felt a chill in his dealings with government and oil-company representatives. More and more he was getting what he called "a Colgate smile and a friendly handshake" from officials who had previously been warm towards him, and he began to worry seriously whether oil interests were preparing to push aside entire bands.

In 1974, Cardinal advised the Indian Affairs minister, Jean Chrétien, that the Indian Association would sponsor an aboriginal-rights case on behalf of the isolated communities north of Lesser Slave Lake, with a view to negotiating a land agreement with Ottawa.

"Certain of the Indian people in Alberta have a claim to that area of land now known as the Athabasca Tar Sands," he advised the minister.

Cardinal coordinated preparations through the Isolated Communities Advisory Board, a grassroots organization that had formed to address the kind of insecurities that people at Little Buffalo were feeling. Its beginnings can be traced to a tall, expansive trapper named William Beaver, who in 1969 began to talk about how to secure a reserve for the 150 people living at Trout Lake—half of them still on the Wabasca treaty list, half of them not on any list at all because of McCrimmon and other circumstances. "We're all the same," Beaver reminded everybody. "Let's make one organization and work together to get our rights." When residents of nearby Peerless Lake asked what was going on, Beaver helped them form a similar association. He did the same at Loon and Sandy lakes, and when the Chipewyan Lake people made inquiries, Beaver suggested that all the bands pursue land and treaty rights together. Because so many people in the interior were classified as "non-Indian," the Alberta government saw the board not as an Indian rights organization but as a Metis association, making it eligible for provincial funding. The board received $50,000 in its first year and $100,000 the next. By the time Cardinal became involved, the board included six communities: Trout, Peerless, Chipewyan, Sandy, Cadotte and Loon lakes. Soon the Lubicon Lake band joined. Cardinal hired researchers to compile historical documents and to interview elders, and he engaged a Calgary law firm to help prepare the case for negotiations.

The toothpaste smiles quickly turned still frostier, tipping Cardinal that Alberta would oppose a land-rights challenge and that federal authorities might do the same. "Somebody in the federal Cabinet took me aside and told me that no matter how much we lobbied, it wouldn't do any good," Cardinal recalls. "In spite of obvious facts that were not being disputed, I was told the only way we could get cabinet's attention on the Lubicon situation and the other isolated communities was a court decision in our favour."

Cardinal and the isolated communities were getting caught in an intense rivalry that had come to dominate national politics: an oil-price dispute personified in tensions between Pierre Trudeau and Peter Lougheed, Alberta's new Progressive Conservative premier. Lougheed had swept to power in 1971, upsetting thirty-six years of Social Credit rule. When world oil prices quadrupled in 1973, he demanded that Ottawa increase the export price of Alberta oil and insisted that most of the increase go to Alberta coffers. Trudeau rejected the call. "The whole country should take benefit from any windfall profits," he said, enraging Lougheed and provoking Alberta motorists to sport bumper stickers saying, "Let the eastern bastards freeze in the dark."

Officially, Lougheed distanced himself from the slogan, but his whole political career was to be characterized by a fierce combativeness towards Ottawa and by an abiding resentment towards what he viewed as central Canadian hegemony. He lumped native people with the federal camp. Since Indians were under federal jurisdiction, and since Indian lands were legally federal lands held in trust, Lougheed viewed the assertion of Indian land rights in the Lesser Slave interior as a kind of federal Trojan horse—a means by which Ottawa could deprive Alberta of some of its oil-rich territory. To ease tensions, federal authorities were assuring Lougheed that Ottawa would not support the Indians unless a court ordered otherwise.

Cardinal pondered his legal options. One was to put the entire aboriginal-rights question before the courts, asking a judge to decide whether the isolated communities held unextinguished aboriginal title to the Lesser Slave interior. Another option was to seek an injunction to halt all oil activity in the interior pending a negotiated land settlement with Ottawa. Either case would be expensive, drawn out and nasty, and in the end Cardinal decided on a procedural route that he thought would be less divisive but that would push both governments at least to take the land question seriously. He recommended that the leaders of the isolated communities file a caveat at the Alberta land registration office declaring a legal interest in their hunting and trapping lands. Such a caveat had no force in law—it couldn't prevent anybody from doing anything—but a notice declaring that the ownership of the land was contested might make some developers nervous, Cardinal speculated, increasing the pressure on both governments to address the issue.

Acting on the recommendation, Lubicon chief Walter Whitehead and headmen of the other isolated communities submitted a caveat on October 27, 1975, formally asking the public to take notice that seven Indian bands north of Lesser Slave Lake claimed an interest in 33,000 square miles of land between the Peace and Athabasca rivers, "by virtue of unextinguished Aboriginal Rights."

"We have no desire to frustrate development," Cardinal told a news conference, "only to share in it." But he warned that if the two governments and the oil industry did not take native people into account, he and the interior bands would take tougher legal action. He wanted to make three points clear, he said. "One, we are not prepared to compromise in our quest . . . for training and development. Two, we are not prepared to compromise in our quest for economic independence. Three, we are not prepared to compromise in our quest to gain an adequate land base for the Indian people of the Isolated Communities who are the original inhabitants of the area."

Unexpectedly, the provincial land registrar refused to register the caveat. On advice from the attorney general's office, he instead referred it to the Supreme Court of Alberta, asking the judge whether he had to file the caveat without proof that the caveators retained aboriginal rights.

The manoeuvre meant that the interior bands faced a court fight after all, and Cardinal applied to Ottawa for legal funding. As trustee of Indian interests, the federal government would help, Cardinal assured the headmen. But there were delays, and on the day of the pretrial hearing, Cardinal was surprised to see two lawyers from the federal justice department in the courtroom. He was even more surprised when one of the lawyers, Ivan Whitehall, said that Ottawa would participate in the case on Alberta's side, arguing that Treaty Eight had extinguished aboriginal rights throughout northern Alberta. Outraged, Cardinal cabled Trudeau, saying: "Your government must instruct the department of justice that it is either to intervene in the case in support of the position of the caveators or not at all." But the federal lawyers proceeded with their intervention, staking out a position from which Whitehall and his colleagues have not wavered since: aboriginal title to the interior can be regarded as extinguished.

More surprises were in store. When the caveat case came to trial on September 7, 1976, the lawyer for Alberta, Howard Irving, asked for a postponement. He said the Supreme Court of Canada would soon be ruling on a similar caveat application in the Northwest Territories, and the decision likely would have a bearing on the Alberta case. The proceedings were adjourned.

The Supreme Court of Canada judges ruled less than three months later. They said that the caveat application in the Northwest Territories was not valid, but suggested that if such a caveat were filed in Alberta, the registrar would have to accept it. Alberta Indian leaders were pleased. The isolated communities had all but won.

When the case resumed, however, the Alberta government lawyer asked for another postponement. Howard Irving said that the government was preparing legislation which, if passed, would have "a very substantial impact on the fileability of the caveat." Again proceedings were adjourned.

The legislation being prepared came to be known as Bill 29, and it revealed to what extraordinary lengths the Lougheed government was prepared to go to subvert native rights over the Athabasca Tar Sands. When the Alberta attorney general, Jim Foster, tabled the bill in the legislature on April 27, 1977, he talked about "tidying the law" and "plugging a loophole" in existing statutes. He said that the law would now read the way the government had always intended it to read. "There is no attempt in this legislation to remove rights," he said.

In truth, the government was preparing to pass legislation to win the court case—a measure almost unheard of in a democracy. Bill 29 would change the wording of the Alberta Land Titles Act to prohibit caveats on unpatented Crown land, and the law would be applied retroactively. (Speaking in an aside years later, Lougheed himself told the legislature that the bill was a direct response to the tar sands caveat. The bill "had to do with the dispute with the Metis [isolated] settlements with regard to their mineral claims and the legal advice we received," Alberta *Hansard* records the premier as saying on April 16, 1984.)

As the bill made its way to final reading, the president of the Isolated Communities Advisory Board, William Beaver, organized a rally at an Edmonton church hall. Guest speakers included author Pierre Berton, director at the time of the Canadian Civil Liberties Association.

"The government says it is tidying up the law," Berton scoffed. "'Tidying up'—that's a wonderful phrase. Take that phrase and fling it back in their faces! Make them regret they ever said it! Next time you see a member of the provincial government, ask him: 'Tidied up any laws today? Planning on any housekeeping with the law tomorrow?' "

But the public all but ignored the issue, and the federal government was silent. Bill 29 passed in May 1977, and when the caveat case reconvened in court, the judge dismissed the application as no longer having a basis in law. Funding for the advisory board ended.

"Totally undemocratic," said Alberta Opposition Leader Grant Notley of Bill 29.

"Discriminatory, immoral and a travesty of justice," said Jim Roberts, president-elect of the United Church of Canada.

"Subtle terrorism," said Burke Barker, a law professor at the University of Alberta.

"A total abuse of power," said William Beaver.

"There was a sense of unreality," Harold Cardinal said years later. "It isn't normal for a government to bring in legislation amending their laws retroactively in the middle of a court session."

The Treaty Eight commission of
civil servants, Mounties and clergymen leaves Edmonton for the
North on May 29, 1899, at around
noon. The commission's failure to
penetrate the Lesser Slave interior
led to early misunderstandings
about the Lubicon Lake Cree. NA-
TIONAL ARCHIVES OF CANADA /C5007

David Laird's mark on history has
faded now, but he commanded attention when he was alive for his
six-foot-four stature and uncom-
monly loud voice. His aristocratic
mien was admired by some people
and ridiculed by others. "Dour
Davie," detractors called him. COUR-
TESY DETSELIG ENTERPRISES

Left, top: Malcolm McCrimmon (*right*) stands aloof from the rest of the treaty-annuity party before leaving Faust on June 3, 1942, the day that he ended the era of benign neglect towards the Lubicon people. Left to right are the flight mechanic; Napoleon L'Heureux; Bishop Langlois; the pilot (*in doorway*); E. Galibois, the clerk; and Pant Schmidt. COURTESY YVONNETTE COMEAU

Left, bottom: Malcolm McCrimmon poses for a staff photo in 1957, when he was Registrar for Indian Membership. "I was a power unto myself," he was to say of his position. COURTESY ANGUS MAC-DONALD

Below: Chief Joseph Laboucan, in the black hat, stands with fellow band members at Lubicon Lake sometime in the 1940s, probably at treaty time. The photograph is part of a collection of old pictures sewn into a scrapbook and kept by band elder John Felix Laboucan. TOM WALKER, *CALGARY HERALD*

Two Lubicon band members sing and beat hand drums at a tea-dance ceremony in 1956. Such occasions, usually held in spring and fall, were a means for the living to seek courage, strength and wisdom from past generations through prayers and offerings. COURTESY ROLLAND SMITH

After the 1956 ceremony, the skeleton of a tea-dance lodge stands on the prairie at Lubicon Lake. Like other northern Cree bands, the Lubicon people believed in a benevolent Great Spirit and feared an evil one. COURTESY ROLLAND SMITH

During a tense exchange on Parliament Hill in June 1970, Prime Minister Pierre Trudeau (*left*) addresses a national gathering of Indian leaders, while Indian Affairs Minister Jean Chrétien (*back to camera*) looks on. Harold Cardinal (*centre, wearing glasses*) tabled "the Red Paper" in response to the government's White Paper on Indian Policy. CANAPRESS PHOTO SERVICE—RAY GIGUERE

Wearing an oil-company insignia doesn't appear to bother elder Summer Joe Laboucan as he relaxes outside his cabin at Fish Lake. "Joe" is a popular name among Lubicon members, and each is known by a nickname. JOHN GODDARD

Terry Laboucan pauses while replacing a broken ax handle at Fish Lake. As an infant, he was bundled into John Halcrow's wagon for the move to Marten River. JOHN GODDARD

Walter Whitehead, the former Lubicon chief, checks a net on Fish Lake, so-called because it is one of the few bodies of water in the territory deep enough to have fish in it. Most of the lakes freeze to the bottom in winter. JOHN GODDARD

6 PICKING UP THE PIECES

AFTER THE Isolated Communities Advisory Board collapsed, members of the Lubicon band urged Bernard Ominayak to serve as chief. It was a pivotal moment. The entire band was still bewildered about outside rules of land ownership—about how a government could sell exploration and drilling rights to people newly arrived in Lubicon territory while granting no rights at all to the people who had used and occupied the land since before recorded time. Band members were awed by the power the government possessed. The laws were the government's laws, the courts the government's courts; and when the courts ruled in favour of the Indians, the government could change the laws. Ominayak knew that securing Lubicon land rights under such circumstances would not be easy. He understood the personal sacrifices that would be required and the amount of time he would be forced to spend away from his young family, but in 1978, at the age of twenty-eight, he let his name stand, and there is a sense in the decision of a man taking up his destiny.

"What choice do we have?" he sometimes says when asked how he carries on. Ominayak has a way of deflecting questions from himself. He shuns the limelight, and even at the height of his renown in the late 1980s, when he was famous in Alberta and well known elsewhere, he managed to remain an enigma. Details of his life are hard to come by, partly because there are no records to draw upon and partly because he has spent much of his life virtually alone in the bush. Only when pushed does Ominayak disclose biographical particulars, and others close to him say little. "The simple way to put it is he really believes in the people he's working for," says a younger brother, Larry, who resembles Ominayak in appearance and demeanour, and who has been a band councillor for as long as Ominayak has been chief. "He believes they should get what they're asking for. That's why he's been trying so hard."

Ominayak was born at Lubicon Lake on April 3, 1950, the first in a family of six children. His earliest memories are of watching his father, George, load a wagon for the autumn trip north to Bison Lake, a three-day ride over muddy, hand-cut trails to the limit of Lubicon territory. The wagon would sometimes sink to its bumpers in mud along the way, and detours would have to be taken around the worst spots. At Bison Lake there was a small settlement. The family would visit there and set their horses free to graze all winter in the surrounding brush, then continue for another three hours by dog sled to the winter cabin.

"I was always trying to go trapping with my dad," Ominayak recalls. At the cabin, he and his brother Leonard played on snowshoes at an early age, practiced shooting with bows and arrows, and hitched up dogs for sled rides. They learned from their mother, Bella, how to snare rabbits and squirrels for fur, which they would clean with moose bones in the evenings and stretch on racks to dry. But Ominayak lived for the times his father took him trapping.

"We never talked that much," he says of the outings. "It was a situation where you had to learn things by keeping your ears and eyes open, always trying to watch what was taking place. It was learning on the job. I started getting to know the area, where to get certain animals and when. I would watch my dad, watch where he would put a trap and how he would set it up. Then one day he said, 'Okay, it's your turn,' and when I tried it, I realized there were a couple of things I didn't know. He just threw this at me, 'Okay, it's your turn,' and I realized watching wasn't good enough, I had to really pay attention. I knew that I was going to have to learn in order to survive."

George trapped an area twenty miles square. Wolf, lynx and wolverine usually brought the best prices, and still do, but mink, fisher, marten, coyote and beaver were all prized as well. Travel was almost exclusively by dog sled. It was slow, and meant extra work harnessing and feeding the dogs, but they rewarded his efforts. "Once, my dad fell through the ice going across the lake with his lead dog," Ominayak says. "Every time he tried to climb out, he broke through again. The dog kept running around and around. Finally it crept close to the edge and gave my dad its paw. Then it backed up and pulled him out."

In spring, the family would return to Lubicon Lake. Ominayak remembers riding a horse through the woods along moose trails and running through the reeds by the lakeshore with Leonard, scaring ducks into the air for their father to shoot at from a canoe. Sometimes Ominayak would go with his mother to pick herbs and berries or to help plant vegetable seeds. When he was old enough, he travelled with the hunting parties, staying behind with the horses as the men fanned into the bush. If somebody shot a moose, it was shared.

"Life was a cycle," he says. To celebrate it, the whole regional band came together at Lubicon Lake twice a year, in spring and fall, for a tea dance—a combined religious, political and social gathering. Men would cut poles to build a tea-dance house, structured like several tepees joined together and walled with canvases and moose hides. "It used to get so crowded we'd take turns going inside," Ominayak says. "Wagons and horses would be parked all around, and sometimes there'd be a second tea-dance house a short distance away."

Like other northern Cree bands, the Lubicon believed in a benevolent Great Spirit and feared an evil one, but the tea dance was also a means for the living to seek courage, strength and wisdom from past generations through prayers and offerings. The ceremony began at sundown. Everyone crowded around the inside periphery of the tent-house, seated on spruce boughs and blankets. Four fires blazed in a row down the middle, representing the four seasons, and all movement around the four fires was clockwise, symbolizing the sun's rotations around the earth. The door flap was at one end, and at the other end sat a medicine man with four drummers, each drum made from a piece of hide stretched over a ring of birch wood and hit with a stick or animal bone. The drummers began with a song to the Great Spirit, the sun, and relatives who had died. Then the medicine man held a plateful of food and tobacco above his head in prayer, placing it afterwards on the fire nearest to him as a sacrifice to the ancestors. As the drumming resumed, four elders danced around the circle. Each picked up one of the four carved staffs standing between the fires, and each carried close to his heart a doll filled with tufts of hair from departed relatives, a signal for the ancestor spirits to return to join the group for the ceremony. After the first dance, a long pipe was passed around and everyone, including children, drew from it. More singing followed, then food was served, heaps of it—moose, duck, goose, bannock and tea—with each family returning part of their share to the medicine man's plate for a second burnt offering to the ancestors. All night long the ceremony continued, until sunrise, alternating between feasting, singing, praying and dancing, with everyone allowed to join in a long pulsating line around the fires.

For Ominayak, seasonal rhythms shifted abruptly when he started school at the age of nine. That fall, his father headed north alone, leaving Bella behind with the preschoolers at Lubicon Lake and sending Ominayak and his brother Leonard to the mission school at Little Buffalo. Both boys were lonely. "Leonard used to cry just about every night," Ominayak recalls. "I didn't cry. I just wanted to do something about it." Several times he ran home, a six-mile trek through the bush. Once, he slipped out after vespers, running through the moonlit woods until he reached home, surprising the rest of the family when they woke up in the morning. But a teacher came to take him back. "It wasn't so much the conditions at the school," he says. "I just didn't want to be away from home."

He remembers once leading the other boys against the class bully. Inspired by a Bible lesson, he and the others bound the bully's hands and feet to a cross that they made with spare lumber and spikes from the coat rack, then they left the boy stranded off the ground for several hours until he was found by one of the teachers. "They used to keep an eye on me," Ominayak says.

To solve the running-away problem, George took Bella and the younger children north with him after Christmas. "We were stuck," Ominayak says. But the next summer George moved the whole family to Little Buffalo so that the children could both go to school and live at home. Ominayak began to enjoy classes more. Rolland and Thelma Smith had left by then—they have no recollection of the boy—but their successors made an impression on Ominayak. They talked about big towns and different types of people: white people and other groups of Indians. And although the Bible lessons sounded strange in some ways, Ominayak says they mostly reinforced what the children were taught at home: not to take anything that doesn't belong to you and to give in return when somebody gives you something. "That was part of the way I was growing up anyway, and when the Bible came along, talking about what was right and wrong, it all coincided," he says. "I learned a lot about respecting any person regardless of age, even if the other person doesn't know as much, and especially to listen to your elders."

The teachers were strict, but Ominayak came from a well-ordered home. On weekdays, everybody was up early and out the door, and after school the children helped their mother by fetching water or chopping wood. Bella couldn't speak or read English and still can't, but she considered schooling for her children vital. "You've got to work if you're going to survive," Ominayak remembers her saying. "And that goes for schoolwork, too."

Community leaders also encouraged the boy in school. They saw from an early age that Ominayak was observant and quick, and some of the hunters who had helped build the mission—people like John Felix Laboucan and his cousins Edward and Summer Joe—began to groom the boy for leadership. The men didn't understand what a government was exactly, or how to approach one, and they saw in Ominayak a chance to develop a leader who could take their case to the outside world.

Ominayak remembers their discussions at tea dances and on other occasions. Lubicon society is patriarchal; the focus is on the men, with status and authority traditionally acquired through hunting ability. Women and children were generally not part of political discussions, and even today no woman has stepped into a leadership role in the community. The hunters would congregate to exchange news of white people causing problems with other bands and to speculate whether settlers might one day move into the Lubicon area. "I don't think anybody really thought white people were going to be coming in," Ominayak says, as though the idea were beyond imagining then. "It was more a matter of trying to settle the thing and trying to get some of the benefits that went along with land, like housing. They kept saying I should stay in school as long as possible."

Encouraged by his parents and the leading hunters, Ominayak did well in school, winning the prize for memory work one year, and advanced with three other children to the vocational school at Grouard, near where Treaty Eight was first signed. The school had a good reputation, taking pupils from all over northern Alberta who might otherwise not have gone beyond the primary grades.

"It was a good school," says Melvin McKenzie of Peace River, who shared an eight-bed dorm with Ominayak in 1967–68. "The meals were good, the teachers were good, and they always had some kind of entertainment going on weekends, like dances or something. We had a hockey team called the Northern Lights and an outdoor rink right outside the dorms." McKenzie remembers Ominayak as a good friend. "He was very smart in school," he says. "He liked music and stuff like that, and he used to go to the dances. He didn't really carry much of a conversation, but if you started talking to him he would answer, and he always liked to help. He'd do anything for anybody, he was that type of guy. He would give his shirt off his back if he had to, and if somebody wanted to stay with him in Little Buffalo for a weekend they were always welcome."

With his twin brother, McKenzie used to drive to Peace River every third or fourth weekend during his one year at Grouard, often taking others who wanted a ride. Ominayak would almost always go, sometimes staying with the McKenzies in Peace River and sometimes managing to get all the way to Little Buffalo, which was open for much of the year by then to four-wheel-drive vehicles.

"He was a very shy guy," says Beverly Mitchell, who with her sister Twiggy often made the trip as well. "If you talked to him he would talk, but I was totally shocked when I first saw him on TV a few years ago—he was always so shy."

Half the school day was taken up with English, arithmetic and other academic subjects, the other half devoted to classes in carpentry, welding and mechanics, courses at which Ominayak did well. After school he sometimes went rodeo riding with a few other boys, led by a dorm supervisor who travelled the summer rodeo circuit. Ominayak has an affinity for horses and still keeps more than thirty of his own in a vast corral across from his house. He remembers his father one year buying a frisky horse at Bison Lake and walking it all the way back to Little Buffalo to be broken. His parents warned him not to go near it, but the trainer didn't show up for days and Ominayak secretly became acquainted. He would approach it, pet its muzzle, talk to it; and when the horse began answering his call, Ominayak put a saddle on it and walked it around. When the trainer still didn't come, Ominayak rode it himself for short intervals, hanging on when it bucked, until he was riding the horse normally. Keeping his secret, he watched with amusement as the trainer gingerly approached the animal only to find it tame.

"The dorm supervisor asked us who wanted to ride," Ominayak recalls. "He said, 'Meet me at seven o'clock and we'll try a few of you guys out.' So I went and he put me on a steer, then a horse, and they bucked and kicked but I was used to it, so he kept after me. He tried to get me and a couple of others into this more, to travel with him in the summer. I had all the equipment and we went to a couple of rodeos. I knew that it was something I could do very well at, but I didn't like the big crowds."

The supervisor, who has since died, also coached hockey and other sports, and as an Indian himself was known as someone who made extra efforts to encourage students he saw as promising. When Ominayak decided to quit school towards the end of grade ten, he went to the supervisor to say good-bye. The man gave him his phone number, offering to give Ominayak a ride back to school if he changed his mind.

"But I didn't like it outside," Ominayak says. "I was homesick. My people were here."

John Felix, Edward, Summer Joe and Ominayak's father all tried to persuade him to return to school after Easter, saying someone would eventually have to deal with the land issue. But Ominayak had made up his mind. He trapped with his dad for two or three years and worked summers with the farming cooperative, gradually accumulating a private herd of nine cows that he boarded there for a monthly fee. Then he noticed people being let go, as Fleuri L'Hirondelle gradually acquired control. Eventually Ominayak was cut too. He and his brother George, the third in the family, sometimes took jobs with a logging outfit southwest of Peace River. Ominayak ran a skidder, his brother a power saw.

Whatever happened, Ominayak seemed to land on his feet. He never looked for work; it came to him. He learned to handle money well, and in every way seemed to be developing as a man of exceptional ability. Soon he took up housekeeping with a childhood friend, Louise Cardinal, a warm, cheerful, hard-working woman who had grown up at Lubicon and Bison lakes and had also gone to the mission school. He built a log cabin for them next to the house he grew up in, not far from the school, and they started a family that eventually included five children: two girls and three boys.

At around the same time, Ominayak began to assume the kind of community responsibility that senior band members had long been urging on him. At the first signs of serious oil activity at Little Buffalo, he was elected secretary to a community association founded by

Fleuri L'Hirondelle, which met occasionally with Alberta officials about local services, or lack of them. In 1975, he beat out L'Hirondelle as the association's president and was soon elected a band councillor as well. Acting in both capacities (the association was later phased out), he became one of the most regular delegates to meetings of the Isolated Communities Advisory Board.

Ominayak almost never spoke at meetings. He watched from the back the way he had watched his father set traps. "I was trying to figure things out," he says. He learned how meetings were run, and how issues were raised and voted on. He also noticed a lack of commitment among many of the people involved, including a few senior ones. Resolutions would be passed and mandates given, but much of the work never got done. Worse, some delegates were more interested in travel allowances than issues, driving to meetings in Slave Lake or High Prairie mostly as an occasion to drink. Ominayak also learned of chiefs taking funds earmarked for their communities and kicking back a percentage to Indian Affairs employees, a scandal Harold Cardinal tried but failed to expose publicly in 1977.

"I started to realize that some of our own chiefs could be controlled," Ominayak says. "I saw that once you attained a certain position, it was tempting to start playing the politician, and that once that happens you're no good to anybody, because you've forgotten your people."

In 1978, he agreed to serve as Lubicon chief, taking up the role that the older hunters had long been grooming him for. Almost immediately, the oil boom began. The last section of all-weather highway from Peace River to Little Buffalo came under construction. Seismic and drilling crews were everywhere. "I was riding on my guts," he recalls. "Everything was happening very fast, and there was a lot of pressure on me. I didn't know which way to move, I only knew there had to be a way, and that's what I was doing—fighting to find a way to try to get this land question settled."

Federal employees kept telling him, incorrectly, that bands without land qualified for no federal funding, so Ominayak took a job as manager at the Cadotte store that the Oblate priests had built. He spent much of his salary driving to meetings in Slave Lake or High Prairie or wherever one was being held: regional meetings of the Metis association, or meetings coordinated by Harold Cardinal in a new push to bring the full aboriginal-rights case to court.

Ominayak would stay until a meeting ended at midnight or one o'clock, then drive home to be at work at nine the next morning. He was working too hard and not sleeping properly, and for a while he was drinking in binges. His brother George had died. The two had been working together at a logging camp, and when Ominayak's work was finished he had returned to Little Buffalo, leaving George to hitchhike home. The next day, the car in which George was riding crashed and George was killed. Partly blaming himself, Ominayak would sit alone for days at a time with a case of Alberta Premium rye.

"I never drank at meetings, and I never lost the intention of doing things to help the community, but I knew I had a problem," Ominayak recalls. "One day I just said, 'That's it.' I woke up with a terrific hangover, coughing blood, and I reached for a twenty-sixer sitting on the counter with three or four inches left in it. I had it in my hand and I was going to take a drink. And I threw it out. Since then I haven't touched a drop."

The clean break testifies to Ominayak's iron resolve, which he was applying equally to Cardinal's renewed drive to assert land rights in the interior. Cardinal had been going through heady times. For eight months in 1977, he had held the top federal Indian Affairs post in Alberta, a controversial appointment because no Indian had previously held such high bureaucratic office. He demoted senior people, initiated stricter auditing procedures and began to investigate dispersements of a $10-million government loan when he suspected chiefs of kicking back money to department personnel. Cardinal was fired, the case left uninvestigated. He resurfaced as head of his own consulting firm, intent on making enough money through native business ventures to take the full aboriginal-rights case to the Federal Court of Canada. By 1979, however, Cardinal's plan was faltering. Ominayak noticed that one of Cardinal's closest associates, Fred Lennarson, no longer seemed to be around.

Lennarson had been "the guy doing all the work," Ominayak says. "I never talked to him at meetings but I would arrive early and Fred was always there. He was always writing and making phone calls, and I knew this guy was trying to do his job." When Ominayak asked where Lennarson was, Cardinal said only that Lennarson had "decided to go in a different direction." When Ominayak asked, "But wasn't that the guy doing all the work?" Cardinal said only, "Yes, that's the guy." Ominayak said he would like to invite Lennarson to work for the Lubicon band. "Fine," Ominayak remembers Cardinal saying, and not long afterwards Cardinal's dream to affirm aboriginal title to the Lesser Slave interior collapsed in a heap of unpaid bills. Barely into his thirties, more or less burnt out, one of the decade's most valiant champions of Indian rights returned home to Sucker Creek to raise cattle.

Night after night, Ominayak called Lennarson at his home in Edmonton, asking questions. Standing outside the Cadotte store feeding quarters into the pay phone, he asked whether oil development could be controlled and how the Lubicon people might secure operating funds like other bands. He asked what the Indian Affairs department did and what the differences between the federal and provincial governments were, the distinction still not clear to him at the time. Slowly, he built a rapport. At meetings with the band elders and two councillors, Billy Joe Laboucan and Ominayak's brother Larry, everyone kept saying, "You've got to convince Fred, you've got to," and Ominayak would say, "I know I've got to." But when he began to ask Lennarson pointedly for help, Lennarson hemmed and hawed. He was considering a job with the governor of Colorado and other options having nothing to do with aboriginal matters. "Bernard was like a trapper going after game," Lennarson recalls. Eventually, he let himself be caught.

7 OUR WHITE MAN

FIRST PART-TIME, then full-time, then double-time, Fred Lennarson applied his extraordinary stamina and intellect to the cause. "The elders call me their white man," he says. "They'll say, 'We'd better check with our white man,' which is how people use experts, and they understand that. I'm their white man." But he is no ordinary white man. Without him it is almost inconceivable that the case of a small, northern Alberta Indian band could have come to international attention and to the forefront of the aboriginal-rights struggle in Canada. He says he was able to help because the band was culturally intact, still functioning well as a society and blessed with an exceptionally talented chief and group of elders. But Lennarson also brought to the case a singular combination of skills and experience. "I'm smart," he acknowledged once. "I know a lot, I have a lot of brain power, I have had a good education and good experience, and I work hard."

Lennarson is six feet tall and hefty, and retains a youthful, boyish presence. His most striking trait is his vigour. He requires only five hours' sleep a night and can function for extended periods on even less, allowing him to accomplish in one day what most people accomplish in two. "We whipped that baby out!" he'll say to express delight at liberating a confidential document; and to describe an astute move by the band against an opponent, he'll exclaim: "All of a sudden this bunch of Indians was jamming up the works!" The informality belies rare organizational prowess. Lennarson has a genius for information gathering and analysis, enabling him to distill great quantities of facts into a clearly defined problem, or trend, or set of developments. He spots patterns most people discern only in retrospect and delineates them with such precision that solutions often become obvious.

To the Lubicon campaign, Lennarson also brought a hard-edged political activism that shocked people who were accustomed to dealing politely with Indian oppression in Canada. Lennarson is a radical in the way that Chicago social activist Saul Alinsky used the term: "Every shaking advance of mankind toward equality and justice has come from the radical. He hits, he hurts, he is dangerous." People in power in Alberta have variously denounced Lennarson as a guru, a communist, a draft dodger, a Black Panther, a member of the American Indian Movement and "the cause of the Lubicon problem." They've been offended by his aggressiveness and they've been spooked at his ability to continue working and travelling and putting out newsletters when he appears to have no income. Their attacks are inaccurate but not wholly gratuitous. Lennarson can be a ferocious combatant, swift to depict people who disagree with him as not merely incorrect but stupid, petty and selfish. He berates many of them by letter, chiding one public official for his "pompous, arrogant ignorance" and another for "the untrue and deliberately manipulative things which you said." He has no patience for soft-pedalling. When an incoming letter begins, "I sympathize with the situation you describe, but . . .", Lennarson is apt to reply, "You are siding with the enemy and should expect to be treated as such" or "Don't expect to get away with prettying up ugly reality with baloney." When one Indian Affairs minister, Bill McKnight, made known through a colleague that he resented Lennarson calling him a liar, Lennarson replied: "Tell him to stop being a liar, then."

Lennarson came to the Lubicon issue in a particularly roundabout way. He grew up as a gifted child of privilege in an enclave of Waukegan, north of Chicago. By the time he was four, he had learned to read, and by the fourth grade he had read all the books in the school library, scoring 167 in an IQ test that year. He was physically adroit as well. He rode a pony, played the violin, organized friends to build tree houses and won every possible badge in Wolf Cubs. But casting a shadow over his childhood was his father's precarious health.

His father, Vernon, was a famous pediatrician. He taught at Northwestern University and the University of Chicago, and ran a large practice. Once a month, he visited a local orphanage and spent every Wednesday at what he called his "well-baby clinic" in a poor black neighbourhood. As a diagnostician, he sometimes saved children other doctors had given up on, and he was considered ahead of his time on matters of diet and preventative medicine. "When I was three, my father had a cerebral hemorrhage and was in a coma for a long time," Lennarson says. "He recovered, and was still incredibly active, but from then on he carried his left arm in a sling and drug one leg as he walked. When I was eleven, he died."

Lennarson was overwhelmed by a sense of injustice at his father's death. He was shocked that such an esteemed, imposing figure could die in his prime. "I sat down and said, 'Hey, what kind of world is this?' " he recalls. "You got bums and drunks and wife beaters and child molesters walking the streets and my father died. What does this mean? What is the nature of life?"

He blamed God, or fate, and turned to the existential philosophers. He studied German to read Friedrich Nietzsche in the original, and in the end prized Albert Camus above the others for his book *The Rebel*, which he still quotes by heart: "To live is to act, but act in the name of what?"

Searching for answers, he tore through adolescence in a perpetual state of rage. He drove over railway tracks when a train was coming, daring fate to take his life. He fought constantly. He hit people with baseball bats and knocked them over with cars. By age sixteen, he had amassed a juvenile police record covering four legal-sized sheets, both sides, almost all involving assaults. "Those were busy days," he says. Authorities were tolerant because of his social standing and because he was still a top student—for a science project one year he built a pulsejet engine and mounted it in a car. But he kept pushing his privileges to the limit. When the school library wouldn't let him take out as many books as he wanted at a time, he organized a schoolwide boycott, turning the question into one of student rights. He discovered he was good at conceptualizing injustice in a way that other people could relate to and at devising popular strategies for action.

"When I was in my junior year," Lennarson says of another early escapade, "the assistant superintendent of the school, a guy named Schaibly, called an assembly to announce new dress regulations. There was a notion that you behaved the way you dressed, that if you wore black leather jackets and jeans you got into fights and all kinds of problems, and if you wore button-down shirts and slacks and wore loafers instead of engineering boots you behaved much better. So Schaibly said there would be no more freak haircuts, and all shirts had to be buttoned up to here, and everybody had to wear a belt, and there would be no more boots or leather jackets. So I raised my hand, which wasn't done at assemblies—there were 2,500 or 3,000 students. I raised my hand, and Schaibly recognized me, and I said, 'Excuse me, sir, but what brand toothpaste do we have to use?' Well, the whole place went up for grabs. Everybody was laughing at him and taking off their belts and unbuttoning their shirts, and the whole serious thing was in a shambles—it doesn't take much to turn 3,000 students into a rebellious group. Schaibly groaned and sent me down to the dean of men. The dean's name was Anderberg and he said, 'Who do you think you are doing these kinds of things all the time, creating consternation around here?' and I said, 'Hey! You got a freak haircut. You got it all growing long on one side, combing it way over. Your jacket is off. Your tie is a mess. Don't tell me how to dress!' "

During his college years, Lennarson attended classes in Chicago's Lake Forest district, one of the wealthiest suburbs in America at the time; but he hung out in the black neighbourhood of Woodlawn on the turbulent South Side. He got to know the merchants and hookers around Sixty-Third and Cottage Grove, and helped to plot combat strategy with a street gang called the Cool Gents. Daily he was rubbing against racism, poverty and social injustice, causing him to start wrestling seriously with ideas about equality. Over time, he became interested in strategies for social change, and as he matured he softened his skepticism towards nonviolence, or what he called "love-everybody-kind-of- stuff," and began to concentrate on no-tions of boycotts and marches and legal challenges as ways to assert human rights.

"I came intellectually to understand concepts that are important to me yet today, and that is that one person's rights are determined by everybody else's rights," he says. "And if that is true intellectually, what does that mean in terms of action?"

Gradually he was drawn to the civil rights movement. By 1960, people across the southern United States had begun to push for desegregation, supported by groups in Chicago and several other northern cities. Lennarson was never a notable member of these groups; he served as a consultant-at-large, travelling widely in the

South and elsewhere as a strategist and tactician, developing relation-ships with people like Jim Groppi of the National Association for the Advancement of Colored People (NAACP) and Stokely Carmichael of the Student Nonviolent Coordinating Committee (SNCC). At meetings and rallies, Lennarson came across most of the prominent activists of the period, and when in early 1965 state troopers savagely beat black marchers in Selma, Alabama, provoking a storm of na-tional protest, Lennarson headed down. "I saw it on TV and deter-mined that's where I had to go," he says. Martin Luther King, Jr., fresh from winning the Nobel Peace Prize, also saw the TV coverage and also went, saying he would lead a second march. For the next several days, attention focussed on Selma. The federal court issued an injunction against King's march. State police moved in. Lennarson was at Brown's Chapel, the march's headquarters, and joined the marchers as they set out for the state capital, Montgomery. Although they got only a short distance, national sympathy was with them, pushing President Lyndon Johnson and Congress to enact new voters' rights legislation.

The events, viewed now as the high-water mark of the civil rights movement, enlarged Lennarson's experience. In the fall of 1965, he enrolled in an elite master's program at the University of Wisconsin in Milwaukee. Urban Affairs, the course was called, a mix of history, economics, sociology and political science applied to urban institu-tional decision- making. The whole class was on scholarships from the Ford Foundation. Lennarson was also married by then to a woman from Lake Forest whose father later became chief justice of Illinois. The first of their six children had been born. He was mixing with interesting people in one of America's most dynamic cities, but perhaps shaping him most profoundly was his involvement with community-action organizations. He wrote his thesis on commu-nity-based social change and developed working relations with Saul Alinsky, the preeminent community organizer in America, famous for the type of tactical flare and audacity that Lennarson would later bring to the Lubicon campaign. "Saul would go regularly to Chicago and I would go regularly with others to meet him there," Lennarson recalls, "and there would be all-night sessions sitting around talking."

Alinsky was no sixties radical. He viewed members of the New Left, the hippie movement and the Yippies (of the Youth Interna-tional Party) not as true radicals but as rebellious youths tilting against established authority. Abbie Hoffman and Jerry Rubin couldn't organize a garden party, Alinsky once said, and he viewed Tom Hayden's protests against world capitalism and the American military establishment as unfocussed and romantic. He scorned flower power. "We've got to get away from reconciliation and friendship," he would say. "Reconciliation is when one side has power and the other side is reconciled to it."

Alinsky's loyalties were to early American radicals such as Tom Paine, James Madison and Thomas Jefferson. He had published his bestselling handbook, *Reveille for Radicals*, in 1946, quoting Jefferson as saying, "a little rebellion now and then is a good thing," and warning Americans that when they ceased to exercise their democratic rights they would lose them. Alinsky distinguished between radicals and liberals. "Liberals protest," he said, "radicals rebel." While liberals fear power and its application, radicals seek power and use it. Radicals hit back. "Radicals become fighting mad and go into action."

To create a community organization is to create a conflict group, Alinsky said, its sole reason for existence to wage war against all evils that cause suffering and unhappiness. Most conflict will take place in orderly and legally approved ways: hard-working citizens organized around boycotts, demonstrations and letter-writing campaigns. But war is not an intellectual debate, he said. There may be times in a war against social evil when the radical must break the rules of fair play. Alinsky believed democracy's shortcomings could best be remedied with more democracy and, as a last resort, armed violence.

Over his long career, Alinsky prevailed as a brilliant tactician, never a violent one. He had a knack for what he called "cutting the issue and freezing the target," an ability to conceptualize a problem in terms that everybody could understand, then identify a culprit against which to mobilize popular opinion. He specialized in a tactic he called "mass jujitsu"—hurting the opponent with the opponent's own superior strength. Large entities such as corporations or city hall tend to underestimate a community group's power, he found, and in the smug dismissal of public concern the adversary becomes a bigger target.

Lennarson practiced Alinsky-style activism in poor neighbourhoods of northside Milwaukee, where he became closely associated with a black Baptist minister named Lucius Walker. Officially,

Walker was director of a job-training and community centre called Northcott Neighborhood House, where he and Lennarson shared a closet-sized office. But both were also involved in a number of community organizations, including the Organization of Organizations, or "Triple-O," a coalition of labour, church and social groups active in civil rights. In 1966, when race riots were sweeping other U.S. cities, Milwaukee's WRIT Radio identified Walker and Lennarson as the most powerful (and most publicly obscure) of the city's leading activists. Lennarson "stays out of the limelight, but is known to police and many Negroes as a force in the Negro community," the station reported in a documentary called "The Civil Rights Leaders— Who Are They?" The report went on to say that "Walker values Lennarson's counsel and the duo easily rank as the most active pair in the civil rights movement in Milwaukee today."

In 1968, Walker moved to New York to establish the Interreligious Foundation for Community Organization, or IFCO, a coalition promoting Alinsky-style community action. Lennarson stayed in Milwaukee. He advanced from community organizing to training organizers to training people who trained organizers. In 1970, he took a contract—almost on a whim, he says—as an urban-planning advisor to the Nova Scotia Cabinet Committee on Planning and Programs. He worked out of the second floor of the historic Carleton Hotel at the foot of Citadel Hill, where Anne Murray sang nightly in the lounge, barefoot and full of promise. He stayed a couple of years, finding that he enjoyed being able to walk home at 4:00 A.M. without getting beaten up. From there, he moved to Ottawa as a consultant to the labour department for a year or so, and was casting around for something else to do when Harold Cardinal called to offer him a job. Spotting a sharp intellect, Lennarson accepted. In 1974, he moved his family to Edmonton and for the next five years the two men saw each other almost daily, sometimes spending eighteen- to twenty-hour days together driving around the province. Lennarson came to know almost every chief in Alberta and helped to organize the isolated communities for the caveat challenge. When Cardinal moved to Indian Affairs as director for Alberta, Lennarson went too, and when Cardinal left Indian Affairs to relaunch the aboriginal-rights challenge, Lennarson followed.

The relationship soured when Cardinal started taking on too much. "Harold was a high-stakes gambler and I'm not," Lennarson says. When grants failed to come through and phone lines went dead, Lennarson found himself differing sharply with Cardinal on how to proceed. During a drive through Peace River one day, Lennarson had Cardinal stop the truck and Lennarson got out, ending the collaboration.

Lennarson reviewed his options. On one hand, he wanted a change and considered returning to the States. On the other hand, he had grown fond of Alberta's wide-open spaces and the subarctic bush country north of Lesser Slave Lake. He had taken his children with him to places like Trout and Peerless lakes the way his father had taken him to the well-baby clinic, introducing them to a culture different from their own. A sense of unfinished business also nagged him. When Cardinal had first told him that the Alberta government was planning retroactive legislation, he had replied, "Harold, that's impossible! You've been watching too much TV." To Lennarson, taking away an Indian's right to file a caveat was like denying a black person the right to vote. Alberta authorities would never contemplate it, he said. And if they did, they would never succeed. When the legislation passed, Lennarson thought again about one person's rights being defined by every other person's rights. The deciding factor was Bernard Ominayak.

"I remember him from the early [isolated community] meetings," Lennarson recalls. "He would sit there and watch and listen, and when it came time to sign something or go someplace, he was always right there doing what he was supposed to be doing. What made him really stand out was that he never claimed expenses. I used to handle that. People would come up and I would pay them from a little budget I had for that purpose. I would write down, 'Joe Blow, $100,' or whatever it was, and quite frankly some people came to the meetings just to be paid mileage. It was part of the way people lived. But Bernard never claimed it, so one night I asked him about it. I said, 'This is what this money is for and unless you're independently wealthy, you should use this to pay for your gas.' And he said, 'I don't believe in taking money from people who are trying to help me.' "

In 1979, Ominayak and Lennarson formed their strange, potent alliance. They seemed so different, yet they easily agreed on long-term strategy. Harold Cardinal's weakness, in Lennarson's view, had been a preference for the master stroke over the well-planned manoeuvre. He had kept adversaries off balance with a nimble intelligence but had never taken time to build an organization. Lennarson advised Ominayak to be methodical.

"If you're going to take on the federal and provincial governments and multinational oil companies, you're going to have to develop capability beyond your own community," Lennarson remembers saying.

"I know that," Ominayak replied.

"It's going to take time, during which you're going to lose ground."

"I know that, too," he said.

Ominayak's steady nature and view of himself as part of a historical process disposed him to want to build a political base, step by step. His differences with Lennarson arose only over style. Lennarson had always worked behind the scenes as a resource, not as a spokesperson. He would prepare a client for a meeting and help evaluate a session afterwards. The client would do all the talking, eventually developing enough experience not to need Lennarson any more.

"I don't want to work like that," Ominayak said. He had always learned by watching, hanging back to study a task before performing it himself.

"Oh, really," Lennarson remembers answering. "And what do you want to do?"

"I want you to talk," Ominayak said. "I want you to keep things moving, and I want to watch. I want to figure things out."

At their first meeting with regional Indian Affairs officials in 1980, Lennarson did the talking. He explained that government support to the band amounted to little more than the five-dollar annuity payments to people still on the official paylist and a social worker driving from Peace River once or twice a month to deliver welfare cheques to a few people in need. The band had no office, no staff, no place to hold meetings, no housing program, no economic-development program, not even a telephone—none of the services other bands received as a matter of course. The officials listened politely with their hands folded in front of them and said that the Lubicon people had no right to Indian programs because the band had no reserve. On his return to Little Buffalo, Ominayak told the community: "Those guys sit across the table and lie just like they're telling the truth."

Lennarson obtained proof that bands without reserves in the

Maritimes and the Northwest Territories were getting government programs. And when the federal minister, John Munro, visited northern Alberta later that year, Lennarson and Ominayak cornered him to extract a promise of four houses as a first step towards federal programming at Little Buffalo.

"Our first victory," Ominayak says.

At subsequent meetings with the department, Ominayak and Lennarson negotiated an annual budget of $276,609 for the fiscal year 1981–82. Ominayak built a band office, hired a secretary, put Lennarson on contract, had telephones installed, ordered the materials for the four houses Munro had promised and hired eight community members to build them. Drawing on other departments he initiated an adult-education course, an educational counselling program for school-age children, a social-assistance program and a means to help community members find jobs. When the Alberta government funded four more houses, he hired another eight community members.

Administratively, Ominayak retained the chief-and-councillors model prescribed by Indian Affairs, allowing him to draw a salary for the first time of $6,000 a year and to pay the two councillors. He also created an unofficial, eleven-member council operating much as the fourteen household leaders had in 1933, when they had all signed Xs to their petition. A cross section of local political interests was represented: status and non-status, key extended families, young and old. Sometimes the councillors met as a group, but mostly they just visited each other, Ominayak constantly passing on information, sampling opinion and staying alert to the rivalries and sensitivities that can be part of a small community. When his two-year term as chief came due, the band tried to vote him chief for life. He accepted a new five-year term.

Lennarson oversaw a socioeconomic survey of Little Buffalo, complete with a census and an inventory of community skills and assets. He sorted through documents amassed by Indian Association researchers in the mid-1970s, numbering and filing every one. He wrote summaries and compiled indices. He drew up budgets, dealt with government departments and frequently travelled north for community meetings.

Within months, the band had gained a measure of control over its own affairs, leaving Ominayak and Lennarson to pursue broader aspects of organization building. But as they had predicted, the band lost ground. A feeling grew among Lubicon members that unless a reserve was established soon, they would be overrun. The pace of oil development in the Lesser Slave interior was exploding.

8 THE MASTER STRATEGY

LOOKING FOR OIL in northern Canada involves large-scale bulldozing, blasting and drilling, all of which can cause widespread environmental damage unless carefully controlled. In the Lubicon area, controls were virtually nil. After 1979, permits were being issued almost as fast as applications were being made, with no environmental or social-impact studies required. Lubicon concerns were systematically ignored. When licence renewals came due on the promised reserve area in 1983, authorities promptly reauctioned them over the band's explicit objections. Fires raged, traps were looted and destruction of trapping equipment became "almost like a competition" among oil workers, witnesses said. The bush economy was being destroyed, and after a while Lubicon trappers came to see the destruction not as a sad, unavoidable consequence of industrial activity but as part of a deliberate government strategy to force people off the land and into settlements to subvert the band's aboriginal rights.

Looking for oil begins with clearing a wide, straight path through the bush in winter when the muskeg is frozen. Two or three workers with a bulldozer mow a twenty-five-foot swath at a rate of one mile a day. Next, a survey crew marks "shot hole" locations. Then the seismograph crew arrives, a parade of up to twenty-five people in an assortment of trucks. At the head of the line are the drill trucks, from which crews bore shot holes sixty feet deep at a usual rate of twelve per mile. A shooter follows to drop a dynamite charge into each shot hole, and line trucks lay cable bearing electrical sensors. When the charges are detonated one after the other, the pattern of sound waves bouncing off the substrata is recorded on magnetic tape in a recording truck. Then the equipment moves on, covering three to four miles a day, supported by camp personnel running portable dormitories and a diner.

If the seismic data show reefs that might be holding oil or gas, workers arrive with D8 Caterpillars to build access roads and to clear a drill site. Rat-hole drillers prepare an exploratory well, and a drilling rig is hauled in and assembled, involving five to ten tractor- trailer units and up to forty workers. Then the serious drilling begins, involving three five- person crews supported by a mechanic, a tool pusher, an electrician, a geologist, an engineer, a mud-company representative, a water hauler and an assembly of cooks and camp attendants. Tankers of fuel, water, cement and drilling mud regularly arrive. If a well is to be tested, or logged, or fished, or fractured, or acidized, crews with special equipment are summoned. Visitors show up from the Energy Resources Conservation Board, the Workers' Compensation Board, various drill-bit supply companies, the cater- ing company, the camp supplier, the drilling company and the parent oil company. Tearing down the rig brings another cycle of hectic activity. If oil has been discovered, downhole and surface equipment is installed; water-separation and storage tanks are erected; and as the oil field develops, so does the network of camps, all-weather roads, service batteries, gathering lines, pipelines and high-tension power cables.

Until the winter of 1979–80, oil and gas development in Lubicon territory had been minimal. In the 1950s, eleven wells were drilled. In the 1960s, the number of new wells roughly doubled, to twenty-three. In the early 1970s, the number doubled again to about fifty, many of them in the Marten River area.

Then the boom hit. In 1979, the Iranian revolution interrupted oil supplies from the Persian Gulf, forcing world prices higher and making profitable the extension of all-weather roads into the Lesser Slave interior. Big discoveries were made south of Whitefish Lake and east of Loon Lake. South of Little Buffalo, the Seal and Slave fields opened. At Marten River, the Golden field was in production. Northeast of Little Buffalo, the Evi oil field was discovered.

Another boost came in late 1980. The federal government an- nounced its National Energy Program, permitting Canadian oil prices to increase semiannually to approach the world price. Reaction to much of the program in Alberta was hostile, but a two-tiered pricing system encouraged new development: one price on oil dis-covered before 1981, a higher price on new discoveries.

In the Lubicon area, exploration and drilling permits commanded the highest prices in Alberta, signalling a storm of new activity. During a single winter in 1979-80, thirty wells were drilled. At least forty were drilled the following year. By 1984, more than four hundred oil and gas wells had been drilled within a fifteen-mile radius of Little Buffalo, and more than one hundred oil companies and subcontractors were working the area.

All the work interfered with trappers. Company signs staked out the bush like sovereign flags: Norcen, Texas Pacific, Mobil, Husky Oil. Gates were erected across roads. Oil company guards hired to keep an eye on rivals forced trappers to sign in and out. Suddenly the bush was colonized by nodding pump jacks, clusters of trailer camps, "No Trespassing" signs and burn-off flares lighting the night sky. Old trails became all- weather roads, one of them passing within feet of a cabin at Fish Lake belonging to Albert Laboucan and his brother, Summer Joe. "I don't feel right that these guys come in and take over," Albert said at the cabin one night late in 1984. "Those big trucks go by until way past midnight and start again early in the morning, shaking us in our beds."

Some of the workers kept dogs that ran loose and chewed fur lying in traps. Bulldozers pushed up snow and debris, blocking animal trails and burying dozens of traps and snares at a time. When trappers started marking their lines with red tape and flags, catskinners would swerve off course to bury them intentionally. In one case, tracks in the snow showed that a bulldozer had followed part of a trapline, burying the traps, then had backed up to bury an offshoot line. Some traps were looted. Edward Laboucan found lynx hair in one of his traps near Otter Lakes, with boot prints visible between the trap and a set of tire tracks. A lynx pelt was worth $400 at the time.

A probation officer in Peace River told Ominayak that several oil-company and forestry workers under his supervision were de-stroying traps on direct instructions from employers. Destroying traplines and shooting animals was becoming "almost like a compe-tition," the officer quoted two Alberta forestry workers as saying. He retracted the testimony under pressure from superiors, but re-confirmed it years later after joining the RCMP. "My department didn't want any heat," he said in an interview, "but there's no question those things were happening."

Terrible fires raged through the territory. In 1980, fire destroyed as much area as in the previous twenty years. Each of the next two years was worse. In the three years combined, fires destroyed 641 square miles of bush, forest service records show. Most of the blazes were believed to have started from natural causes, but not all, and Lubicon members hired to fight the fires twice complained of being ordered to stand idle as flames flared out of control. One of the two fires burned a large area east of Marten River at Joker Lake. The other destroyed a huge swath of territory north of Fish Lake.

"I had to laugh at myself today," John Felix Laboucan said north of Fish Lake one night. "I used to have a heck of a time getting all my fur onto the toboggan, but today all I had was one little bag of squirrels." Fire had destroyed much of his trapping area, including two of his five cabins, along with food, traps and equipment. He had been doing all right on the untouched part, he said, until oil companies pushed farther into the area. In the previous two months, he had caught one fisher, one marten, three beavers and some squirrels. "I don't know what to do," he said in Cree. "I love trapping. I don't want to quit. But with all the trucks around it's getting dangerous even to run my dog team."

All trappers found themselves working harder for diminishing returns. Statistics gathered by Kenneth Bodden, a wildlife specialist at the Boreal Institute for Northern Studies at the University of Alberta, showed that the average family made more than $5,000 from trapping in the winter of 1979–80. Earnings dropped to $4,000 a family the following year, to $3,200 the year after that, to $800, to $400, to almost nothing. Moose kills for the community numbered more than 200 the year before the boom. The numbers dropped steadily to 110, 101, 27, and down to 19 by 1983–84. With trapping gone, there was almost nothing to turn to but welfare, which rose from 10 per cent of the work force to 90 per cent during the same four years.

"By the winter of 1982–83," Lennarson wrote, "the previously viable traditional economy of these aboriginal groups was for all practical purposes totally destroyed."

≈

Throughout the Lesser Slave interior the oil boom drove native hunters and trappers from the bush to live on welfare in the seven isolated communities. Alberta authorities did nothing to impede the process. Rather, they gave oil companies unrestricted access to the region, so readily facilitating the boom that Lennarson began to wonder if driving native people from the bush was an intentional government objective. He developed a theory about a "master strategy." Distilling evidence from a range of sources, he speculated that provincial-government advisors had devised an elaborate legal strategy, linked with oil development, to defeat any further assertion of native land rights in the interior.

The strategy, as Lennarson explained it to the mailing list, had two main parts. The first had to do with building a legal case that the interior bands no longer held land rights because they no longer used the land. The logic flowed from a judgment issued in 1980 by the Federal Court of Canada involving the Baker Lake Inuit of the Northwest Territories. The ruling suggested that to prove unextinguished aboriginal title in Canada, a native society must prove that its members continue to pursue a traditional way of life on land that their ancestors used and occupied. The ruling was not definitive, but it implied that Alberta's legal position would be strengthened every time a native person of the interior gave up trapping in the face of oil development.

The second part of the master strategy, as Lennarson explained it, involved changing the legal status of all land in the interior so that no Indian reserve could be created there. Alberta officials openly argued that the interior had become legally "occupied" by oil companies. The significance of the word "occupied" can be found in the Alberta Natural Resources Act of 1930 (sometimes referred to as the Land Transfer Agreement because it formally transferred all federal Crown land in Alberta to the Alberta government). Under the act, Ottawa can ask Alberta to set aside new Indian reserves only on "unoccupied Crown lands." In 1984, Alberta's native affairs minister, Milt Pahl, told the legislature that "the definition of 'unoccupied' would be 'without a competing land use or surface lease.' " No unoccupied Crown land, he suggested in the same speech, remained in the Lubicon area for a reserve.

Whether a master strategy for the region literally existed will likely never be known, but what is certain is that massive oil development served the Alberta government's legal interests against the Lubicon and other bands in the Lesser Slave interior. Every permit sold, every well drilled, every work crew installing itself both drove native trappers from the bush and strengthened oil-company "occupation" of the territory.

At Little Buffalo itself, government actions were so ruthless that no theories were needed to help people understand what was going on. From 1979 to 1984, the Alberta government of Premier Peter Lougheed pursued a multifaceted program involving several cabinet ministers and departments to assert provincial jurisdiction over the community. The aim was to turn Little Buffalo into a legally "occupied" provincial municipality so that it could never be established as a reserve.

The government's first move at Little Buffalo came in the fall of 1979 as the oil boom got underway. Senior people in the municipal affairs department secretly designated Fleuri L'Hirondelle, the local Metis farmer, as a "provincial advisory councillor." A kind of puppet regime was being installed. L'Hirondelle was still farming the promised reserve land, and he viewed Lubicon efforts to secure their land rights as contrary to his interests. His new job was to represent the community in all dealings with the Alberta government, bypassing the elected chief and council.

L'Hirondelle's first official act, also conducted in secret, was to ask that something called the Land Tenure Program be applied to Little Buffalo, a request that Municipal Affairs Minister Marvin Moore publicly approved on April 23, 1980. Under the program, residents were entitled to purchase a two-acre lot for a dollar, Moore announced. Sixty lots would be surveyed and made available. Other details were withheld, however, and the significance of the announcement was not immediately understood by band members.

Four days later, snap elections were called for the position of advisory councillor and for membership to a local land-tenure committee. On the basis of a tiny turnout, Fleuri L'Hirondelle declared himself the democratically elected councillor and chairman of a committee that included his son Chester and three close friends. With government help, committee members worked out a street and residential plan. They divided Little Buffalo into two-acre lots, some of them forming odd geometric shapes to accommodate the original random settlement pattern. Moore approved the plan, and on

January 16, 1981, he quietly signed ministerial order 651-81, changing the official status of Little Buffalo from "unorganized Indian settlement" to "provincial hamlet."

"It's very clear what's going on," James O'Reilly, a lawyer for the band, said when more information about the moves finally surfaced. Changing the status of the community was an attempt to change "unoccupied Crown land" into "occupied Crown land" under the terms of the 1930 Natural Resources Act, he said. And trying to sell residents two-acre lots for a dollar was a way of having the Lubicon people legally admit that they didn't already own them. "The government wants to make sure the area around Little Buffalo never becomes a reserve," O'Reilly said.

Survey crews soon staked out a town site. Road crews followed. Footpaths and cart trails became gravel streets with street signs saying "Ominayak Road," "Calahasen Road" and "Laboucan Crescent," as though the settlement was any other Alberta municipality. Veiled harassment began. Ominayak arrived one afternoon at the site of a new home that he was building and saw a bulldozer roll through his backyard, taking out a poplar grove that would have sheltered his house from the north wind. When he asked the catskinner what he thought he was doing, the man apologized, saying he had made a mistake, he was supposed to be making the road a little farther away.

Municipal affairs employees from Edmonton next began to canvass the settlement door-to-door, selling two-acre lots for a dollar. They used Fleuri L'Hirondelle and his wife, Rose, to translate and explain the application forms. Forty-nine people signed their names or Xs, but many said later that they hadn't understood what they were signing. One woman, Martha Whitehead, said she thought she had applied for a house trailer. Another said she thought she was getting free firewood. Irene Laboucan had carefully listed the names of her four children, thinking she was completing a census form. "I didn't really understand it," thirty-one-year-old Joe Laboucan told a newspaper reporter. "I signed a couple of papers. I never read them."

When Ominayak asked that the program be suspended until the land dispute was settled, the minister, Marvin Moore, refused. Land tenure and land claims are unrelated, Moore repeatedly told Ominayak in writing. Moore's legal advice came from Howard Irving, the lawyer who had handled the caveat case for Alberta and who was Lougheed's top legal advisor on aboriginal matters. "Everybody is free to live as before," Moore wrote. "No pressure will be brought to bear on anybody."

But the assurances proved short-lived. In August 1981, Moore wrote to Ottawa saying that Little Buffalo could never be part of a reserve. "The hamlet of Little Buffalo being occupied Crown land would not be available for treaty purposes," he said.

As residents continued to resist the land-tenure program, outright threats and intimidation began. The telephone and electrical companies refused hookups to householders without land tenure. Building a house or shack or corral suddenly required a development permit. The Northlands School Division of the Alberta education system approved a new school over objections from the elected school board in Little Buffalo; the board viewed the school as another attempt to assert provincial jurisdiction. Northlands also levied a "supplementary school tax" on all residents, including recognized status Indians whose education costs were already covered by Ottawa. Provincial property-tax notices arrived at every home, whether the owner had signed for land tenure or not. The tax went with hamlet status, municipal affairs employees said. Ominayak got a bill for $250, with a warning that a 15-per-cent penalty would be levied against late payment, or personal belongings seized. In correspondence and public statements, provincial officials began calling Lubicon people "trespassers" and "squatters on Alberta Crown land."

"These people are legally squatters," said Robin Ford, assistant deputy minister of municipal affairs and overseer of the land-tenure program.

Another issue arose. A resident named Peter Sawan, who had allied himself with the L'Hirondelle family, worked up a petition supporting the land-tenure program in the spring of 1984. Fleuri L'Hirondelle had died the year before and his son Chester had become advisory councillor, but Sawan viewed himself as a community spokesman as well, especially among non-status members. Sawan's father had lost the family's Indian status by taking scrip, making Sawan non-status, or what he called "Metis." He made the rounds with a petition saying, "We the Metis of Little Buffalo Hamlet wish to have the Land Tenure Program in the community." It was signed, said Sawan, by 27 people representing 141 community residents.

Ominayak denounced the petition as a forgery, but Premier Lougheed tabled it in the legislature at once. "We have received a communication from the Metis people," he announced, and he read the last paragraph into the record: "What will happen to all of these Metis people if the Lubicon Lake Band succeeds in getting a Reservation in the Little Buffalo–Lubicon Lake areas? Someone has to speak for their rights now."

Lougheed appointed himself as that someone. "I wish it were simpler, but it isn't," he told the legislature. "I think that letter should be tabled to make sure that we have a fair presentation of both sides."

Little Buffalo is split, the premier said, introducing an argument that was to confuse the Lubicon issue in the public mind for years. Because of the McCrimmon removals, scrip and other circumstances, about half the residents of Little Buffalo remained without official Indian status. Almost all of them considered themselves Lubicon band members and were accepted by each other as such, but Lougheed portrayed the non-status residents as "Metis," lumping them with the L'Hirondelles and saying that the community was split fifty-fifty. Promoting such a view served Lougheed in two ways. First, by standing up for the "Metis," he could portray himself as a defender of community members, not just of oil-company interests. Second, he could portray the issue as a dispute between factions at Little Buffalo rather than a struggle for land rights.

"So when we talk about fairness and equity on this issue," Lougheed told the legislature, "let's keep in mind the fairness and equity of other people who are living in that area. It's our responsibility as a government to balance that fairness and equity. I think that in all fairness and equity [the Metis] position should be presented to this House as well. They're equally Alberta citizens."

Ominayak and Lennarson watched from the visitors' gallery as Lougheed lamented the community division. "Let me assure you that you have no need for concern," Ominayak wrote Lougheed the next day in a letter drafted by Lennarson. "The vast majority of non-status people in Little Buffalo are participating in the land claim. Our genealogical research indicates that most of them are entitled to both land and status. Should any of them not be entitled to land and status in their own right, they will be welcome to share our land, as they always have."

Ominayak also sent Lougheed a petition sponsored by John Auger, another non-status member of the community. It included fifty-two signatures representing most of the people that Sawan had claimed supported him. "Our real position," Auger said, "is that we claim aboriginal rights to our traditional area, along with the members of the Lubicon Lake Indian Band, and we strongly support Chief Bernard Ominayak."

Lougheed did not table the second petition. Instead, his government circulated figures indicating that the Metis population formed a slight majority in a divided Little Buffalo: 170 Metis people living alongside 140 Lubicon Indians.

Threats and intimidation against Little Buffalo residents continued. Education Minister Dave King announced that the government would proceed with the school despite local opposition, saying, "Forget for just a moment the question of the reserve. There are children up there who need an education and they deserve to have their education provided for them in an adequate facility."

Johnny Johnson, the forestry superintendent in Peace River, wrote to Lubicon resident Dwight Gladue saying that Gladue must either buy a lot for his new house through the land-tenure program or take out a provincial-government lease. Gladue stuffed the letter into a drawer. Four months later, the deputy minister of renewable resources in Edmonton, Fred McDougall, threatened to remove Gladue, his wife and four children from their home, saying: "Pursuant to Section 46(1) of the Public Lands Act, a person who occupies public land and is not the holder of a disposition authorizing him to do so shall be deemed a trespasser and any improvements [such as a house] created by him are the property of the Crown."

Fred Facco, the director of land dispositions in the forestry, lands and wildlife department in Edmonton, threatened John Auger, sponsor of the second petition, saying: "It has come to the department's attention that you have constructed some fences and corrals in LSD13 and 14 of section 11-86-14-W5th Meridian on Crown land on the north side of the road directly across from your place of residence. As I can find no record of any authority granted you [to do so] . . . you are hereby notified . . . to remove those fences and corrals . . . within sixty days." Auger, who had built the corral six years earlier, let the deadline pass. Nine days later he got a visit from Brian MacIntosh of the same department, who said Auger would either have to apply for a government lease for the land or dismantle the fences. "Nobody will take down those fences unless they take me away first," Auger told him.

The Lubicon people stood firm. By the end of 1984, they had rolled back the land tenure program to fourteen applicants, including the L'Hirondelles, Peter Sawan and a native couple who had recently moved to the area. The Lubicon community ignored all permit requirements, returned all tax and tax-arrears notices, left their homes and corrals standing and defeated the school proposal. When provincial officials threatened to dismantle three new homes deliberately built outside hamlet boundaries, Lubicon hunters strolled into the meeting with loaded rifles—a gesture that kept the province from calling in the bulldozers.

"I thought of Marten River," says George Seeseequon, one of the homeowners outside the boundaries. He had finally moved from Marten River of his own accord, only to have provincial authorities threaten his new home.

For a while, residents of the six other isolated communities also resisted land tenure, after provincial authorities expanded the program throughout the interior. By 1984, the Alberta land-tenure secretariat had spent nearly $8 million on roads, power lines and surveys in the interior, but few householders had applied for the two-acre lots. "Repeated visits made it clear that Trout Lake, Peerless Lake, Chipewyan Lake, Loon Lake and Cadotte Lake would not request program delivery," one official reported gloomily. "They either saw no need for the program or preferred to concentrate solely on negotiations with the federal government."

Over time, however, all six communities crumbled. Hunters and trappers were driven off the land by oil work throughout the interior and forced onto welfare in the settlements. Land-tenure lots were sold, provincial schools were built and advisory councils were created to undermine elected band leaders. At Loon Lake, oil-company workers bought two-acre lots and took up residence. At Trout and Peerless lakes, summer sports fishermen arrived in droves at newly created provincial parks, competing with the domestic fishing of band members.

On the evening of March 10, 1986, an event at Peerless Lake signalled how badly conditions in the isolated communities had deteriorated. A drinking party got underway at the home of Eliza Netawastenum, and when the drinkers ran low on liquids, someone broke into the new provincial school to steal a four-litre jug of photocopying fluid. Thirteen people drank from it. Six of them died of methyl-hydrate poisoning.

"In the days that followed," a feature article in *Maclean's* magazine said, "reporters from all over flew in chartered planes to the marshy airstrip at Trout Lake, and then drove 30 km along a dirt road to Peerless Lake to cover the funerals and ask the 350 inhabitants— without success—how people could want to get drunk so badly that they would drink duplicating machine fluid."

Lennarson was not as mystified.

"The tragedy at Peerless Lake is clearly a direct result of social and economic disruption, dislocation and disintegration caused by the Alberta Provincial Government's deliberate campaign to systematically deprive these aboriginal people of their aboriginal land rights," he wrote to Lubicon supporters. "It comes as no surprise to those who've been following developments in the area. Moreover no one should be surprised by other, equally horrific events which will inevitably occur as this genocidal process continues."

9 GENOCIDAL CONSEQUENCES

STATE-SPONSORED SUBJUGATION of native peoples is generally thought of in Canada as a barbarity that happens elsewhere. Few people were prepared to acknowledge the enormity of what was taking place in the interior, and Alberta news organizations carried few reports on events anyway. Looking for an audience, Ominayak, Lennarson and band elder Edward Laboucan travelled to a global assembly of the World Council of Churches at Vancouver in 1983, their first move to bring the case to international attention. Through Lennarson's former Milwaukee associate, Lucius Walker, they arranged to brief a number of senior people, capturing particular interest from Anwar Barkat, director of the council's program to combat racism. Barkat asked for more information, and after receiving thousands of documents at his headquarters in Geneva, he wrote a blunt seven-page letter to Prime Minister Trudeau, stating dramatically: "In the last couple of years, the Alberta Provincial Government and dozens of multi-national oil companies have taken actions which could have genocidal consequences."

Barkat chronicled events surrounding the land-tenure program and quoted statistics on lost trapper earnings. "The situation of the Band and Band members is thus desperate," he wrote. "They know no other way to live. They have no money, many have never been out of their traditional area. Many speak only Cree. Many neither read nor write. None have completed Grade 12. Those who try to pursue a different lifestyle will both deny their heritage and break their traditional bond with the land, an essential legal requirement of their aboriginal claim. They are literally in a struggle for their very existence as a people." Barkat urged the prime minister to extend the band financial, political and legal help, and to begin land-rights negotiations immediately.

The prime minister's office referred the letter to the Indian Affairs minister, John Munro, who was already familiar with the case. Twice Munro had urged Alberta politicians to ease up on the band. He had asked Marvin Moore to suspend the land-tenure program pending land-rights talks and had asked Milt Pahl, the native affairs minister, to explore issues with band and federal representatives as a prelude to formal negotiations. Both overtures had failed, but after Barkat's letter Munro tried again.

He asked that Pahl set aside the promised 25.4-square-mile reserve, "given the urgency there exists about setting up a reserve for this band if it is to survive as a group and preserve its identity." The allotment would be a first step towards an overall land settlement to be reached in negotiations, Munro said. He also proposed that both governments contribute to a special housing and infrastructure program for the reserve, and urged Alberta to establish a wildlife conservation regime with the band to balance "the incessant encroachments of development on what the band feels are its traditional wildlife lands."

Pahl rejected the appeal. "The Alberta Government is continuing to review its entitlement policy," he replied.

Munro followed with an impassioned plea, making clear that he knew exactly what was happening. "I must point out that within the last few months the Band's situation has become progressively worse," he wrote to Pahl in February 1984. "As a result of the encroachment of industrial development in the Lubicon region, the autumn [moose] harvest was negligible. The threat to the Band's traditional lifestyle is even more pronounced. If this Band is to survive as a group and is to preserve its identity, a reserve is urgently needed."

Again he asked that the province set aside the promised 25.4 square miles as a first step and concluded, "The Governments of Canada and of Alberta have the responsibility to ensure that every conscientious effort is made to relieve the Band's suffering. At the very least, we should be motivated by a sense of social justice and provide a land base for their reserve. I believe we cannot wait until after the historical and legal analyses are completed; thus, I must request again that the Government of Alberta consider my proposals immediately."

Again Pahl refused. "As you are aware," he replied obscurely, "the Province of Alberta is obliged to provide unoccupied Crown land to the Federal Government to enable Canada to fulfill its treaty obligations to the Indians of Alberta. The Province of Alberta is willing to honour its legal obligations."

Munro gave up. He was prepared to ask for Alberta's cooperation but not to demand it. Instead, he turned his attention to his ultimately unsuccessful bid to replace Pierre Trudeau as Liberal Party leader. When asked during the campaign about Lubicon, he said that the band was no worse off than many other bands. "There are [other] cases just as bad," he told a television reporter. "I could take a television crew to fifty or a hundred places shockingly bad . . . . We're trying to do the best we can with the limited resources that we have, with a program that is admittedly seriously underfunded."

With Munro fading from the scene, Ominayak and Lennarson turned again to the churches. Archbishop Ted Scott, primate of the Anglican Church of Canada, agreed to head a fact- finding mission to the Lubicon area, bringing with him four leading Anglican, Lutheran, United and Roman Catholic clergymen. Almost as soon as they arrived, an oil-company truck nearly ran them off the road. "We found ourselves subjected to the harassment that band members say happens to them continually," Scott told a news conference afterwards in Edmonton.

"In the short time we were there, the violations of human rights became apparent to us," Scott also said. "The traditional economy, which we believe was intact a few years ago, is in a state of ruin. The trust and confidence in the social structure of the band and in the elders is being severely tried. Everyone is very confused about the sudden lack of control over their lives. Unity amongst the people is being threatened from without."

Scott didn't repeat the phrase "genocidal consequences," but his tour provoked the first spate of widely disseminated news coverage of the band's circumstances. The CBC television program "The Journal" aired a hard-hitting documentary that began with host Barbara Frum saying, "Tonight, a story of political neglect and bureaucratic deceit." The *Globe and Mail* ran a full-page Saturday feature under the headline "The last stand of the Lubicon." An editorial in the same paper said that "meaner treatment of helpless people could scarcely be imagined." The *New York Times* ran a lengthy story from Little

Buffalo on page two, with a map, two photographs and a headline that said, "Caught up in an oil rush, a Canadian tribe reels."

≈

In the face of such publicity, a curious self-deception took hold among Alberta government officials. Cabinet ministers and senior civil servants denied, sometimes ridiculed, the reports. Lougheed himself had no comment. Neither did provincial lawyer Howard Irving nor Municipal Affairs Minister Marvin Moore. People who had issued band members threatening letters, such as the deputy minister of renewable resources, Fred McDougall, and the director of land dispositions, Fred Facco, similarly refused to be interviewed. Over time, however, a number of officials consented to talk about their role in events, including Native Affairs Minister Milt Pahl, a rookie member of the government who was taking most of the heat.

As Pahl reacted to events, his position seemed to evolve. He stated several times in the legislature that the Lubicon band might be entitled to land but not to the subsurface rights that automatically go with a reserve. Later he went further, saying that the Lubicon area was legally "occupied" by oil wells and drilling leases, not available for reserve purposes at all. When asked if he meant the province would never grant the Lubicon people a reserve near Lubicon Lake, Pahl replied that Indian bands are "certainly somewhat nomadic" and said, "Let's face it, there's a heck of a lot of unoccupied land in northern Alberta." Ultimately, Pahl arrived at the Malcolm McCrimmon position. He took to calling the Lubicon band "the people of Lubicon Lake who claim to form an Indian band." Confidential government research showed the number of true Lubicon Indians to be "less than a dozen people," he said—not enough to warrant a reserve.

Mostly, Pahl confined his remarks to the legislature, but in April 1985, he consented to a forty-minute interview at the close of a first ministers' conference on aboriginal rights in Ottawa. As the premiers and other delegates filed out, Pahl sat himself in Lougheed's chair at the conference table. "There is no factual basis for the allegations of cultural genocide and harassment and all of those things," he began defensively. "An all-weather road went in there in the late fifties, early sixties. And at the request of the people there, not the oil companies."

"The all-weather road to Little Buffalo?"

"Late fifties, early sixties," he repeated.

"It was finished in 1978."

"I was up there in the early sixties," he said. "I was over it. An all-weather road. Those people weren't isolated at all."

As the hall emptied of stragglers, Pahl talked about the rights of Metis residents and the need for a school. He referred to the Lubicon people as "squatters." He said the reason he refused to set aside the 25.4 square miles, as Munro had asked, was because "there is a dog fight over the numbers" of band members.

"What are your numbers?"

"Our numbers were based on a genealogical study," he said, "indicating there were less than twelve people [who] could not be traced back to other bands."

"Fewer than twelve? How many?"

"Nine. And the reason those couldn't be traced back is because their parents were illegitimate, okay?"

"How does Ottawa's study get 347 and you get 9?"

"Basically, there's a dog fight," Pahl repeated, letting his face drop. "The sad part is there is a community up there under a lot of serious stress. There's the Metis people. There's people who think they might be band members, they might not be."

"Nine Lubicon Indians—who are the rest?"

"Well, they're either Metis or non-status," Pahl said. "And what does non-status mean? It means Metis. It means Albertans. Let's call them native Albertans by and large, but Albertans first and foremost. And life goes on."

"How can they make the transition from bush life if you don't recognize them as native people with special needs?"

"Albertans are eligible for a lot of programs," he said.

≈

Only Pahl tried to say that the all-weather road to Little Buffalo was finished by the early 1960s, but other Alberta officials proffered facts that turned out to be less than accurate. One such official was John Kristensen, executive assistant to Pahl for his single term of office and afterwards director of social policy coordination at the federal and intergovernmental affairs department. Kristensen supported Pahl's story that Little Buffalo residents had asked for the road in the first place, and he went further, saying that Ominayak himself had requested the road as secretary to the community association in the early 1970s. Kristensen frequently referred to Ominayak pejoratively as "Bernie" or "Chief Bernie."

"The road was to be built at a certain rate over a certain time period and Bernie asked that construction be accelerated," Kristensen said. "The argument was that since the road was already on the drawing boards, why couldn't the community benefit earlier?"

"Can you substantiate that?"

"Probably."

A week later, Kristensen forwarded three documents. The first was a 1973 letter from the deputy minister of transport concerning the proposed construction of a ten-mile section of road east from Three Creeks—the first phase of an eventual fifty miles of new road to Little Buffalo. "The people of Cadotte Lake and Little Buffalo are continually pressing for service," the letter says, refuting Pahl's contention that the road existed by then and failing to show that Ominayak requested a road.

The second document concerned a meeting held late in 1973 at Peace River, attended by representatives of thirteen government departments and "Metis representatives" from Little Buffalo and Cadotte Lake. Ominayak is not mentioned, and only government people are quoted as saying an all-weather road is needed.

"It was voiced by Mr. Whitmey [of the Peace River Health Unit] that proper roads into these two communities were required above all else, and stressed this priority," the paper said. "Mrs. Campsall [also of the health unit] repeated the need for the high priority of an all-weather road . . . . Mr. Lockwood and Mr. Jardine of the Department of Social Development also voiced their concern over the lack of proper roads into this area."

The third document summarized a 1975 meeting at Peace River attended by twelve government people, William Beaver of the Isolated Communities Advisory Board and representatives from Cadotte and Little Buffalo, including Ominayak as secretary-treasurer of the Little Buffalo Farming Coop. Under the heading "Roads," the minutes said: "It has been reported that highways will not have sufficient monies to complete the road to Little Buffalo. If road is not completed it could postpone power reaching Cadotte Lake this year. Local people should write local MLA pressing for road completion." There was no mention of anybody from Little Buffalo requesting a road and no sign of government determination to build the road for the communities instead of for the oil companies.

"Not precisely what we were looking for," an attached note from Kristensen's office said.

≈

The person sending the tax-arrears notices to Little Buffalo residents was Neil Gibson, manager of assessment and taxation at the municipal affairs department in Edmonton. An excitable man close to retirement age, he kept getting up during an interview to point at maps or to fetch copies of statutes and regulations.

"I, personally, most likely could agree with the Lubicons," he began. "But the legislation says if you own a house you're liable for taxation, because somebody's got to pay for the schooling of your kids, for your roads, your ambulances, your recreation, your streetlights, all your municipal services. See what I mean? My role here is not very significant except I'm doing my job by saying, 'Hey, you owe us taxation because you're a resident of our municipality.' "

For nearly an hour, Gibson talked about his "philosophy of tax assessment." Essentially, it involved "creating taxation growth" so that communities like Little Buffalo could develop and prosper. "Those people in the hamlet will want to become a village!" he said. "They'll want to incorporate! They'll want to run their own affairs! They'll want to elect their mayors and their reeves and their councillors!" He spoke dreamily of taxing homes with cedar-shake sidings and triple- car garages.

"Mr. Gibson—these are trappers in homes with no running water."

"Those taxes are still created," he said. "If you don't own land, you're considered a squatter, but you still get a notice for your skid shack or mobile home or whatever—it's all covered in the Municipal Taxation Act. You know what they say, 'Death and taxes.' Nobody gets away from taxation."

"Does it not strike you as heartless to go into a bush settlement where people have lost their livelihood and declare the place a hamlet—"

"That's not Neil's doing."

"—and have Neil send them tax assessments—"

"That's my job."

"—and threaten them with penalties and removal of their homes?"

"Because that's my job," said Gibson, not backing down. "If special exemptions are required, the politicians must make them. And if they do so, I will be the first to say, 'Hey, don't tax them.' But until then, my job is to set mill rates and collect taxes. I'm not a lobby group. My hands are tied."

After a prolonged silence, Gibson stood up, groping for a lighter note on which to end.

"I, personally, was in this country thirty-five years ago," he said, approaching a wall map of the interior. "Back in 1951. Tar sands exploration. We drove out of Three Creeks in a half-ton, a fourteen-hour trip in those days if you didn't hit the ditch, 'cause it was all just bulldozed trails. We saw lots of moose and everything else and that whole way of life, and I personally knew of those people living in there at the missions and what not. I was up at Wabasca and all the way up to the Buffalo Head Hills [near where Ominayak's father trapped]. I'm well aware of their plight and most likely I would be the most sympathetic to their cause if it came down to it."

He fell silent for a moment, as though suddenly aware that he was contradicting his pose as the naive official just following the rules. "I'm just doing my job," he said again firmly. "To me they're no different from any other ratepayer."

≈

The job to implement the land-tenure program at Little Buffalo belonged to Robin Ford, the assistant deputy minister of municipal affairs. He is an articulate and self-assured man—"not the kind of person who is insensitive to community situations," he said evenly.

Ford came to Edmonton via Dar es Salaam and Nairobi, where he had worked for seven years with the International Labour Organization on employment and rural-development programs. Afterwards, he worked briefly for the federal Indian Affairs department, arriving at Alberta municipal affairs in 1979. At that time, he said, there was concern that land tenure was not being introduced "sensitively" at Little Buffalo. The person in charge was "pushy" and "female" and "not an easy lady," he said. "Something came down from the premier, who had a personal interest in this thing, saying, 'Well, what's happening?' and nothing had happened."

Ford was asked to take charge. He expanded the land-tenure program to the entire Lesser Slave interior and over time developed firm views about the program's benefits. Land tenure was created to meet the special needs of northern natives, he said. Granting hamlet status was a way to deliver badly needed services. Little Buffalo was split between Indian and Metis residents, and the Lubicon band was merely "a very arbitrary creation of Indian Affairs at some point in time." In an apparent reference to Lennarson, he said: "My general experience in native communities in Canada has been that if there's a problem, look for the white man."

Ford also started to say that there was no connection between the government's attempt to impose land tenure and the band's attempt to assert aboriginal rights.

"It was very, very clear on the land-tenure applications that this grant of land was totally without prejudice to any future land claims," he said authoritatively. "Marvin Moore made very clear back in 1980 that improvement in services was entirely separate from anything in terms of the change of the status of the land."

"I've seen the correspondence."

"Well?"

"Moore also wrote that Little Buffalo is now occupied Crown land and cannot become part of a land settlement."

Ford stopped cold.

"Yes," he said. "Well [pause] I don't have any [pause] as I say [pause] I think the only way to really address that situation [pause] it could have been addressed [pause] it was addressed in other communities, and, you know [pause] I guess maybe the correspondence speaks for itself."

≈

Of the more than two dozen Alberta officials interviewed about government actions at Little Buffalo, only one displayed pangs of conscience. She was Barbara Deters, public-relations officer for Jim Horsman, the deputy house leader and minister of federal and inter-governmental affairs. After 1986, Horsman also became attorney general and native affairs minister, making Deters the key provincial government contact for reporters on Lubicon Lake. Because her job was to feed the government line, she was often prone to giving false information such as "Bernie was born at Whitefish Lake" and "Who are the Lubicons to claim one-tenth of Alberta?" But Deters is an outgoing, curious person, and as she learned about the case she showed signs of uneasiness. On hearing of Marten River, she expressed dismay, and she refused to believe at first that deputy minister Fred McDougall was calling Dwight Gladue a "trespasser" and claiming Gladue's house as Crown property. While discussing the so-called community split, her jaw literally dropped when she heard that Josie L'Hirondelle, the original Metis settler at Lubicon Lake, had been a long-time supporter of the reserve quest.

Late one night, Deters phoned wanting to talk. She seemed to be struggling with something. For two and a half hours, she swung between defending her government's actions and questioning them.

"I read a circular going around Europe that the band killed 419 moose in 1979–80," she said.

"The figure was 219."

"Well, holy smokes, that's still a lot of animals, a hell of a lot to consume," she said. "I didn't know how big a moose was so I looked it up in my children's encyclopedia—this is a big animal. It weighs as much as a car. Did they have the capacity to store all that? Or did they overkill?"

Minutes later, Deters swung around.

"I don't want to do in the Lubicons, for heaven's sake," she said. "I'm a good old Ukrainian girl from Vegreville. I went to school with Indian kids. I've spent time at Lac la Biche Pow-Wow Days. I have a friend who is Indian, an incredible designer. You may have seen me in some of her clothes. My kids have friends who are Indians. They stay over at my place. If I'm being duped, I'm appalled."

Then she swung again.

"No, I can't believe that part about a master plan. I've been to all kinds of meetings at the lowest level and the highest level, I've been privy to all sorts of information, and I can't imagine a concerted effort. It's not something I'm familiar with. If I honestly believed that were happening, I'd start my own business or do something else, but I just don't see it."

And swung back.

"I don't like everything I hear. Some of the stuff ends up being fairly heavy-handed and quite unacceptable to the ordinary guy, but maybe in the scheme of things it's acceptable to the government."

Deters eventually left the government to start her own public-relations firm, but for the next several years she continued to disseminate the government line. In reply to routine inquiries, she continued to issue an "information package" suggesting that the Lubicon people were from Whitefish Lake and referring to the reserve promise as "an administrative notation." A document she especially pushed for a while was the *Special Report on the Complaints of the Lubicon Lake Indian Band*, which concluded that the "genocidal consequences" charge from the World Council of Churches had "no factual basis."

≈

The special report was the work of Alberta's ombudsman, Randall Ivany, who undertook the investigation in 1984 at the request of the official opposition. It was to be his last assignment before retiring at the end of a ten-year term. He began awkwardly. He defined his frame of reference in the narrowest way possible, saying he had no power to investigate land claims, no power to study political motives and no power to examine oil-company activity; he could only inquire as to whether Alberta civil servants were properly doing their jobs. "Genocide is an attempt to eradicate a species, and I don't believe that is happening here," Ivany also said the day he accepted the assignment.

"We wonder what Dr. Ivany means," Ominayak replied in a news release, "when he refers to us as a separate species."

In his report four months later, Ivany said there was no evidence that forestry workers acted improperly when fires at Fish and Joker lakes burned out of control in 1982. Fires that threaten timber stands should receive higher priority than those threatening "only scrub bush," he said.

While traps and snares certainly were being destroyed, Ivany said he couldn't say for sure that they were being destroyed deliberately by provincial employees.

Problems with the land-tenure program had to do with "poor communication." Ivany said he could neither prove nor disprove that people had been misled about what they were signing, but conceded that using Fleuri and Rose L'Hirondelle as interpreters raised legitimate "concern about bias."

Whether people such as deputy minister Fred McDougall had acted properly in threatening to remove people's homes, Ivany said he wasn't sure. But he found there was nothing wrong with trying to get a new school for the community. "The quality of education can only be improved by providing an appropriate new facility," he said.

At the outset of his report, Ivany said he could not address the "genocidal consequences" charge. "Much of what was contained in the World Council of Churches' letter referred to an aboriginal land claim," he wrote. "That issue, of course, cannot be investigated by the Ombudsman for Alberta, because it is beyond my jurisdiction."

But he addressed the charge anyway. "During my investigation, I was able to find no factual basis for it," Ivany wrote. "I have not been provided with any evidence either from members of the Band or from other sources, that could substantiate such a serious accusation."

The report, said Milt Pahl, meant that charges of genocidal consequences "have been put to bed."

"No evidence for genocide charge," one newspaper headline read. "Lubicon band not in jeopardy," said another.

Three years later, in the summer of 1987, Ivany agreed to an interview at the University of Alberta in Edmonton. He had an office at the law school there, where he ran the International Ombudsman Institute, a research and publication centre that he had founded and for which he had won the Order of Canada. When he talked he leaned back expansively, puffing a pipe, but his remarks were oddly bitter. "My experience with the Church on these issues is they make a lot of noise, they have very few facts straight, and what good they do in the long run, damned if I know," he said.

Before he was ombudsman, Ivany had been a senior Anglican clergyman, the dean of All Saints' Cathedral in Edmonton. He was a conservative, at odds with Archbishop Ted Scott, and hostile towards the World Council of Churches for involving itself in social issues. On his retirement as ombudsman, Ivany expressed expectations of being named a bishop, but reaction to his Lubicon report had helped dash that possibility. Representatives from all the major churches denounced the report variously as "narrow," "one- sided" and "disturbing."

"The Church is a funny institution," Ivany said. "It reminds me of the story of a former bishop of London when he was being installed. He walked in and took a look at the clergy and congregation who were assembled and said, 'At last the sea gives up its dead.' And that's my view of the House of Bishops of the Anglican Church. My relationship with them, to say the least, has been strained since this report. But they only want one side." Reaction from fellow Anglicans hurt the most, he said. "I have never seen an organization that could show such hatred and viciousness as these people. I suppose they had to get their kicks some way."

The longer Ivany talked, the more reckless he became. "There is financial involvement in the Lubicon from the American Indian Movement," he said, referring to the organization famous for confronting police at Wounded Knee, South Dakota, in 1973. "I also know that at least one of the Lubicon advisors was involved in the American Indian Movement and came here directly from the United States."

"Are you talking about Fred Lennarson?"

"I think that is the name, as a matter of fact," Ivany said. [Lennarson had come to Alberta via Nova Scotia and Ottawa, and says he has never been associated with AIM.]

"How much money is involved?"

"In the neighbourhood of three to four million dollars."

"Over how long a period?"

"It started a long time ago."

"That's hot news."

"Of course it is," Ivany said. "Now, none of this can be proved but I had sufficient information to convince me this was the situation. During the investigation, I had access to certain papers and files. People in government are aware of this, although they don't publicize it."

"Who is your source?"

"I can't tell you that," he said. "But we're talking millions of dollars."

"Did you know that the band took out bank loans for $700,000 cosigned by the James Bay Cree?"

"I didn't hear about a loan, I just heard about a lot of money."

"Could the bank loan be the money you heard about?"

"Could be," Ivany said.

"Maybe you're talking about something else."

"Not necessarily."

"So maybe there's nothing to the AIM thing either?"

"It's no secret that Lennarson was with the American Indian Movement."

"In what capacity?"

"I have no idea."

"Can you substantiate any part of what you're saying?"

"The comments were made to me."

"What is the American Indian Movement, by the way?"

"Well," Ivany said, taking a long draw on his pipe, "I really don't know. And I don't know much about the James Bay movement either."

A year after the conversation, Ivany died of cancer. Another year later he was discovered to be a crook. In a writ filed in the Alberta Court of Queen's Bench in 1989, he was accused of having borrowed $250,000 from the charitable Gladys and Merrill Muttart Foundation of Edmonton when he was a director. He had pretended to put the money towards a child-abuse study pending receipt of a federal grant, the writ said. But there was no study. Ivany had credited the funds to his own account instead, and in 1987—at around the time of the interview—he had embezzled $301,356.05 from his own ombudsman institute to repay the loan and interest. As director of both the charity and the institute, the writ said, "Ivany conceived a plan to fraudulently or otherwise wrongfully raise or convert money to satisfy his personal indebtedness." In June 1990, representatives of the institute, the charity and two chartered banks agreed out of court to split the loss.

10 TRUSTING THE LAW

"THE LUBICON PEOPLE will have their land rights affirmed," James O'Reilly, the band's lawyer, would often say. Through the worst years of the oil boom, he repeatedly assured band members of a fair hearing in the Canadian courts. "It may take time," he would say. "We may not get everything. We may have to go all the way to the Supreme Court of Canada. But ultimately the courts will recognize the band's right to land."

O'Reilly can be an eccentric, at times comic, figure. His shoes are often scuffed, his tie is sometimes askew and a lock of unruly dark hair tends to fly across his pate as he rushes around. But in court, he is meticulous and unrelenting. When a big case is underway he works day and night, often rising to the kind of tough, powerful oratory that makes for high drama. "This band has a will to survive!" he once told the parliamentary standing committee on aboriginal affairs in his courtroom style, nearly shouting as he wound his right arm through the air. "It has a resiliency that has amazed me, and that has amazed many other Canadians, and the fight will get worse. A warning to the government of Canada: the Lubicons will not go away! Their advisors will not go away! I personally am committed to rectifying this particular injustice if it is the last piece of work I do!"

Although he lives in Montreal, O'Reilly came to the Lubicon case early. In 1979, Harold Cardinal sent Lennarson on a research trip across Alaska and the Canadian North to see how other native groups were pursing aboriginal rights, and Lennarson returned saying, "The James Bay people have things to teach us." The James Bay Cree and the Quebec Inuit had negotiated a breakthrough aboriginal-rights settlement under which they retained the measure of self-determination they deemed necessary to continue as distinct peoples. O'Reilly was their lawyer. He had won an upset decision in Quebec Superior Court that got talks moving in the first place and had served as legal advisor to the Cree during negotiations on the final agreement. The deal, signed in 1975, had established O'Reilly as one of the leading native-rights lawyers in the country. In early 1980, Cardinal and Lennarson flew to Montreal to hire him for an aboriginal-rights challenge to the Athabasca tar sands.

"I told them I thought they had a strong aboriginal-rights claim," O'Reilly recalls. "Even though a treaty had been signed, these bands had not been signatories."

At the very least, he told them, the isolated communities had an overwhelming claim to unfulfilled treaty rights. The Lubicon case stood out as particularly strong, he said. Ottawa had recognized the Lubicon people as a distinct Indian band and had provisionally set aside a reserve in 1940.

"I couldn't get over what a clear claim they had to a reserve and how they had been left with absolutely nothing," he remembers. "My wife said, 'Don't get into another James Bay,' but the inequities just seemed so flagrant I figured it wouldn't be too tough."

Two months later, O'Reilly filed a suit on behalf of the Lubicon band as a test case for the isolated communities. In the Federal Court of Canada, he asked that the court either affirm the Lubicon people's aboriginal rights to their traditional territory, or, if the court held that such aboriginal rights had somehow been extinguished, affirm the band's right to a reserve and $1 billion in compensation for lost lands and treaty benefits. He named as defendants the federal government, the Alberta government and ten major oil companies operating in Lubicon territory.

Among the lawyers for the other side, O'Reilly faced two seasoned adversaries. Representing Ottawa was Ivan Whitehall, the justice department lawyer who had argued against the Indians in the caveat case, staking out Ottawa's position that Treaty Eight had extinguished aboriginal rights in all of northern Alberta. Representing the province was Howard Irving, the premier's legal advisor on the caveat case, the retroactive legislation and the land-tenure program.

Irving and the oil-company lawyers argued procedurally, saying the federal court had no jurisdiction over them. The judge agreed. The band could sue the federal government and federally owned Petro-Canada in federal court, the judge said. But the band must sue the Alberta government and the other oil companies in an Alberta court.

Following the decision, O'Reilly filed parallel aboriginal-rights suits in the federal and provincial courts. In an effort to avoid a court struggle altogether, he also helped to prepare a brief sent to Indian Affairs Minister John Munro, asking that land negotiations begin soon and requesting a loan to help all seven isolated communities prepare for such talks. Munro agreed in writing to appoint a negotiator and to advance $1 million. But three weeks later he reneged, saying only that he had "experienced difficulty in coming up with necessary funding," part of Munro's on-again, off-again pattern of support.

At the federal Office of Native Claims, officials conceded quickly that the Lubicon people had been treated shabbily by Ottawa. "Unless something is done immediately to assist those people, there's a danger that as a cultural group they might not exist much longer," said one of the directors, Bob Connelly, echoing Munro's statements of the period. The band appeared entitled at least to a 25.4-square-mile reserve with mineral rights, Connelly and others said. But like the justice department lawyers, claims officials regarded the case as an outstanding treaty entitlement, dismissing the band's aboriginal-rights position.

The distinction was significant. In federal jargon, an outstanding treaty entitlement is called a "specific claim." The category applies to aboriginal groups who have signed treaties but whose reserves for various reasons ended up smaller than they should be. The Lubicon people wished to negotiate a "comprehensive claim" based on aboriginal title. They had never signed a treaty, which to them meant that they continued to hold aboriginal rights to lands they traditionally used and occupied. In exchange for ceding their lands to Canada, band members wished to retain a reserve, establish a modern community settlement and create the means to make the difficult transition to a diversified economy based on agriculture, small business, and wage employment in the oil and forestry industries. The band also sought compensation for the destruction of the bush economy by $5 billion worth of oil work.

With the two sides deadlocked on how to proceed, O'Reilly launched a further legal action. In February 1982, he asked the Alberta Court of Queen's Bench to order an injunction against the work of ten major oil companies and the Alberta government in Lubicon territory until the land dispute was settled. He asked the court to stop all oil work within a sixty-square-mile area centred around the promised reserve lands, order strict controls on work within a wider 900-square-mile area, and apply sufficient controls over work in the rest of an 8,500-square-mile territory to allow hunting and trapping to continue at some level.

To pay for the suit, the band again approached Ottawa for money, and after months of delay Munro again turned down the request, saying: "The litigation does not fall within the approved criteria." The department also cut the band's annual operating budget in half, from $101,736 to $51,460. Band members could expect little help from the department, said the director of operations for Indian Affairs in Alberta, as long as they pursued an aboriginal-rights position. Ominayak later was to obtain bank loans totalling $700,000 cosigned by the James Bay Cree, but when the case began the band had nothing. Undaunted, O'Reilly flew to Calgary at the expense of Byers Casgrain, the large Montreal law firm to which he was attached through most of the 1980s.

"Certainly our case is overwhelming on the 25.4 square miles and very strong on the surrounding area," O'Reilly said confidently at the time. "We are almost certain to get some kind of injunctive relief."

O'Reilly had cause for optimism. His career in native rights had gone spectacularly well to that point, and major decisions had gone in the Indians' favour. As a young lawyer at the prestigious firm of Martineau Walker, O'Reilly won the first Indian case he took on. Andrew Delisle, chief of the Mohawk community of Kahnawake immediately south of Montreal, had hired him in 1966 after federal authorities expropriated a piece of land for St. Lawrence Seaway construction, then transferred it to Quebec for a road. O'Reilly helped win the return of four hundred acres of land and $700,000 in compensation. "He took it to heart," Delisle says of O'Reilly's handling of the case, and O'Reilly stayed on as lawyer for the Kahnawake Mohawks.

When Pierre Trudeau swept into office proposing to revise the

Indian Act, Delisle and O'Reilly rushed to get involved. Delisle secured federal funding to create committees around Quebec. The committees later amalgamated as the Indians of Quebec Association, with Delisle as president and O'Reilly as legal advisor. They held meetings with forty-two bands across the province to discuss legislative revisions, but found that people had other issues on their minds: better living standards, larger reserves and greater control over their own affairs. They talked of wanting their rights to hunt, fish and trap affirmed in the Canadian constitution.

People also raised questions about land rights, sending O'Reilly and a colleague into the archives, where they researched colonial regulations on the fur trade and discovered a rich body of law favouring protection of Indian lands. In a series of papers, O'Reilly laid the basis of his pioneering work in native-rights law, and when Jean Chrétien released his White Paper on Indian Policy in 1969, O'Reilly joined the outcry. "Before any change is brought about," he told the annual meeting of the civil liberties section of the Canadian Bar Association, "Indian rights [must] be first determined and recognized."

As debate intensified, Delisle became chairman of a national committee on Indian rights and treaties. He and O'Reilly travelled the country meeting chiefs, researchers and association presidents, hearing concerns and helping Harold Cardinal and others form the National Indian Brotherhood. O'Reilly loved the work. He enjoyed the combination of history, geography, politics and spirituality that was bound up in Indian issues, he says, and liked fighting for justice for the underdog. "I kept saying to myself, 'How come these people who once had all of Canada are now the rejects of Canadian society?' I felt something had to be done."

In the spring of 1971, his fateful opportunity came. Quebec Premier Robert Bourassa announced Quebec's "project of the century"—a series of hydroelectric dams along La Grande River in northern Quebec involving widespread flooding and the diversion of four major waterways. In southern Quebec, the idea was popular. The project would create 125,000 jobs in its first phase, Bourassa said, contributing to Quebec's economic self-sufficiency and ascendant national pride. In northern Quebec, the news raised alarm. The plans took almost no account of the 10,000 James Bay Cree and northern Quebec Inuit whose lives would be seriously disrupted.

The Cree asked O'Reilly to help fight the project. He hesitated. His law firm was acting for the James Bay Development Corporation, the hydroelectric company involved. To take the Cree case, he would have to leave the firm. He was married, the second of his three children was on the way, he had a mortgage on his home, and the chances of winning the case looked terrible.

"It was a total risk," he recalls. "We would be bucking a huge trend. But after a couple of months I decided my place was with the Indians. A tough decision in some ways, but easy in terms of following one's principles." After establishing a new firm with a couple of friends, he took the case with Jacques Beaudoin, a Quebec City lawyer he had known at the Indians of Quebec Association. With lawyers for the Inuit, they made a bid to stop construction at James Bay pending the settlement of native rights. "And we all embarked on an exciting adventure," O'Reilly says.

Preliminary arguments were heard in late 1972 in Quebec Superior Court at Montreal. Teams of lawyers for the Quebec government, Hydro-Quebec and the James Bay Development Corporation said they could show in one afternoon that Indian title to northern Quebec did not exist. O'Reilly replied that it did, pulling out the archival documents he had unearthed over the years, starting with King George's Royal Proclamation. After four days of arguments, Mr. Justice Albert Malouf ruled that the native groups had some apparent rights and were entitled to a hearing. O'Reilly's documents, the judge said, "show without doubt that the Government of Canada recognized that Indians were entitled to exercise rights in the territory described."

The full injunction hearing took a year. It was extraordinary in the way that hydro dams are extraordinary—for sheer dimension. Witnesses testifying: 167. Exhibits filed: 312. Pages of court transcript: 10,000. At stake was the future of Quebec's northern native peoples. Also at stake was Quebec's centrepiece megaproject to which the premier himself had attached patriotism, prosperity and his own political career.

"The most important case I've ever handled," Malouf says in retrospect. "It was also a beautiful experience because we were dealing with the customs and habits of the aboriginal peoples of this country."

Among lawyers, Malouf is called "the Sphinx" for the impassive expression he assumes in court, but he is also known for his compassion, particularly in minority-rights cases. He listened carefully as O'Reilly argued that the Cree and Inuit retained rights as original inhabitants of the territory, that hunting and trapping constituted a way of life for them, and that serious interference with that way of life compromised their existence. "He started opening my eyes," Malouf says of O'Reilly. "He cited judgments going way back—to the nineteenth century and before—and laws adopted by the colonial government. He had all this at his fingertips and was quoting chapter and verse . . . . After hearing something like that for a few days your eyes start to open up, and I realized that this would have great importance and that it would last a long time."

Malouf began taking notes in court, and on weekends he prepared summaries of the evidence and legal questions raised. When the hearing ended he worked all summer and into the fall preparing his judgment, which he delivered in both English and French—the first time a Canadian judgment was written in both official languages.

"The rights of the Cree Indian and Inuit populations have never been extinguished," he ruled, forcing a stop to construction on the James Bay project pending a full aboriginal-rights trial, a process expected to take another two years. Quebec's financial loss was less important than the devastation to native people if the plans weren't changed, he said. "I find it difficult to compare such monetary loss to the damages which such a large group of people will suffer."

The ruling "shook the country," as Malouf later put it. He had come down firmly on the side of the Cree and the Inuit, and the judgment followed two ground- breaking court decisions elsewhere. One came from the Supreme Court of Canada. Six of seven judges hearing the aboriginal rights case of the Nishga people of British Columbia affirmed that English colonial law in the province had recognized Indian title to land. The six judges were split on whether Nishga title had since been extinguished, and the seventh judge threw the case out on a technicality, but Prime Minister Trudeau saw the significance of the ruling. "Perhaps you have more legal rights than we thought you had when we did the white paper," he told the Union of British Columbia Indian Chiefs. "The judgment," he said in the House of Commons, "has indicated new possibilities for [the Nishga people's] legal rights."

In the other decision, the Dene chiefs of the Northwest Territories won the first round of their caveat application. Mr. Justice William Morrow of the territorial Supreme Court ruled that notwithstanding Treaties Eight and Eleven, "there is sufficient doubt on the facts that aboriginal title was extinguished" in the Mackenzie Valley. He said the chiefs should be allowed to file a caveat claiming title to the land—a ruling that was to be overturned in the Supreme Court of Canada, but which led to comprehensive land-rights negotiations with Ottawa.

Reaction to the Malouf ruling was swift. Lawyers for the James Bay project asked that the judgment be suspended pending appeal, and the Quebec Court of Appeal immediately complied. The public interest as determined by the Quebec government takes precedence over the interests of a minority, the appeal judges said. One week after the Malouf decision, dam construction resumed.

The appeal court would later fully overturn the Malouf judgment, but by then its political ramifications could not be ignored. With O'Reilly still legal advisor to the Cree, Ottawa opened land-rights negotiations with the Cree and the Inuit, talks that led to the landmark James Bay and Northern Quebec Agreement of 1975. Under the agreement, aspects of the hydro project were modified to protect prized wildlife areas, and the native groups retained the measure of self-determination that they deemed necessary to continue as distinct peoples. The Cree kept 2,000 square miles of reserve land and exclusive hunting-and-trapping rights over 25,000 square miles. They won a guaranteed income plan for trappers and a form of aboriginal self-government: control over their own education, health and police systems. They also agreed to an estimated $150 million in compensation, expected to free them from the tutelage of Indian Affairs and lay the basis for a new local economy. The Inuit settled for similar terms.

"We are almost certain to get some kind of injunctive relief," O'Reilly said confidently as he arrived in Calgary for the Lubicon application.

Preliminary arguments began in September 1982. O'Reilly and his Calgary associate, Ken Staroszik, faced more than a dozen government and oil-company lawyers, including Howard Irving acting for Alberta and Ivan Whitehall observing for Ottawa. But as in the James Bay case, the defending lawyers proceeded casually at first. They said the court shouldn't hear the case because the Crown enjoyed immunity from injunctions, and they argued that no irreparable damage was being caused—the animals would come back.

O'Reilly went all out. "Crown immunity emerges from the archaic principle that the King can do no wrong," he began in a presentation that was by turns sarcastic, amusing and professorial. He recounted the history of the band's neglect, describing how the original inhabitants of the territory had come to be considered "strangers in their own land."

"Your Lordship is representing the Queen as a fountain of justice," O'Reilly said. "This is a court of equity and I respectfully submit that on an equitable basis Your Lordship . . . can look at the entire history, the circumstances in which particular applicants find themselves . . . and can on the basis of purely equitable relief suggest a remedy." Over the next several days he cited Indian rights case law and, for the first time, the Constitution Act of 1982, which states: "The existing aboriginal and treaty rights of the aboriginal peoples of Canada are hereby recognized and affirmed."

Lawyers for Alberta and the oil companies stuck to procedural arguments, raising a total of seven technical objections to the application. The presiding judge, Mr. Justice Gregory Forsyth, decided to hear the objections at two separate sittings.

Forsyth had come to the bench from the oil industry. In the 1970s, he had been the senior litigation lawyer for the Nova Corporation of Alberta, when it was called the Alberta Gas Trunk Line Company Limited and owned most of Husky Oil Ltd.—a company with operations in Lubicon territory although not one of the ten defendants in the case. Far from being sphinxlike, Forsyth is convivial, constantly interrupting lawyers with jocular asides. When O'Reilly once referred to the band's white binders and the government's black ones, the judge interjected that he hoped O'Reilly wasn't reading symbolism into the colours. When an oil-company lawyer began a lesson in fur-bearing animals, the judge said he knew what beavers can do to a golf course. And when the lawyer said a lynx pelt can fetch up to $400, the judge remarked: "If your wife has ever been in a fur store and looked at lynx coats you will appreciate the popularity of them."

Forsyth heard the first set of objections in early November, at the start of the 1982–83 drilling season, taking two weeks to deal with a matter that is commonly dealt with in one or two days. He dismissed the objections, siding with the band.

He heard the remaining objections in early December, taking three months to deliver a judgment. It came in early March 1983, as another drilling season was being completed. Again he dismissed the objections.

The full hearing got underway in September 1983, a year after the start of preliminary arguments. O'Reilly wanted to call witnesses and file exhibits as he had done at the James Bay hearing—Ominayak and other band members were in court through the entire case—but Forsyth allowed written evidence only. In compliance, O'Reilly tabled scores of documents. He argued that the Lubicon people make up a distinct aboriginal society trying to pursue a traditional way of life on land that their ancestors had used and occupied since time immemorial. Most band members still speak Cree, he said. Most can't read or write. Many depend on horse teams and dog sleds to get around. Hunting and trapping remain essential to the Lubicon way of life, O'Reilly argued, a way of life that determines how people feed themselves, organize their time, relate to each other, educate their children and deal with basic questions of life and death.

Affidavits sworn by six elders offered details on the tea dance, food sharing, the seasonal round, birthplaces, grave sites, boundaries with other bands and the location of major trails, cabins and former settlements.

Affidavits from Chief Ominayak described the seismic and drilling work, including the busy trucking of gravel, water, fuel and construction equipment. The roadblocks were described, along with the overrunning of traplines and the recent scarcity of game. "These damages and effects cannot be valued in terms of money," Ominayak said in the sworn statement. "We believe we are threatened with extinction as a people."

In one of ten outside papers solicited by the band, Kenneth Bodden from the Boreal Institute of the University of Alberta submitted figures showing the steady drop in moose kills and trapping income. He also showed that hunting and trapping as a way of life made economic sense for Lubicon members, at least until 1982. Rather than work for wages, people are better off hunting for their food in winter and taking temporary wage work in the off-season, the paper said. "Subsistence activities are significant in the economic structure of the community and vital to the social well-being of its inhabitants."

Ben Hubert, a Yellowknife zoologist, found that each active oil well destroys two to four acres of moose habitat, plus an equal amount for oil gathering, processing and production, plus land for roads and pipelines. "Unless vigilant and prudent management action is taken, the moose population over the entire hunting/trapping territory of the Lubicon Lake band is threatened," he said.

Affidavits from two forest ecologists and a geologist included detailed maps with data on everything from timber stands to gas deposits, offering a comprehensive picture of the advance of exploration and development, and the extent of the damage to date. Peter Dranchuk, a petroleum engineer teaching at the University of Alberta, concluded in his report: "The Reserve Area and the area surrounding it comprise one of the most, if not the most, active oil and gas exploration and development areas in Western Canada."

James Smith, a New York ethnologist and specialist on the western woods Cree, submitted a paper exploding the notion that Cree peoples expanded westward from Lake Winnipeg only after acquiring guns through the fur trade. Government lawyers were suggesting that the Lubicon people had not occupied their territory "since time immemorial," a point with legal implications on the aboriginal-rights question. But Smith traced the migration theory through the journals of early explorers, finding that it had gained credence mostly by successive travellers quoting previous ones. Studying a wealth of anthropological, historical and linguistic evidence, he established that while the Swampy Cree were indeed migrating during the fur-trade period, other woodland Cree groups populated areas as far west as Peace River long before European contact.

Joan Ryan, head of anthropology at the University of Calgary, predicted the worst. Oil development, if unchecked, would initiate a downward social spiral among band members, she said in an affidavit. Loss of food and income would cause a decline in health and living standards. Ties based on food sharing would be severed. Former providers would turn to alcohol. "The experience of other native land-based societies confronted with development is applicable to [the Lubicon]," she said. Money would not solve the problem, but money plus time to develop a new economy would give band members a chance to survive as a distinct people. The process would take two generations, she said. Maybe longer.

Lawyers for Alberta and the oil companies argued that the

Lubicon Cree had no right to hunt and trap on lands "occupied" by oil companies. The high welfare rate at Little Buffalo, they also said, indicated that the Lubicon Cree no longer followed an aboriginal way of life. "Indians and Inuit people have abandoned their ancestral way of life and adopted the white man's ways," the defence lawyers said. "The clock cannot be turned back."

Since the Indian way of life did not exist, no irreparable harm could be done to it, the lawyers argued. On the other hand, irreparable harm would be caused to the oil industry if an injunction were imposed, they said. Oil companies would lose between $450 and $500 million a year—more than $1.2 million a day. The Alberta government would lose $90 million a year in royalties.

The decline in the wildlife harvest was a natural phenomenon having nothing to do with oil work, lawyers for the oil industry and Alberta also said. An infestation of winter ticks had caused moose numbers to decline. Lack of forest fires in some areas and an abundance of fires in others had both led to a lack of moose browse, but development work would help solve the problem, they said. "Oil development in the past few years . . . is not a cause of any reduction in the numbers of moose up there," said Howard Irving's partner Ev Bunnell. "In fact, it's an enhancement of the habitat for those animals" when forest land is cleared.

Reduced fur catches, defence lawyers said, could be explained by "natural cycles" in animal populations, a reduction in effort on the part of trappers, fur-price fluctuations that might affect trapper motivation, and possible overtrapping in previous years.

In other arguments, the lawyers for Alberta and the oil companies said that the Lubicon people were part of the Whitefish Lake band. They also said that if an injunction were imposed against the ten defendant companies, activities of smaller companies would increase in the area, nullifying the effect of an injunction. "No case law," one lawyer also argued, "has been brought forward to support the proposition that a particular way of life is a legal right that can be protected by way of injunction."

On the final day of the hearing, Chester L'Hirondelle and Peter Sawan entered the courtroom as O'Reilly was rising to give his closing remarks. They had a lawyer with them who asked that they be allowed to file affidavits. The statements said that many people in Little Buffalo opposed the injunction application, fearing that they would be forced from the area if a reserve was created.

O'Reilly struggled to maintain his composure. Speaking softly, he called the last-minute intervention "astounding." He was all for letting minorities have their say, he said, but the deadline for affidavits had long since expired.

The judge invited other lawyers to comment. Those for the oil companies were quick to say they knew nothing of the matter and wished to remain neutral. Howard Irving, acting for the Alberta government, chose his words carefully. "My Lord," he said, "my knowledge is a little bit more detailed than that of [the other lawyers]. I shall tell Your Lordship that about Wednesday of last week, I received a communication through my client [the attorney general] that several of the non-status people were concerned and wanted to make representations, and could they make them through me? And my answer was no, if they chose to do anything of this sort, they'd have to have their own counsel. That's the sum and substance I know of it." Irving also said that the Crown had "no objection to [L'Hirondelle and Sawan] being added as a party."

"I cannot believe, My Lord," O'Reilly said, "that the attorney general of Alberta is not a party to having these people coming in at this stage."

"That is a fairly serious allegation to be making," said the judge.

"It is, My Lord," O'Reilly replied. "I have never seen anything like that in all my practice."

Forsyth allowed the late submissions. During a recess, O'Reilly's colleague Ken Staroszik turned to Irving and said that slipping in a couple of affidavits at the last minute was pretty sleazy. Irving said he had nothing to do with it, to which Staroszik replied, "That's a bunch of baloney." Then Irving, who stands six-foot-two, shoved Staroszik, who stands five-foot-three and has one artificial leg, sending Staroszik stumbling backwards. Lennarson surged forward, Irving tensed, and O'Reilly leapt between them.

Mr. Justice Forsyth rendered his decision on November 17, 1983. He did not call the session "a beautiful experience," and he expressed no wonderment at "the customs and habits of the original peoples of this country." Rather, he showed annoyance that the hearing had lasted "twenty full days" and included "numerous lengthy affidavits . . . cross examinations . . . consideration of a mass of historical articles, maps and charts, and genealogical tables."

The key question to consider, the judge said, was this: "Is oil work causing the band irreparable harm?"

"No," he decided, dismissing the injunction application. If oil work goes ahead and the band later proves aboriginal title, Alberta and the oil companies could make up the band's losses with money. No form of interim injunction was warranted, he ruled: not on the total area, not within a fifteen-mile radius of the community, not on the promised reserve land at Lubicon Lake.

"The evidence of life style being affected is limited to a few individuals who hunt and trap," Forsyth ruled.

"One thing is clear," he also said. "This is not a case of an isolated community in the remote North where access is only available by air on rare occasions and whose way of life is dependent to a great extent on living off the land itself. The twentieth century, for better or for worse, has been part of the Applicants' lives for a considerable period of time."

Forsyth said he wished to comment further. Unlike Malouf, who had found it difficult to compare monetary loss to human suffering, Forsyth said granting an injunction would have caused Alberta and the oil companies "large and significant damages" and "a loss of competitive positions in the industry." As the band was in no position to repay the companies should the band fail to prove aboriginal title, he said, stopping the oil work was not appropriate.

The judgment was the most extreme one possible short of saying the band had no claim to territory at all, said O'Reilly.

One month later, Forsyth presided over a discussion of court costs. Lawyers for Alberta and the oil companies said their expenses, later estimated at $200,000, should be paid by the band. Forsyth agreed. He ordered the band liable for all costs of the injunction application, including the costs to hear both sets of procedural arguments, which the defendants had initiated and the band had won.

Forsyth also ruled that the band must pay costs "in any case." This meant that the band had to pay the costs even if it later won its aboriginal-rights case, affirming that the government and oil companies had been trespassing.

The band didn't have to pay right away, Forsyth said, but the oil companies and the provincial government could demand immediate payment at any time. "A legal sword of Damocles," Lennarson called the arrangement, which meant that the band's adversaries could at any time seize funds raised for an appeal.

"We are presiding at a requiem," O'Reilly told the hearing on costs. "I feel like our learned friends want to take the corpse out of the coffin and stab it again and put it back in the coffin."

On appeal, Forsyth's rulings stood. The Alberta Court of Appeal upheld them in a unanimous decision written by Mr. Justice J. A. Kerans, who said that the band's affidavits were "permeated with hyperbolic claims of cultural harm." If the band eventually proved to be the rightful owners of the territory, he also ruled, the oil companies could restore the band's way of life with money damages. The band could, "if successful at trial, gain through damages sufficient moneys to restore the wilderness," Kerans said.

Band members were "stunned" by the outcome, says Ken Staroszik, who with O'Reilly had travelled frequently to Little Buffalo to brief the community on developments in the case as it dragged—because of delays—into the longest injunction application in Alberta history. "We told them to have faith," Staroszik recalls. "This wasn't their system. They had no way of relating to it, and we kept telling them to trust us, that the system was fair and equitable, that it was going to protect them. They put their faith in a system not their own while the oil companies continued to pound their traplines, and for them the result was like a betrayal. It was like a cruel joke."

"It's obvious," O'Reilly said of the judges of both courts, "that they did not believe the Indians. Their views were anchored in the sort of non-native Alberta tradition, which is that the Indians don't have a particular way of life, that that whole way of life has disappeared, and the problems they were experiencing in hunting and trapping couldn't have been caused by white men, but must be due to some kind of natural cause or the fault of the Indians themselves, and that this whole thing was essentially a put-up job on the part of the lawyers and the Indians."

The decision, said Nigel Bankes, a law professor at the University of Calgary, suggested that native people must fit the noble savage image to have rights. In an independent assessment published by the Canadian Institute of Resources Law, he said the case showed that "aboriginal peoples of Canada have rights so long as they remain in a fossilized or primitive state, but their rights are progressively diminished to the extent that they avail themselves to the benefits and burdens of the twentieth century."

O'Reilly asked the Supreme Court of Canada to hear a further appeal, but the court refused. He applied a second time, an audacious move but warranted, he said, because of a new ruling by the British Columbia Court of Appeal. The ruling had granted the Clayoquot and Ahousaht bands on Meares Island an interim injunction against logging pending a trial on aboriginal title. Appeal courts in adjacent provinces were contradicting each other, creating in O'Reilly's view an important issue for the top court. But the application was again refused.

"A dark day for the Canadian judicial system," O'Reilly told reporters at the time. "As a lawyer, I've always felt the Supreme Court was a beacon guiding the Indians on major cases . . . . But when you look at the whole record it's not very good."

11 SPECIAL ENVOY

"I HAVE ONE QUESTION on my mind all the time," Ominayak often used to say. "How long can we hold together?"

He was referring to the stress of the oil boom and government pressures, and the frustration of getting no relief from the courts. The sole hopeful sign for the band was that popular support appeared to be growing. Ominayak and Lennarson had been devoting more and more time to building the broad political base they had deemed essential over the long term, waging what they called a "public education campaign."

Essentially, it began on December 3, 1982, when they drove to Slave Lake one night to speak to a parliamentary subcommittee on native self-government. "I've never talked in public before," Ominayak began softly. "And you can understand that it is very difficult for me to talk about local government when we are faced with a battle for our survival as a people."

The appearance led to a hearing before the parliamentary standing committee on aboriginal affairs in Ottawa five months later, where Ominayak and Lennarson told of being refused legal funding and of having the band's operating budget cut in half.

"We need help immediately," Ominayak said. "If we don't receive it, we will not survive as a people."

Twenty-two listeners approached Ominayak after the session asking for more information. Lennarson took their names and addresses, creating the basis of what he came to call "the Lubicon support network" or simply "the mailing list." After every public appearance, Lennarson continued to add names, using the list to get news to people whether reporters were on the story or not, and maintaining a presence for the band in the minds of people living far from northern Alberta. He sent copies of Neil Gibson's tax-arrears notices, Lougheed's remarks on the "Metis" question, Forsyth's judicial decision, and his own sixty-one-page rebuttal to the Randall Ivany report—five pages longer than the report itself.

Sometimes the material was stridently worded. "The Alberta Provincial Government is trying to wipe us out because they want to steal our traditional lands," said one early, fourteen-page letter to Prime Minister Trudeau. "They have made clear that they are prepared to use all of their legal, political, financial and governmental power to wipe us out. They also made clear that they are prepared to do absolutely anything they can to wipe us out."

The signature was Ominayak's but the style was Lennarson's, and people would be surprised on meeting Ominayak to find him so soft-spoken. A few supporters suggested that Lennarson lighten his tone. Some advised Ominayak to speak more aggressively. "Keep it short," others said. Packages of between ten and twenty pages were going out as often as twice a week. One mailing ran to a hundred pages.

"People were telling me I was absolutely out of my mind," Lennarson says of the early mailings. "They were telling me nobody would read it, nobody could handle it, nobody would pay any attention. They said, 'Keep everything to four sentences.' 'Put everything into a slogan with a logo.' " But Lennarson stuck with what he knew. "This is a fight for justice, not a marketing venture," he would say. "A slick PR campaign is exactly the image we want to avoid."

On airplanes and in hotel rooms, Lennarson would hunch over a lined yellow notepad writing summaries for the mailing list in his scratchy handwriting. Once finished, he would read them aloud to Ominayak, who would comment on ideas and suggest changes. Lennarson would then rewrite, often going through the process several times until both were satisfied with content.

Completed drafts would go to Terri Kelly, Lennarson's office manager since his Milwaukee days. She is an unsung hero of the Lubicon campaign, a highly organized woman originally from Greybull, Wyoming, population 2,000. "People growing up in Wyoming are not usually interested in social-justice of any kind," she says, but her grandfather was a legendary character called Yellowstone Dutch, whom she describes as "a rebel, a social-justice advocate and a very unusual type of person who was comfortable with everybody and with dogs." Kelly adopted his independent spirit. As a student at Carroll College in Montana, she enrolled in a new national youth program called Vista—Volunteers in Service to America—a kind of domestic Peace Corps that paid young people a subsistence wage to work in poor pockets of the country. "I said, 'I'll join that,' and ended up six weeks later in an apartment building in South Chicago that had twice the population of my hometown," she recalls. After cursory training, she was assigned to a black neighbourhood of downtown Detroit where she lived through the race riots of July 1967. A transfer to Milwaukee landed her at Northcott Neighbourhood House. Lucius Walker had moved to New York by then, but Lennarson was directing a vocational-training program in the vicinity, and Kelly quit Vista to work for him. She has been part of his operation almost continuously since, moving with the business to Halifax, Ottawa and Edmonton. The basement offices of her home in south Edmonton contain a complete set of band archives and the all-important photocopying machine, mostly operated now by her teen-aged son, Pat, and his neighbourhood friends.

In its first five years, the mailing list expanded to more than six hundred individuals and organizations. It extended across the country to parts of the United States and to ten countries in western Europe. It became a kind of chain letter. One Canadian church organization summarized the material for its own mailing list of eight hundred people. In New York, the Interreligious Foundation for Community Organization did the same for its mailing list of three hundred. Other groups incorporated the material into their newsletters, bringing regular Lubicon news to thousands of socially conscious readers.

"It's our muscle, it's our capability, it's our army," Lennarson would say of the network. "The provincial government can try to write off the World Council of Churches as a bunch of communists, but they can't write off a United Church congregation in Banff!"

≈

In the fall of 1984, Lennarson called the support network into action for the first time. The federal Progressive Conservative Party under Brian Mulroney had won a landslide election victory over the long-reigning Liberals, bringing David Crombie to Indian Affairs as the new minister. He was an odd choice for the job, a city populist once hailed as the "tiny perfect mayor" of Toronto. At Lennarson's urging, Crombie was soon inundated with what one federal official called "bushels of mail" on Lubicon.

At the end of November 1984, Crombie arranged to see Ominayak. The minister was visiting the Sturgeon Lake reserve south of Peace River to hear from twenty-seven regional chiefs assembled there, and at the noon break he led Ominayak down a corridor to a storage room, where they cleared a space for themselves. Ominayak handed him a two-page paper. "Points for Discussion," it was titled, listing sixteen subheadings under which Lubicon land rights might be addressed. Crombie studied them from a semistanding position, leaning forward with one foot on a chair. The paper asked that a reserve be created at Lubicon Lake, calculated at 128 acres per person, or one square mile for every five people, as specified in Treaty Eight, and asked that the band be allowed to determine its own membership to end the inequities of McCrimmon's rules. The paper also requested that the band be given a say in wildlife management and environmental protection over its traditional lands, that a comprehensive socio-economic development package be negotiated and that compensation be awarded for past government neglect and the destruction of the band's hunting and trapping grounds.

By then, Crombie had begun assigning high-profile people to study especially intractable or pressing Indian issues. "Special envoys," he called them, because they reported directly to him. Emmett Hall, a former justice of the Supreme Court of Canada, had set off for the Whitedog Reserve in northwestern Ontario to determine damages to the Grassy Narrows and Islington bands from mercury pollution. Murray Coolican, a Halifax consultant and son-in-law of former Conservative leader Robert Stanfield, prepared to open hearings to find a fresh approach to settling aboriginal-rights cases. Frank Oberle, a Tory backbencher, had begun to address unfulfilled Treaty Eight promises with a view to designing a model for native self-government. Other envoys were taking on other tasks, and the minister's staff chart had begun to resemble a molecular diagram: atoms careering through disparate orbits around a nucleus that was Crombie himself, the entire structure floating self-contained and free of the department. Looking up from Ominayak's paper, Crombie said, "I think it's time to make a deal."

Crombie appointed a special envoy on Lubicon: E. Davie Fulton, a reserved, unfailingly courteous man with impeccable credentials. "Fearless Fulton" he was once known as, for his unshakable integrity and adherence to principle. He had been justice minister from 1957 to 1962 under Prime Minister John Diefenbaker, was twice a contender for the party leadership, and had served as a justice on the Supreme Court of British Columbia. In short, Fulton was a pillar of the Tory establishment, a mentor to the whole generation of Conservative politicians then coming into power. Prime Minister Mulroney, External Affairs Minister Joe Clark, and the Tory leader in the Senate, Lowell Murray, had all worked for him.

Two episodes with the bottle late in his career forced Fulton's resignation from the bench, but his handling of events further exemplified his unfailing sense of right and wrong. On a Saturday evening in 1979, he drove drunk through Vancouver, nicked a car, drove on, rear- ended another, got arrested, convicted and fined $500, and had his licence suspended. When he realized what he'd done, he publicly confessed his error, apologized to the two drivers and praised the arresting policeman for "exemplary behavior." Two years later, a Vancouver hooker coyly cited "Davey F." as a client in a squalid autobiography called *The Wendy King Story*. Fulton sued and King confessed in court that she had never met Fulton; but the stress of the ordeal got to him. He was caught driving impaired a second time. "I thought I had drinking under control but obviously I didn't," he said later. After a few days in jail and treatment for the drinking problem, he emerged to join the Vancouver law firm of Swinton & Company, where Crombie tracked him down.

Fulton was sixty-nine years old by then, still vigorous and still with one of the most incisive legal minds in the country. He arrived in Little Buffalo on the evening of April 9, 1985, spending the night with John Felix Laboucan at Laboucan's tiny bungalow, the only government representative ever to stay overnight in the community. He helped feed wood into the stove and used the backyard outhouse. When Ominayak came around the next morning, Fulton and Laboucan were washing dishes together and smiling, neither apparently bothered about not knowing the other's language.

Soon Fulton and Ominayak were flying northwards in a helicopter over Lubicon hunting and trapping territory. They reconnoitred the crisscrossing seismograph lines, the pipelines, the roads, the colonies of yellow-and-white ATCO housing units and the scores of nodding pump jacks painted bright playground shades of red, blue and orange. Fulton expressed surprise at the extent of the work.

"I have seen the terrible effects of development," he told about thirty community members gathered that afternoon in a tiny meeting hall stuffy with cigarette smoke and moist socks. "I want to try to do something about it."

Fulton outlined his program. After hearing from the band, he proposed to seek reaction from provincial and federal officials. He would also meet oil-company representatives, members of the L'Hirondelle family and leaders of the other isolated communities. He would then write a "discussion paper," laying out everyone's side of every issue. Afterwards, he would bring the band and the two governments together to negotiate a resolution of differences. The discussion paper would be ready in two months, he said. Direct talks would be underway in three.

Fulton came across as gentlemanly and intelligent, but there was an imperiousness about him that irritated Ominayak at first, perhaps more so because of the terrible hardships the band faced at the time. An odd friction developed. When Fulton said he hadn't had much experience with native claims but had a sense of what was just and fair, Ominayak said that working with someone from the government who was just and fair would be a new experience for the band. He also said that the Alberta government, with Ottawa's complicity, was trying to crush the band, causing Fulton to snort dismissively and slap the air with the back of his hand.

"I think they thought I was just another person who had come along as a gesture—to take up time and defuse the strength of their claims and so on," Fulton said later of initial tensions.

"Everyone came up to me at the break saying, 'Kick him out,' " Ominayak recalls. "But I thought, 'Maybe this guy should be given the opportunity to get screwed by Alberta, too.' "

Ominayak decided not to count on Fulton. As the envoy left for Edmonton and Ottawa, the band became involved in something called the Spokane Relief Caravan, one of a number of events during the Fulton period that sprang from the band's ongoing public-education campaign.

The caravan idea came from David Lundean, an Episcopalian minister in Spokane, Washington. He happened to see a filmstrip on

Lubicon circulating among U.S. churches and invited himself to Little Buffalo for a first-hand look. In return, he invited Ominayak to Spokane, and while other congregations were raising money for starving people in Ethiopia, Lundean launched a food drive for the Lubicon Lake Cree.

Response was overwhelming. During Lent of 1985, at around the time Fulton got started, the food drive engaged the energies of churchgoers and boy scout troops throughout eastern Washington and neighbouring Idaho and Montana. Lundean raised five thousand pounds of brown rice, three hundred pounds of beans, seventy-five cases of apples and nearly three tons of canned goods along with clothing, toys and first-aid supplies. Estimated value: $12,000. To deliver the goods, he led a caravan of thirteen cars and trucks on a weeklong round trip to Little Buffalo with news conferences along the way at Fort Macleod, Calgary, Edmonton and High Prairie.

The Spokane Relief Caravan rolled into Little Buffalo at dusk on April 15, a week after Fulton's first visit. "We have a certain amount of pride and it's hard to take something like this in a way," Ominayak told the visitors. "But the reality is we need all the support we can get." When the goods were unloaded, most band members were too shy to take anything. Apples, onions and other perishables had to be distributed door to door. Many who did take food left small dona-tions of money. At a community meeting, members voted to create a cooperative store with the remaining goods, an alternative to a grocery run by the L'Hirondelles.

Fulton stayed clear of the relief drive and its accompanying pub-licity, but two other issues soon arose demanding his intervention. The immediate one was money. The band was $1.5 million in debt on its loans for legal fees and other costs, plus interest, and the bank was demanding payment. Crombie had promised to cover the debt as an advance against an eventual settlement, but officials at the treasury, justice and Indian Affairs departments were blocking the move. Ottawa should not cover the band's legal costs, they argued, because the band sued before exhausting all avenues of negotiation.

Fulton studied the dispute and sided with the band. He asked that Cabinet approve the funds at once, not as an advance but as an outright grant. "It is not putting it too strongly to say . . . that if [the band] had not started Court action in 1982, which was 42 years after the original [reserve] promise, nothing would have been done for them to this day," he later wrote.

Months passed with no response. Finally, the band sued Crombie for breach of trust, asking $2.25 million in damages. The band dropped the suit when Crombie came up with the promised $1.5 million—not as a grant, as Fulton had recommended, but as an advance against a final settlement.

A second issue arose. The Union Oil Company of Canada announced plans to build a pipeline across the promised 25.4 square miles, parallel to an existing line.

"We intend to stop construction of this pipeline any way we can," Ominayak told a news conference in Ottawa. "If these major construction projects are allowed to continue in our traditional area, there will be nothing left to discuss." For the first time, Ominayak also talked of taking "direct action," including a possible "effort to block truck transport of oil-company equipment and supplies into our traditional area." At his side to express support were Anglican Archbishop Ted Scott; the national chief of the Assembly of First Nations, Georges Erasmus; the grand chief of the James Bay Cree, Ted Moses, and two opposition members of Parliament—Keith Penner of the Liberals and Jim Manly of the New Democrats.

Fulton also sought to suspend the project, realizing that new pipeline construction at the heart of Lubicon territory could jeopardize his work. "I have recently been making every effort that I can think of, by representations to both the Government of Alberta and the Government of Canada, to prevent the application going forward while this inquiry is under way," he wrote at the time.

The Union Oil people appeared unmoved. In statements from Los Angeles and Calgary, they downplayed the land-rights question by addressing an environmental one. "We are using an existing right-of-way right beside a road and an already existing power line to minimize environmental impact," one company representative said.

Lennarson cut the issue. "A line has to be drawn," he wrote the mailing list. "The purpose of the proposed pipeline is to transport oil from a major oil field which Union has developed in the Band's traditional area while the question of the Band's legal rights has been before the courts."

Demonstrations broke out in front of Union Oil offices in Calgary, attracting widespread news coverage, editorials and letters to the editor, all of which generated further meetings, rallies and letters.

Band members prepared to block roads to pipeline construction crews in Lubicon territory.

The company backed down. Faced with mounting public pressure, a company spokesman in Calgary announced a suspension of pipeline construction through the 25.4-square-mile area until the land dispute was settled. In addition, the company agreed to consult the band on wildlife and environmental concerns during pipeline construction outside the promised reserve area and to hire band members for construction clean-up work. Union Oil wants to be "a good friend and neighbour" to the band, the spokesman said. It was the band's first successful use of Alinsky-style mass jujitsu.

In early December 1985—a full year after the Crombie-Ominayak meeting—Fulton distributed what he called his "discussion paper." It was an exceptional document. Another investigator might have seen unbridgeable gulfs between parties: at one extreme, the province recognizing nine band members; at the other, the band asserting aboriginal rights to an enormous territory. Fulton didn't pretend that he could bring together the two positions, but as he laid out the views of each party on each issue, he began to see ways to accommodate various essential interests. He assumed good will on all sides, was careful not to scold anybody for the current mess and used words such as "equity," "generosity" and "fairness" to soften some of the entrenched legal and bureaucratic language in the dispute.

Previous talks had always foundered on terminology, with Ottawa calling the case a "specific claim" based on treaty entitlement and the band calling it a "comprehensive claim" based on aboriginal rights. Fulton viewed the debate as unproductive. He understood that the band considered assertion of unextinguished aboriginal rights to be crucial in the quest for a fair settlement. He also understood that neither Ottawa nor Alberta was prepared to recognize unextinguished aboriginal rights in an area covered by treaty. Such recognition had been granted in the Northwest Territories, but never in a province, and neither government was prepared to set the precedent. To break the impasse, Fulton tried to show that the band was owed a generous settlement under provisions of Treaty Eight and the Natural Resources Act of 1930.

While the band used an aboriginal-rights argument to insist on some control over wildlife management, Fulton showed how the demand could be seen as a treaty right. And while the band asserted an aboriginal right to compensation for lost hunting and trapping, Fulton showed how compensation could be owing under Treaty Eight and the act, both of which he said guaranteed Indian rights to hunting and trapping over Crown lands. Fulton acknowledged that there was an "enormous" difference between a specific and a comprehensive claim: if the Lubicon people proved aboriginal title they could be owed more than $1 billion. But he said he felt certain that a settlement fair to all parties could be reached through treaty entitlement.

In eighty-eight pages, Fulton addressed four principal areas of dispute as outlined in Ominayak's original brief to Crombie: reserve size, band membership, wildlife management and cash compensation.

The first two items—land and membership—were inextricably linked: the more band members, the bigger the reserve. Fulton laid out the respective positions. Alberta would honour the original promise of 25.4 square miles except if the band insisted on more, in which case Alberta would offer nothing. Ottawa recognized 182 status Lubicon Indians, for a reserve of 36.4 square miles, and was prepared to recognize more people if they met certain membership criteria. Band representatives said membership was not negotiable. Everybody of Lubicon descent living in the Lubicon area must be recognized as a band member, a number which at that time stood at 427, entitling the band to a reserve of 91.4 square miles.

Fulton held that the band's position was essentially correct and just, implicitly rejecting the notion that the community was split between Indian and Metis residents. He suggested that Alberta hand over the promised 25.4 square miles and that the federal government pay Alberta for the rest of the land. The exact amount of land could be worked out in negotiations, but would likely be close to what the band had determined. Ottawa should pay Alberta, Fulton said, because the failure to carry out the reserve promise of 1940 was "entirely the responsibility of Canada." Full subsurface rights to the reserve should go to the band as well, he said. As for the L'Hirondelles, Fulton held that the family's claim to the coop lands had merit but was irreconcilable with the band's, and that the band's rights must take precedence. The L'Hirondelles should be compensated for surrendering their interests, he said, with other lands, or money, or a combination of both.

Regarding wildlife resources, Fulton again laid out the respective positions. The band proposed a management program to be run jointly with the province. It would ensure that oil work proceeded at a level that would allow at least some band members to hunt and trap. Quotas on fur catches would be part of the regime at least until animal stocks were restored, and maybe elk could be introduced to make up for a decline in moose. Oil and gas extraction is compatible with a continued hunting and trapping life for some band members provided that care is taken by both sides, band representatives said. Alberta and oil-company representatives expressed guarded acceptance of the band's proposal. Ottawa officials said they were in favour if Alberta was.

Fulton endorsed the band's wildlife-management proposal and went further. He said that if an irreconcilable conflict were to arise between oil interests and wildlife interests, the protection of wildlife must take precedence. If an oil company wanted to build installations vital to its operations, but which might destroy a breeding ground vital to hunters, the wildlife area must be protected even if the company went bankrupt. "There must be acceptance of the paramountcy of the Band's interests as the guide" to wildlife management, he said. Taking an apparent shot at the Forsyth judgment, Fulton added, "It is the continuation of wildlife which is threatened by development, not development which is threatened to the point of extinction by the continuation of wildlife."

Fulton went further still. He noted that freedom to hunt and trap over unoccupied Crown lands is a right guaranteed to Indians in Treaty Eight. The Indians "signed the Treaty only on receipt of assurances that they would be 'as free to hunt and fish as they would be if they never entered into it,'" Fulton quoted Commissioner David Laird as saying. Fulton also quoted the Natural Resources Act of 1930 as stipulating that "Indians shall have the right, which the Province hereby assures to them, of hunting, trapping and fishing for game and fish for food at all seasons of the year on all unoccupied Crown lands." Most of Lubicon territory remained "unoccupied" despite exploration leases and oil wells, Fulton said. And if Indians had a continuing right to hunt and trap on unoccupied lands, "then surely they have a continuing and pressing interest in the maintenance of the resource—the wildlife—without which that right becomes a mockery."

Compensation issues took up almost half the report. The band claimed compensation in nine categories, the leading three of which were nonreceipt of treaty benefits from 1899, nonreceipt of government programs and services from 1899, and loss of livelihood from hunting and trapping since the onset of oil development. Both governments indicated a willingness to discuss some compensation items.

Fulton strongly supported the three main claims and lent qualified support to the others. Regarding lost treaty benefits, he said that "due to the failure by Canada to discharge its obligations" the band did not receive its full entitlement to annuity payments and went without other treaty entitlements such as livestock, farm implements and hunting and trapping equipment. The band was deprived not only of the capital value of the items but also of the annual income to which their use would have given rise. "A debt normally carries interest until the date it is paid," he also noted, concluding that "when a final calculation can be made a considerable sum will be found to be due."

Regarding nonreceipt of reserve programs and services, Fulton said, "it seems that in principle the Band has a valid claim." He cited computer calculations that Lennarson had provided, showing the value of Indian programs for each year from 1899, plus annual interest and inflation. The sum: $167 million. Whether 1899 or 1940 should be accepted as a starting date and whether Lennarson's method of calculation should be accepted as the official one remained matters for discussion, Fulton said.

Regarding lost livelihood from hunting and trapping, Fulton rejected arguments made before Mr. Justice Forsyth that ticks, natural cycles or the laziness of trappers were somehow responsible for a decline in the moose and fur harvests.

"The hard fact is, of course, that the decline in the annual harvest commenced with, and has continued during, the period of active development—that is the evidence," Fulton wrote. "On the other hand, while there has been reference to natural cyclical changes as an explanation, there has been no hard or scientific evidence that such a change was due or was in fact taking place. I have flown over the area and have seen what is involved by way of seismic grid lines driven through this previously wilderness area in a criss-cross pattern, and of installations dotting the previously unlittered landscape .... The weight of the evidence is that the decline in harvesting from hunting and trapping is not attributable to the coincidence of a cyclical change, which is speculative, nor to a sudden disinclination on the part of Band members to pursue their traditional means of living, which is not proven, but is due to the impact of development which is an established fact, which coincided with the onset and continuance of the decline, and which decline is consistent with the known fact that many of the species of wildlife population involved here are averse to such human intrusion and interference." Alberta should compensate the band for loss of livelihood from hunting and trapping, he concluded. He mentioned no figure.

Fulton supported the band's other claims to compensation with varied degrees of enthusiasm. The claim to money that Alberta collected for exploration and seismic leases on the 25.4 square miles was "very strong," he said. He also urged Ottawa to pay in full the band's legal and other costs related to the preparation of its case. The band's claim to all oil and gas revenues so far collected from the entire traditional area he saw as more problematic—the amount would be huge. But the band might be willing to drop the claim, he suggested, if "a generous recognition and satisfactory resolution" of the other claims were reached.

While giving remaining issues less prominence, Fulton praised the band's proposal to govern itself in matters of education, health, policing, wildlife management and subsurface development. "It is desirable that the Band should be given, and should assume, the widest powers of self-determination and self-government to enable its members to realize the concept of the preservation and continuance of their way of life as an Indian community," he wrote.

Fulton had taken far longer than the original three months he had predicted for the first stage, but his discussion paper brought to the Lubicon case the kind of intellectual rigour and emotional detachment that had not been evident since Mr. Justice W. A. Macdonald investigated the McCrimmon removals.

Band representatives were pleased. "We had many tough discussions with Mr. Fulton, and disagreed with him on many things, but he never once gave us reason to doubt his integrity or his sincerity," Lennarson wrote. "He earned our respect and our trust." Ominayak, Lennarson and O'Reilly objected to Fulton's attempt to characterize the Lubicon case as an outstanding entitlement under Treaty Eight, insisting that the band retained unextinguished aboriginal title. But they said they respected what Fulton was trying to do.

Reaction in Edmonton was hostile: the Alberta government did to Fulton what Ominayak had predicted at the start. On December 10, 1985—four days after receiving the draft discussion paper—Milt Pahl called a news conference to announce that the Lubicon case was settled.

"Alberta's land offer to the federal government to resolve the treaty land entitlement claim of the Lubicon Lake Indian Band has been accepted," he announced. He and David Crombie had agreed to create a Lubicon reserve of 25.4 square miles, Pahl said. In exchange, the band would sign a release saying its "claims against Alberta had been finally and completely dealt with." Pahl also said that "Fulton's job is now done, his involvement over. The province plans no further meetings with Mr. Fulton."

Fulton called the announcement "a great surprise," and Crombie protested weakly that he had agreed to no such deal. He would accept transfer of 25.4 square miles only "as a first step to resolving the issue," Crombie said, while telling Fulton to continue "full steam ahead."

But by then Crombie was losing control of his portfolio. People close to events say that his deputy minister, Bruce Rawson, had grown unhappy about having special envoys operate from his budget but beyond his control. The Fulton inquiry particularly irritated Rawson, insiders say. Rawson is an Albertan. He had worked for the Lougheed government as a lawyer, then as a top civil servant, and during his time in Ottawa he commuted home to Edmonton on weekends. When the discussion paper came out, Rawson went to see Milt Pahl, telling band representatives afterwards: "I don't see Fulton as playing a useful future role."

Fulton submitted a polished draft of his paper to Crombie in February 1986. In it he made two further recommendations to speed discussions. He also asked that talks begin immediately between the band and Ottawa—without Alberta—on land and membership. And he suggested that if talks broke down over native title, Crombie should refer the question directly to the Supreme Court of Canada. Going through regular court channels would be "very lengthy and exceedingly costly," he said.

Crombie left Fulton hanging. He thanked Fulton for his suggestions but didn't respond to them in detail. Crombie also refused to make the discussion paper public. Within weeks, almost all the other special inquiries ended too, with the exception of Emmett Hall's, which had started first and which settled the Grassy Narrows case in a way all parties considered fair. What made Crombie abandon the inquiries is not known; he refused all comment. Maybe he lost some of his initial enthusiasm. Maybe he realized that he couldn't ignore his large bureaucracy indefinitely. Or maybe Indian Affairs just wasn't his thing after all. In April 1986, he was reassigned to become secretary of state and minister of multiculturalism, portfolios that demanded he spend lots of time in Toronto.

Following the inquiry, Fulton kept public statements to a minimum. He took pains to maintain the disinterested posture that characterizes his discussion paper. Years later at his Vancouver law office, however, he left no doubt that he felt the band had been unfairly treated.

"I had the impression when I first heard from Fred Lennarson that the band's position was extreme, that that sort of thing couldn't have happened to them and that, well, they were just overstating their case," Fulton said in his deliberate manner. "But I came to the conclusion as I looked into it . . . that there has been a grave injustice done to these people . . . a really almost incredible injustice, which demands that we try to remedy the matter in the most generous way."

Without referring directly to the Forsyth decision, Fulton said that spending time in Little Buffalo had been a revelation to him. "I had not previously come into contact with any band which led what you might call a primitive life—a life of hunting and trapping as their primary means of livelihood," he said. "The Lubicons had been deprived of it shortly before this inquiry started as a result of the oil and gas development, but until that time—I learned from them and I saw—they had been leading a true Indian way of life dependent on vast territories for their support. That means of livelihood was interrupted, without any alternative being made available, and I came to appreciate what sort of nightmare that must represent to them."

12 A NEW FOCUS

EARLY ONE SUNDAY MORNING in August 1985—with the Fulton inquiry still underway—six young people from Little Buffalo and Cadotte smashed a car head-on into a pickup truck on the road to Peace River. Both vehicles burst into flames. The truck driver, who was from outside the area, threw himself free of the wreckage and survived, but the six young people were burned beyond recognition. The eldest was twenty-one years old, the youngest thirteen. Some of them had been drinking.

The depth of grief at Little Buffalo and Cadotte was almost beyond imagining. The crash not only killed the six young people but also marked a kind of official beginning to a general societal breakdown. "Everybody knew a tragedy was coming," said band member Steve Noskey. "It was a matter of where and when."

The sorrow was intensified by complications with government authorities. RCMP officers in Peace River seized the charred remains of the victims for formal identification, and when the task proved too difficult, officials flew the pieces to Edmonton. Mourners became confused about what was happening. Nearly a week passed before the six sets of black chunks were shipped home in small boxes, which were then placed in regular caskets and carried in a long line of pickup trucks to the cemetery.

Further grief arose when the mother of two victims tried to sell a moose hide to help pay for two caskets. The sale of moose hides tanned naturally over a fire had long been a source of income for Lubicon women, as had the sale of items made from the hides—jackets, gloves, vests and moccasins. But provincial authorities now insisted that Lubicon women have a special licence, or "tag," to be purchased from the Alberta wildlife department. Band members saw the tag system as part of the strategy to assert jurisdiction over their lands. Rather than compromise the band's position, the woman forfeited the sale.

Within months, a string of other tragedies occurred.

A six-year-old girl playing unattended with a bullet and a cigarette lighter blew away part of her intestine.

A mother of seven children fell asleep with a cigarette and burned herself alive. She was alone at the time, drinking.

A woman shot a drunk man when he tried to rape her. He survived and went to jail.

A father of six children committed suicide with his hunting rifle, the first suicide in memory among the Lubicon Lake people. He had been living alone since leaving his family a couple of months earlier. "I lost my husband," said the man's distraught widow not long afterwards. "He was forty-five years old. He believed in the old way of life. Trapping was very important to him because that was the only way of life he knew. There was some cutlines [seismograph lines] running through his trapline—quite a few. He was depressed and he drank a lot."

The deaths signalled a decline at Little Buffalo, the beginning of the downward social spiral that anthropologist Joan Ryan had predicted during the injunction application before Mr. Justice Gregory Forsyth. But the deaths also stiffened people's resolve. The shock of six young people burning alive followed by a series of other tragedies incited band members to take steps to reverse the trend. More than ever, people felt motivated to prepare for life in a land of few moose and many oil wells. They began to develop detailed proposals for negotiations with Ottawa and took steps to regain control of their lands pending the commencement of talks.

For years, band members had been turning over ideas about what kind of reserve community they might establish once the land question was settled. In a way, the discussion had been going on at least since 1939, when Alexis Laboucan and others talked with Schmidt and L'Heureux. "Their leader, Alexis Laboucan commented on their ability [to] hunt following the game where it goes but stating their willingness to learn agriculture," L'Heureux reported. "They wish their children educated," he also wrote. As oil work escalated through the early 1980s, the band held periodic meetings to develop plans. A population of 450 people would entitle them to a reserve of ninety square miles, if the Treaty Eight formula were applied. They selected a site of that size at Lubicon Lake. The boundaries encompassed the original 25.4 square miles at the lake's west end, took in the northern and eastern shores, and embraced a wide swath of land to the south with good patches of prairie soil and stands of spruce.

Midway along the south shore, a peninsula of high ground juts into the lake. Band members talked about building the core of a new Lubicon settlement at its crest. They discussed clearing enough trees to build a school, a band office and a whole cluster of other public buildings, including a health clinic, a community store, a day-care centre, a community hall and a hockey rink. Homes, people also decided, would be spread out Indian-style along the lakeshore in either direction.

"What will we eat?" people asked.

Edward Laboucan suggested buffalo. He remembered coming across buffalo skulls as a child and noted that Bison Lake and Little Buffalo drew their names from former herds in the area. "If they survived here once, maybe they could do so again," he said.

Soon members talked about clearing farmland south and west of the lake for crops. They talked of introducing cattle and actually did start a buffalo herd. James O'Reilly sold stock certificates to his law partners and their secretaries, raising $5,100—enough for five buffalo cows and one bull, with a frisky bull calf added free of charge when it jumped uninvited into the trailer. Band members built a cedar-rail corral near the existing band office, later adding a huge wire-fence enclosure south of Little Buffalo. Within five years the herd had grown to seventeen head.

Education was important, people also said. They discussed ideas for a vocational training centre and maintenance shop, from which they imagined would flow a variety of agricultural enterprises and small-business ventures, such as gravel crushing and cement making for the oil companies.

By 1985, many of the band's ideas were developed enough that Ominayak submitted them in a five-year plan to E. Davie Fulton. But it needed fleshing out. If the proposals were to be placed on the negotiating table, they had to include how many lengths of sewer pipe would be needed, how many tonnes of gravel for the roads, and how much everything would cost.

To come up with some numbers, Lennarson turned to Richard Plodzein, an old high-school friend from Waukegan. Plodzein was a planner and cost estimator in skyscraper construction who had helped to build office towers in Houston, St. Louis and Chicago. "I figure out how something can be done and for how much," he says. He talks just like Lennarson, in the same Chicago accent and with the same knack of expressing complex ideas in street vernacular.

Plodzein had worked in northern Alberta before. In 1977, Lennarson called him in Chicago to say that the Indian Association of Alberta needed somebody to run a project of Harold Cardinal's to help native people benefit from oil development. The Oil Sands Economic Development Corporation, it was called. Plodzein became general manager for seven years, running courses on small-business planning. Steering clear of sawmills and hotels, he concentrated on enterprises such as groceries, laundries, gas stations and welding shops. "I found that the kind of entrepreneurial person who will spend the amount of time and effort necessary to run a trapline, which is a lot of work, is going to make the kind of effort needed to run something like a grocery store," he says. Training sometimes was slow and the dropout rate was high. But the program helped establish 150 businesses, 85 per cent of which were still making money after five years. Plodzein returned to the United States, then headed north again in 1986 when Lennarson asked him to flesh out Lubicon reserve plans.

"Reserve planning is an ad hoc situation 99 per cent of the time," Plodzein says of what he has seen elsewhere. "You start out with a barn and it ends up as the band office, and you need something next to it so you put a school. There's no planning, there's no layout, there's no aesthetics, there's no form or function. There's just a hodgepodge that requires everybody to criticize you because the sewage treatment plant ends up next to the school and everything looks and smells bad."

Plodzein undertook to transform the band's ideas into numbers that could be tabled at negotiations with Ottawa. He began with a population figure. He calculated what 450 people might need in the way of roads, sewage, water, electricity and housing. Then he started thinking about a school. He thought about what the student-teacher ratio should be and how many rooms might be needed, and when he realized he didn't know anything about the requirements for a modern school he looked for help, eventually calling Bruce Koliger of Koliger Schmidt, an Edmonton architectural firm.

"I called him up cold and said I'd really enjoy sitting down and getting some ideas—could he spare someone?" Plodzein recalls. "And I ended up spending a whole day with four senior people, including a design man named Yoshi Natsuyama who had just won a national award for a school he designed at a Metis settlement. They took the list of buildings we were working on and said, 'We can help you with this, we can help you with that,' and when it came to talking about roads and water they brought in an associate firm for half a day to talk about civil engineering."

Plodzein has a talent for generating interest and enthusiasm. Soon he had Natsuyama camping with him for three days at Lubicon Lake to study the peninsula site. An agronomist volunteered to go along to take soil samples. Almost everywhere he turned, Plodzein found entrepreneurs and government officials not directly responsible to Indians willing to help the band develop its plans.

While visiting a prison farm to ask about irrigation, Plodzein found the manager to be "crazy about saskatoon berries," a bush fruit that Lubicon women had always mixed with pounded moose meat. The manager told Plodzein about how the band could join a cooperative to become saskatoon-berry farmers, with access to harvesting machines, a processing plant and a hybrid berry that was big, juicy and disease-resistant.

Officials at the vocational training branch of the education department opened their files to Plodzein. They gave him equipment prices on every vocational school in the province and helped design a school tailored to the band's specifications.

Help on ideas for raising cattle and growing grain came from Jerry Darichuk, a former schoolteacher and farmer who had become Alberta's most successful dealer of John Deere farming equipment. Plodzein met him through Lennarson's sons, who competed with Darichuk's sons at high-school swim meets.

"Jerry sat down as a teacher and laid out a lesson plan for me," Plodzein says. "He took me around for a week talking to grain farmers. Successful ones only. He didn't want me to see anything that was poorly done. We'd drive down the road and stop at a beautiful place, I'd meet the wife and kids, and the guy would open up his books for me and everything. Then we'd go into the field and look at the equipment, the crop-rotation plans, the grain-storage buildings, and I'd find out all about how he saved on fuel, how he avoided fertilizers. Then we'd go to another guy and he'd have a little bit different method. Then we did cattle. We met guys who walked through cow crap all day long and they'd explain to me how to pick out a sick cow."

Plodzein compiled detailed estimates on community construction and economic development. Plans for the cow-calf herd alone ran to forty pages, with specifics on land clearing, cultivation of grain and forage crops, and the construction of a combined veterinary clinic and slaughterhouse. Plans for the vocational centre included a maintenance facility for road graders and farm machinery, and a work place where roof trusses and other housing parts could be prefabricated in winter. He worked out costs for a saskatoon-berry orchard and a wild-rice operation. He wrote requirements for a coin-operated laundry, an eight-unit motel and a community store complete with butcher shop, grocery, dry-goods space, hardware inventory and gas station. He also worked out proposals for a gravel- crushing business and a portable concrete batch plant to produce oil-drilling pads.

"Everything was geared to self-sufficiency," Plodzein says. "People would grow the grain to feed the cattle, which would be slaughtered in the slaughterhouse and sold in the community store." He budgeted for hiring outside specialists, but the local vocational training centre would give band members a chance to learn most skills themselves eventually, including how to maintain the farm machinery and other equipment. "Nobody suggested setting up a factory to build computer parts. Nobody decided to go into the entertainment business, or make bingo halls for everybody across North America. Nobody decided to grow grain as a cash crop because that's high tech and pretty much beyond the reach of the community. But they decided, 'Yeah, we'll grow some grain for the animals. We'll own the land and the equipment. We won't be debt-loaded to the gills. We'll put it in the ground and if it rains that'll be good.' That's not dreaming. That's an aggressive approach to taking charge of one's life."

Specific plans gave the band a new focus. In a struggle that often showed no tangible progress, Plodzein's numbers helped to sustain hope. And plotting reserve boundaries on a map aroused the same feeling of possessiveness that the original reserve promise had inspired in band members in 1940. The ninety square miles became the reserve the Lubicon people were fighting for.

In mid-1986, the band moved to assert control physically over the area. Ominayak announced that all oil companies were required to ask the band's approval before going ahead with any new work in the traditional Lubicon area. He also declared the ninety square miles a resource-company-free zone. (Until then, a few seismic lines had been cut, but companies had mostly left the area around the lake alone—whether out of deference to the land dispute or because prospects appeared poor.)

Band members began to patrol the lake area and elsewhere to see that the rules were being followed. Under other circumstances, the companies might have laughed off the move, but the showdown with Union Oil and a number of other run-ins had taught both the companies and the provincial regulatory authorities that the Lubicon people were serious. Officials at the Energy Resources Conservation Board ordered all companies applying for new work in Lubicon territory to check with the band first.

"I started getting calls from very put-upon, upset oil-industry people," says Plodzein, who handled inquiries for the band in addition to his estimating work. He would tell callers about the band's aboriginal interest in the area and ask the location and nature of the proposed job. He would then call Ominayak. If the project was outside the ninety square miles and did not interfere with grave sites or a trapper's cabin, Ominayak would approve the project and mark it on a wall map with a coloured pin. Sometimes Ominayak wasn't at his desk, and sometimes a trapper would have to be consulted as well, but a routine developed in which Plodzein could answer a company in less than twenty-four hours.

All work outside the ninety square miles Ominayak routinely approved. In one case, a company asked to blast seismograph lines through Little Buffalo itself, two of the lines running directly through people's homes. The company offered compensation. "I figured Bernard would never go for it," Plodzein recalls. "But he thought it over and said, 'Little Buffalo is outside the ninety square miles—let 'em do it.' " Ominayak stipulated only that no work be done within three hundred metres of a house or corral. He also turned down the money. The rules were imposed not for money, he said, but to assert a principle.

"After a while the oil people started to soften," says Plodzein. "You could tell by the lowering of tension in their voices. I would start giving them the pitch and they would say, 'Yeah, I understand all about it, I have to do this and this,' and I would say, 'How did you know?' and they would say, 'Oh, the word's around.' They had all decided that meeting the band's requirements was what they had to do."

In the enlightened atmosphere, a few companies started hiring band members for clean-up and forest reclamation work. Band member Steve Noskey organized a small subcontracting company of three crews, with about five people each, to bid on jobs and carry them out.

"They didn't want handouts," says Michael Allen, then head of community relations for Alberta Power Limited, one of the first companies to hire Lubicon workers. "They saw themselves as trying to get into business development. They didn't want to be involved with environmental destruction or the exploitation of the oil resources, but they did want to be involved with reclaiming, so we hired them for reclaiming."

The superintendent was so pleased with the work, Allen says, that Alberta Power hired Lubicon crews for a job near Fort McMurray, well outside the Lubicon area. Oil companies also hired Noskey's crews. By 1987–88, the second year of operation, the Lubicon company was doing fifteen to twenty jobs a winter and showing a profit of $100,000.

Trouble arose only when a seismic team was caught violating the ninety square miles. In mid-January 1987, Steve Noskey, on a routine patrol of the area, came across signs of clearing work at the northeast corner of the lake. He located the crew and established that its members worked for Sonics Exploration Ltd. of Calgary. He asked the crew to leave. The head of the crew phoned Ominayak, who also asked them to leave. The boss then called the RCMP to complain of harassment.

Soon three RCMP officers arrived in Little Buffalo to say that Sonics had a duly executed permit to conduct seismographic testing and that band members would be in violation of Alberta law if they interfered. Ominayak explained the situation. The Lubicon people recognized neither Alberta's authority to issue the permit nor the RCMP's authority to police the area in question, he said, showing the officers piles of permit applications from companies working in Lubicon territory. "We are acting under our own lawful authority, which is the only lawful authority in our area," Ominayak said.

The police backed off. "This is a political matter, not a police one," the ranking RCMP officer replied. "I'm recommending to my superiors that they tell Sonics to get out."

Flushed with a sense of accomplishment, band members formally voted to eject the trespassers.

"We're not looking for violence, but we are prepared to do whatever it takes," Ominayak told reporters. "The area is clearly marked now. We've got signs up. We've got guys out there steadily looking and one access road is blocked. We're going to let these guys know we mean business."

Sonics quietly withdrew.

13 BOYCOTT

A FORMER SASKATCHEWAN grain farmer named Bill McKnight succeeded Crombie as Indian Affairs minister in the spring of 1986.
His mandate, people close to him said, was "to lower expectations
raised among the Indians by Mr. Crombie." McKnight began with
Lubicon expectations. Shortly after assuming the portfolio, he
confirmed E. Davie Fulton's departure by appointing a "federal
negotiator" to deal with Alberta and the band.

The negotiator was Roger Tassé, an Ottawa lawyer and former
deputy minister of justice distinguished for having helped to draft the
Charter of Rights and Freedoms (and, more recently, the Meech Lake
Accord). On Lubicon, Tassé took a hard line. Ottawa would accept
the official band list of 196 status Indians—up from 182 due to natural
increase—for a reserve of 39.2 square miles, he said. From there, he
was prepared to negotiate upwards. "I have a number in my head and
it will come out during the course of negotiations."

"Membership is not negotiable," Ominayak replied. "I can't bar-
gain away my own people."

In response, Tassé travelled to Little Buffalo "to develop a feel"
for the band and its outlook. When he arrived, nearly fifty people
confronted him on the membership issue. Tassé protested that he was
there to learn, not to negotiate, but people insisted that he address the
issue. A community meeting was called. Tassé repeated that Ottawa
would deal only with a band list approved by the Registrar for Indian
Membership. As for people not on the list: "If they go to court and
prove that they have any rights, then we might be able to provide land

for them," he said.

"We invite you to come back to our community when you get a mandate to deal with us as one people," Ominayak replied.

As the meeting adjourned, Tassé wandered over to Steve Noskey, assigned as Tassé's driver for the visit. "Tassé came over to me trying to be friendly and sympathetic," Noskey recalls. "He mentioned that the federal government was prepared to negotiate immediately with the status people. He was suggesting that I was foolish to let the non-status hold the status people back. He assumed that I was status. I told him, 'Mr. Tassé, I know what you're trying to do. You're trying to divide the status and non-status, but that's not the way it works around here. Status and non-status doesn't matter.' I also told him I was non-status. He stared at me and I could tell he was thinking, 'I've just put my mouth where I shouldn't.' "

Tassé returned to Ottawa saying he hadn't seen any "genocide" and that the band was "jacking up its membership." Later, he suggested that Lubicon hunters were the cause of their own problems. "They could have overhunted," he said. "You cannot just go on and kill and kill and kill. You need to manage the resources if you want them to survive."

As Tassé hardened his line, all conventional avenues of addressing the land question appeared to close. In Edmonton, Don Getty succeeded Peter Lougheed as premier without changing the province's policy on Lubicon. In the federal and Alberta courts, the aboriginal-rights suits appeared destined to be, as Fulton had put it, "very lengthy and exceedingly costly." Sensing that time was on the government's side, Ominayak and Lennarson searched for a way to pressure Ottawa to pick up where Fulton had left off. They began to toy with the notion of creating an international campaign for Lubicon rights.

"Would it helpful to you if we organized a boycott?" one of the Spokane people had asked during the relief caravan. The group had noticed promotions in their area for the Winter Olympic Games scheduled to be held at Calgary in February 1988. At first, Ominayak and Lennarson saw more problems than advantages in a boycott campaign. "Is it prudent to go after something that verges on motherhood?" they asked themselves. "Is it tactically possible?" Allies belonging to churches, labour groups and political parties were equally unenthusiastic, but as conventional avenues of discussion closed, the notion of calling an international boycott of the Calgary Olympics gained appeal. "It's a high-risk strategy but we're in a high-risk business," Lennarson eventually concluded. "It's a tactical opportunity we have to seize."

The games were nearly two years away, assured of a long run of publicity. Targetting them could gain the band a long run of publicity as well. As Lennarson explored the idea, he noticed that almost everybody helping to plan the games was oil-connected and Tory, linked however indirectly to the destruction of Lubicon territory. Peter Lougheed, the retired premier, was honorary chairman of the Olympic organizing committee. The active chairman was Frank King, vice-president of Turbo Resources, a petroleum company that the Lougheed government had rescued from bankruptcy in 1983. Bob Brown, president of a Turbo subsidiary, was named a committee member, along with Terry Roberts, Lougheed's former campaign manager, and George deRappard, who had held Alberta's top civil servant job under Lougheed. Also on the committee were Bob Niven, John Lecky and Bob Laidlaw, all oil-company executives. And a cabinet committee to coordinate Alberta government involvement in the games was being chaired by Al Adair, who was the band's representative in the legislature and a supporter of the land-tenure program.

In March 1986, band representatives made a last-ditch effort to open talks. In Ottawa, they met Roger Tassé and the deputy minister of Indian Affairs, Bruce Rawson, asking that bilateral negotiations begin at once, as suggested by E. Davie Fulton. Rawson insisted that Alberta be represented. The band insisted that Alberta be excluded. Rawson walked out, saying, "This meeting is a nullity."

A week later, Ominayak called for an international boycott of the Winter Games. "The Calgary Olympic Games are being organized by basically the same interests that are committing genocide against the Lubicon Lake Indian people," he said in a news release. "We believe that the people of the world need to know . . . the truth about the situation in Alberta, the truth about the interests behind the Calgary Olympic Games, the truth about their lack of respect for human rights, the truth about their lack of basic human decency, and the truth about the horrendous effect their development activity is having upon the aboriginal people whose land and resources they are stealing."

Games organizers laughed. "This thing is so ridiculous that it's difficult to believe," said Jerry Joynt, vice-president of communications for the organizing committee. "Our connection with the Lubicon Lake Indian band is zero."

But if the connection seemed vague at first, organizers themselves soon made it clearer. Television rights to the games had been sold at a record price, motivating organizers to think of colourful Alberta images that might be projected to the world. Oil and gas installations made poor viewing, they decided. Indians and their accoutrements would be better. One early suggestion for the opening ceremonies was to have Indians in war paint ride into the stadium on horses to ignite covered wagons, terrorizing white people posing as early settlers. "Lots of pizazz," the head of the ideas committee, Bill Stinchcombe, said approvingly. But the idea was dropped when one native leader replied, "We'll agree only if the white guys inside the burning wagons are from the organizing committee."

Other suggestions on the Indian theme went ahead, however. Organizers had a giant tepee built at McMahon Stadium over the cauldron bearing the Olympic flame. They conceived what they called "an Olympic Pow Wow" of Indian drumming and dancing. For winning athletes they had Olympic medals produced that featured an Indian headdress of skis, two types of sleds, a biathlon rifle, a speed-skate blade, a hockey stick and a ski pole. "The ski pole in the ear may be more symbolic than the designer of the medal knows," Lennarson said.

As the central attraction to an arts festival accompanying the games, organizers also announced a major exhibition of North American Indian artifacts. Forget Not My World, it was to be called. It would be held at Calgary's Glenbow Museum and include the earliest and rarest items from museum collections in Europe and the United States. Normally, the Glenbow couldn't hope to mount such an elaborate production. Dozens of museums would have to be approached. Costs would be enormous: $2.6 million. But the Olympics were not normal circumstances. Games organizers embraced the idea and arrangements were made to have Shell Canada Limited contribute $1.1 million as the show's exclusive corporate sponsor.

Shell was one of the major developers in Lubicon territory. The museum, Lennarson also noticed, was as oil-connected and Tory as the rest of the games organization. The Glenbow was founded by a Calgary oil millionaire, Eric Harvie. Operating capital came mostly from the Alberta government and from an endowment established jointly by the government and the Harvies. One of the museum's honorary co-chairmen was Eric Harvie's son, Donald. The other was Alberta Premier Don Getty. The chairman of the board of governors was David Tavender, a law partner of Jack Robertson, who had been the senior oil-company lawyer opposing the Lubicon band before Mr. Justice Forsyth. Also on the board was Harold Millican, a former Lougheed advisor and a member of the Olympic organizing committee. Others included the president of Gulf Oil, the president of Rozsa Petroleum, the director of Intercity Gas Corporation, the chairman of British Petroleum Canada, the managing director of the Independent Petroleum Association of Canada, the president of Wellore Resources and the ex-president of Bodiam Resources. Among the people listed as Glenbow "fellows" was Mr. Justice Douglas McDermid, one of the three appeal-court judges who determined that the Lubicon wilderness could be restored with money damages. Among the financial contributors to the museum, Lennarson counted fifty- six companies that were also listed in the Canadian Oil Registry.

Lennarson cut the issue. "The irony seems painfully obvious," he wrote the mailing list. "A display of North American Indian artifacts to attract people to the Winter Olympics is being organized by interests who are still actively seeking to destroy Indian people: namely, the Alberta Government and its oil-company allies. The Band will therefore be writing these various museums asking that they support the Band's boycott of the Calgary Winter Games by refusing to loan these artifacts at this time." The overall games boycott was still on, but the focus became Forget Not My World, a show whose title suddenly acquired new irony.

≈

The director of the Glenbow Museum, Duncan Cameron, responded to the band's initiative the way Union Oil executives had responded earlier: he underestimated the band's political strength. He was also less than straightforward. He changed the show's title to The Spirit Sings, and denied that Forget Not My World had been the title in the first place. A museum curator in Germany quoted Cameron as saying that the Glenbow had reached an agreement with the band about the show, which was not the case. A French curator quoted Cameron as saying that native groups across Canada supported the exhibition, after every major Indian organization in the country had announced the contrary. To a Danish museum, Cameron wrote: "The Lubicon Lake Band has taken a position that the Olympics, in general, should be boycotted . . . but we have no information or reason to believe that the Lubicon Band has specifically suggested a boycott of the Glenbow exhibition." Cameron then denied writing any such thing: "We have known from Day One that the Olympic boycott encompassed the entire project and we've never told anyone anything different."

With his every move, Cameron turned himself into the perfect target for mass jujitsu. He became stubborn and hot-tempered. He shouted at curators, blew up at reporters, and at an international conference in Buenos Aires flew into what witnesses called "a mad tirade."

The conference was convened by the International Committee of Ethnological Musea in the fall of 1986. An ethnologist from the National Museum of Copenhagen, Torben Lundbaek, told delegates about being asked by the Glenbow Museum to lend artifacts and about being asked by the Lubicon Indians not to lend. Lundbaek went on to describe "the long history of repression of the Lubicon Lake Indians," the committee's newsletter reported afterwards, and to explain why he agreed with the band's use of the games to attract international attention. Invited to give the museum's side, Cameron told delegates that the games offered a unique opportunity to organize a show of exceptional quality that would heighten awareness of Indians. A debate followed.

"Unfortunately this degenerated into a mad tirade of reproaches from the management of the Glenbow Museum to the European Musea," the committee's secretary, Harrie Leyten, later wrote. Cameron, she said, accused Lundbaek and others of being "influenced by a handful of excited Indians." Cameron then "left the meeting abruptly."

In his absence, delegates drafted a resolution that they later described as designed to support the band without citing Lubicon specifically. "Museums which are engaged in activities relating to living ethnic groups should, whenever possible, consult with the appropriate members of those groups," the resolution states. "And such museums should avoid using ethnic materials in any way which might be detrimental and/or offensive to such groups." The position was later also adopted by the committee's parent body, the International Council of Museums.

≈

The first curator actually to boycott the show was James Smith, the New York ethnologist who had supported the band at the injunction hearing. The Museum of the American Indian, where he worked, holds the world's largest collection of North American Indian artifacts, and until his death in 1990, Smith was the world's leading scholar on the Cree peoples of northwestern Canada. One of his contributions was to establish that, contrary to popular belief, Cree groups existed throughout the western woodlands prior to the fur trade, a finding that he reported in the authoritative *Handbook of North American Indians*, volume six, published by the Smithsonian Institution in 1981. Almost as soon as the book appeared, Lennarson phoned Smith to ask how the findings applied to the Lubicon people. Smith said no field work had been done in Lubicon territory and proposed to do it himself.

He was fifty-six years old at the time—a probing, talkative, dryly witty man who had spent half his life studying the Cree and Ojibwa peoples of northern Manitoba and Saskatchewan. During his visit to the Lubicon area, he sometimes sat all night listening to what band members call "whisky-jack stories"—sometimes risqué, often humorous mythological tales with a wide cast of characters. Traditionally, the stories were told for entertainment and instruction. "The easiest bit of field work I've done in my life," Smith later said of one particularly good session with John Felix Laboucan, using Joe T. Laboucan as interpreter. "He sat there and gave a very informal lecture for an hour and a half on exactly every subject I wanted to cover."

There is little doubt that Cree people inhabited the area prior to 1763, Smith concluded, citing the date of the Royal Proclamation, the legal definition of "since time immemorial." He also came away with a deep affection for the people he had met and excited about further research possibilities. Lubicon society was more intact than any other boreal society he had encountered, he said. And he suspected that he had discovered a variation on a pattern of cross-cousin marriage, one of his special interests. He made plans to return the following year to pursue the research.

Back in New York, Smith nearly burned to death in his apartment. He must have left a cigarette burning in the living room when he went to bed, and his dog, Thea—part German shepherd, part Siberian husky—must have woken him, or dragged him out of bed, because he was found unconscious in the bathroom by firefighters at 6:00 A.M. "Anthropologist saved by dog," the *New York Post* headline read. Serious burns covered half his body. His ears and fingertips went black and fell off. He regained consciousness momentarily, then slipped into a coma for five weeks. Thea was dead.

Smith underwent half a dozen major operations and forty-five surgical procedures to repair the damage. He suffered two heart attacks and had part of his lungs removed. But he looked on the bright side. "When my hair grew out there was not a speck of grey," he said. Within months he was back at work, first one day a week, then two. Within a year of the fire he was working five days a week and beginning to type again. When the Glenbow called to ask Smith to lend eighty-four items to the Olympics exhibition, Smith said he would be pleased to cooperate. When the band called a boycott, however, Smith changed his mind.

"Anthropology is kind of a weirdo science," he said reflectively at the time. "Our subjects are not insects, or dead dinosaurs, or stars a zillion miles away. Our subjects are people. And while one does want to retain a certain amount of scientific objectivity, we must also take into consideration the rights of Indian people. To cover up injustices with an art exhibit I think is inadequate. Am I partisan? I don't know. I just know I couldn't lend to the Glenbow after the band asked me not to."

Smith's decision had a tremendous impact on the museum world. To mount international exhibitions, directors depend on mutual cooperation. They borrow and lend items frequently, assuming debts among each other and collecting favours. None had honoured a boycott before; none had faced one. So when Smith—backed by his director and board of trustees—announced that he would not lend to the Glenbow, other museums took note. Authorities at the University Museum in Pennsylvania wavered, consulted Smith, then pulled out too. The Peabody Museum at Harvard University followed.

One by one, European museums also began to withdraw—partly influenced by Smith's example, partly offended by Cameron's behaviour. Torben Lundbaek of Denmark was the first, writing to Cameron saying simply, "The National Museum will not be able to contribute to the exhibition."

"Like many other museums in Europe," wrote Ernst Kläy of the Musée d'Histoire in Berne, Switzerland, "we are also compelled to withdraw our agreement for a loan . . . . We deplore the fact that you have omitted informing us adequately about the seriousness of the boycott and the grievances aired by the Lubicon band and other native Canadian groups, as well as about the growing of worldwide support for the boycott."

"We regret," wrote Tom Svensson, acting director of the Ethnographic Museum in Oslo, "that we have to cancel our former agreement to lend six Inuit artifacts." Citing the Lubicon boycott and the Buenos Aires resolution as reasons for the decision, he added that "when a controversy with such far reaching implications connects to a particular exhibition, it seems to us that the original purpose of the exhibition has been lost."

The show, wrote Felix Valk, director of Rotterdam's Museum voor Volkenkunde, risked being seen "as a kind of cover-up, a nice façade hiding the real world of today's native peoples."

≈

To give the boycott a further boost, Lennarson urged Ominayak to go to Europe. He was being invited to make a tour by leaders of the European Support Groups for North American Indians, an activist coalition of anthropological and human-rights organizations in twelve countries. O'Reilly had addressed the groups earlier in Luxembourg. Now they were making Lubicon top priority.

Ominayak has no taste for travel. More than a few days away from Lubicon territory and he starts suffering from fatigue, headaches and nausea. He gets homesick. "I remember when it was a big deal just to go to Peace River and Slave Lake," he said once, "and then later ending up in Edmonton and finding out there are a lot of other people out there in the world, all rushing around all over the place and you don't know what's going on. I never thought, even after four or five years as chief, that I'd ever be in Europe or any place outside of Canada at all." But with other avenues still closed, raising international awareness appeared to be the only way to carry the Lubicon case forward.

Ominayak flew to Europe in the fall of 1986 with an entourage that included Lennarson and his wife, Avis, Edward Laboucan and his wife, Josephine, two representatives of the Indian Association of Alberta and a reporter from the *Edmonton Journal*—all scrambling to meet a tight train schedule through seven countries in fourteen days. They stopped in Vienna, Bonn, Luxembourg, Paris, London and a number of other cities in between, met at every juncture by local supporters handling all arrangements.

The trip was "really hectic," Ominayak said later. "We had meeting after meeting and we were just making it, or sometimes late, and I don't like to be late for meetings." He met ministers and deputy ministers, museum directors, officials on national Olympic committees and political activists. He met the Austrian sports minister and German Green Party activist Petra Kelly. The work paid off. Every stop generated local news coverage and introduced the Lubicon issue to reporters scheduled to cover the Winter Olympic Games.

For months the coverage continued. Every museum to withdraw, every statement of support issued, every denial from Cameron created another news item for Alberta newspapers and broadcast stations, keeping the Lubicon issue constantly in the public eye. National reporters picked up the story, issuing periodic updates on the number of museums pulling out of the Glenbow show.

Public backlash appeared nonexistent as a series of scandals dampened enthusiasm for the games. Television executives complained of substandard media housing being built by ATCO Ltd., owned by a longtime Lougheed friend Ron Southern. Competing developers complained that the $60-million contract had been awarded unfairly through Lougheed, who subsequently was named to ATCO's board of directors. There were other controversies. The ticket manager of the games was charged with fraud after overcharging American customers. A new road to the ski slopes was said to threaten elk habitat. Up to half the seats to main events were found to be set aside for dignitaries and sponsors. And half of Calgary's taxi drivers declared solidarity with the Lubicon boycott, claiming "a common frustration in dealing with governments" over cab-licence restrictions. Even a member of the International Olympic Committee was critical of the Calgary organizers. "They screwed up the ticket sales, they screwed up the press centre, they screwed up the accommodation," said IOC vice-president Richard Pound of Montreal. "The problem I've had with Calgary is that they don't seem to realize that this is an international event and not a Stampede for people with funny accents."

As the boycott gathered momentum, games organizers stopped laughing. They began their own countercampaign, also with an international dimension, planned with officials from three federal departments: Indian Affairs, External Affairs and the Department of Fitness and Amateur Sport. The *Calgary Herald* obtained censored copies of memos from the planning sessions; among them were three memos titled "Lubicon Update," "Lubicon Visit to Europe" and "Lubicon Boycott." Both Bruce Rawson and Roger Tassé attended at least one meeting to discuss "economic development for Indian bands resulting from the Olympic Games." One memo stated the intentions of the meetings bluntly: "A program strategy is to continue to try to gain some native friends." Six months later a "native participation program" was announced, featuring a national native youth conference and promising $1.5 million in economic spin-offs from the games.

The memos also contained references to a "communications strategy . . . to de-link the games from any native land claims issues." The strategy extended to Canadian embassies in Europe. Brian Watson, deputy director of arts promotion at External Affairs, publicly called the boycott "no big deal," while acknowledging that diplomats in several countries were working to contain the damage. Museum directors in Paris, Copenhagen and Stockholm who had announced they would not lend to the Glenbow complained of "tremendous" and "phenomenal" pressure from Canadian diplomats. The Paris director of the Musée de l'Homme eventually succumbed, citing "great political pressures to loan." In a further attempt to defuse the boycott, Canadian diplomats circulated a Lubicon "fact sheet" to European news agencies. Canada regrets, it said, "that the band has chosen [the boycott] to reach a more generous settlement of its claim in Alberta."

Behind all the manoeuvres and public statements lay a sense of exasperation that the Lubicon issue seemed to be building, not fading away. The normally affable mayor of Calgary, Ralph Klein, went from saying, "Anyone can protest anything in this city," to saying, "It is totally unfair for Ominayak to hold the city of Calgary ransom."

≈

Ominayak recognized Klein's lament as a cry of pain and returned to Europe to keep the pressure on. Nine months before the games, he and Lennarson attended the third annual congress of the European Support Groups for North American Indians in Vienna. The groups share a common stated goal: "To eliminate cultural bias and build understanding in Europe for the native peoples of North America." Independently, they publish magazines and put on exhibitions furthering the awareness of native peoples. They inform news reporters about native issues and help to organize trips for native leaders wishing to visit Europe. The Vienna meeting was to be the largest so far—120 delegates from twelve countries. On the agenda were land-rights issues at Big Mountain, Arizona, and in the Black Hills of South Dakota. But the top item was Lubicon.

"There are three reasons why we are focusing on Lubicon," the conference organizer, Peter Schwarzbauer, said at the time. "First, it is an emergency case. If a fair settlement can be reached soon, Lubicon society stands a chance of recovering. The second reason is that many people believe genocide of Indians is a thing of the past, something from the last century, but the Lubicon situation shows it is a problem of today. The third thing certainly is that the Lubicon are much better organized than other Indian groups we know. If there were no Fred Lennarson to keep up the continuous work and package things in a way that white society understands, we would not be concentrating on Lubicon. The information puts us in a position to do something. When the Canadian embassies send information to reporters and museums, reporters call us afterwards and we are able to respond."

Ominayak arrived at the conference in a cheerful mood. Travelling still did not agree with him, but he recognized a number of people this time. Among them was Frank Kressing, a graduate student at the University of Tübingen, West Germany, who had visited Little Buffalo and written a book in German about the band. John van Tilborg, a Dutch member of the European Parliament, had both visited Little Buffalo and dined with Roger Tassé in Ottawa, saying afterwards: "I was shocked. Europeans have the impression that Canada is one of the few countries of the world taking human rights seriously. Then you see what they did and you are really shocked." Manfred Kaufmann, an ethnology student at the University of Vienna, had visited the Lubicon area on a research trip, telling an *Edmonton Journal* reporter afterwards, "I'll never forget the sad look on Edward Laboucan's face when he walked out of the bush empty-handed."

Other delegates appeared equally well informed. Naila Clerici, a professor of American history at the University of Genoa, Italy, who publishes an eighty-page magazine called *Teepee* three times a year, was reporting on the congress for national Italian radio—"to inform the public about issues I feel are important," she said. Claus Biegert, a journalist from Munich who had cowritten *A River Drowned by Water* about the James Bay Cree, was arranging to be in Calgary to help German reporters cover the Lubicon angle on the Winter Games.

"I want to thank all of you people here for coming," Ominayak told delegates on the second night of the congress. He showed a video of the 1984 television documentary produced by CBC's "The Journal" and answered questions from the centre of the room with everybody gathered around him. "The Lubicon people have survived off the land all these years, but since the oil companies have come in, they've destroyed the whole environment, therefore destroying our way of life, which is hunting and trapping," he said. "Today 95 per cent of the people are living on welfare. We had our first suicide within the past year. That never happened before. We're going to get to a stage where even if we win, we would have lost because of the social problems beginning now. We've tried to deal with the courts and through the political process and we haven't reached a solution, and now our backs are against the wall. When you have such strong enemies, your only power base is the public at large, and that's why we have to appeal to the public as often and as far away as possible."

Delegates decided on a boycott "action plan." Twelve of them from ten countries established a Lubicon Network Committee to identify all museums lending to the Glenbow show and influence their directors. Delegates resolved to write the Vatican, which had agreed to lend three items, and to inform local athletes, sports journalists and politicians about the boycott. To draw further attention to the band, delegates also decided to demonstrate on October 12—Columbus Day—outside Canadian embassies.

Seven months before the games, the United Nations Human Rights Committee in Geneva announced that it would hear the

Lubicon case. The band had filed a formal complaint in 1984 charging that Canada was violating the Lubicon people's right to self-determination and that the band had exhausted all domestic remedies in trying to stop the practice of cultural—if not physical—genocide. After examining evidence from both the band and Canada, the committee ruled that "there are no effective remedies still available to the Lubicon Band" in Canada, upholding one of the band's central arguments following the court disputes and the Fulton inquiry. While appearing to reject the self-determination argument, the committee also ruled that the complaint was admissible "in so far as it may raise issues under article 27 or other articles of the Covenant."

Article 27 pertains to the denial of cultural, linguistic and religious rights, and was the article cited in a landmark decision involving Sandra Lovelace. She was a Maliseet Indian from New Brunswick who lost her Indian status by marrying a non-Indian, and who as a "non-Indian" remained barred by Canadian law from her reserve of origin even after the marriage dissolved. A decision by the human rights committee in her favour under article 27 compelled Canada to change the Indian Act in 1985, allowing Indian women to retain Indian status no matter whom they married.

In its preliminary ruling on Lubicon, the committee also asked that Canada "take interim measures to avoid irreparable damage to Chief Ominayak and other members of the Lubicon Lake Band" while the full complaint was being heard, and to submit within six months "written explanations or statements clarifying the matter and the remedy, if any, that may have been taken."

Ottawa ignored the "interim measures" request and began an exchange of submissions that was to delay a final ruling for years.

"In judicial terms," Lennarson told the mailing list, "this decision by the UN Committee on Human Rights can be described as a decision that there's a serious case to be heard . . . . Canada has thus not been adjudged guilty of genocide by the world community, but has at least been called to account."

≈

Six months before the games, a health crisis arose at Little Buffalo. A baby was diagnosed as having tuberculosis, prompting provincial medical authorities to screen other people in the area for exposure to the disease. Of 358 people screened at Little Buffalo, 47 were found to have active TB. Many others were found to be infected and at high risk of developing symptoms. Altogether, 107 people at Little Buffalo—nearly one third of those tested—were put on medication against the disease, making the outbreak one of the worst in Canada since the Depression.

Tuberculosis is a lung disease that usually spreads through coughing and thrives among people whose physical resistance is low from substandard living conditions, poor diet and stress.

"They have outside privies and no running water and that is not conducive to good hygiene," said Graham Clarkson, a consulting medical officer for the Peace River health unit.

"Crowding is a factor," said John Waters, director of communicable diseases for the Alberta community health branch. "So is their socioeconomic condition and their diet."

Treatment of the disease involves a nine-month period on antibiotics that can cause vomiting, hives, fever and liver problems. The health department sent one nurse to Little Buffalo to dispense medicine and explain possible side effects. Band members said later that the nurse spent the day in a medical trailer and complained that nobody was coming to see her. Asked why she didn't visit the sick people in their homes, the nurse said that the roads were too muddy. Ominayak said that the roads were muddy for the sick people, too. He expelled Alberta health authorities from Little Buffalo and arranged for three federal nurses, including two specializing in tuberculosis treatment, to do the work.

"If it was a non-native community, we'd have doctors and nurses coming out of our ears," Ominayak said. "A lot of our people are really frustrated about the whole damn thing."

"What's happening," Lennarson wrote the mailing list, "is a repeat of what happened in other North American aboriginal societies upon contact with Western Europeans—introduction of diseases in a population of people with little built up resistance, destruction of the traditional economy and way of life and replacement of it with a welfare economy and way of life, replacement of a time-tested traditional diet with a typically inadequate welfare diet."

≈

In the remaining months before the games, Ominayak continued to travel. He remained shy, continuing to display signs of nervousness in front of crowds, but he was determined to tell what was happening at Little Buffalo. Technically he was still the local chief of a small, isolated band, but as his fame grew he became regarded as a kind of national hero. "The fight that we're in is a fight for all native people," he would say, linking the Lubicon struggle to the larger struggle for aboriginal rights and calling for a united effort. In Masset, B.C., a provincial assembly of chiefs rose in a standing ovation the moment he entered at the back of the hall. At Kahnawake, near Montreal, the Mohawk people raised $1,000 for the Lubicon band in a spontaneous passing of the hat after hearing Ominayak speak. At the Blood reserve southeast of Calgary, people held a rarely performed "honour dance" to recognize Ominayak's contribution to aboriginal rights. His face was painted, an eagle-feather headdress was placed on his head and a Blackfoot name was conferred on him: Gaday-skougkh-omee, meaning "man with no land."

There were other tributes. In New York City, Lucius Walker honored Ominayak at a twentieth-anniversary dinner for the Inter-religious Foundation for Community Organization, citing Ominayak's "valiant, creative and effective" leadership.

At McGill University, Professor Bruce Trigger told three hundred students that "Chief Ominayak and the Lubicon people have become the conscience of our nation." Trigger, one of the country's most prominent anthropologists, had noisily resigned as honorary curator at Montreal's McCord Museum of Canadian History after discovering it was lending to the Glenbow show. "When we ponder how the Lubicon people should be dealt with," he told a lecture with Ominayak present, "we ask nothing less than what sort of society we want to see in Canada as a whole."

The biggest event of the period was a rock concert in Calgary starring Buffy Sainte-Marie. In the host city of the games, the heart of the Alberta oil industry, nearly 2,400 people all but filled Jubilee Auditorium for a concert "in support of the last stand of the Lubicon." Thirty Lubicon members drove from Little Buffalo to attend. Many had never seen a city before.

"The Lubicon people will go back tonight to a level of poverty never known before in their history," said the master of ceremonies, Roland Leitner, a member of the Calgary support group organizing the event. "But they will take with them the knowledge that people care. That people care in Calgary. Just as people care in Edmonton.

As people care in Toronto. In New York. Boston. Germany. Austria. France. Italy. Norway. Sweden. People all over Europe know that the people of Lubicon Lake deserve better. They know that the people of Lubicon Lake deserve the acknowledgement of their aboriginal rights and the land promised them almost fifty years ago. And we can make it happen. With help and support, we can do it. By coming out tonight we have taken the first step."

Leitner asked the band members to stand. A spotlight picked them out in the middle of the auditorium and band members started waving to the darkness around them. With the emotional level steadily rising in the hall, Leitner called Ominayak from the wings. The crowd rose to its feet.

"We don't have much to sing about," Ominayak said unsteadily. "But we're really, really grateful to see people such as yourselves show us that you are concerned enough about us to be here."

≈

Eighty-eight days before the 1988 games, a cross-country torch relay began from Signal Hill, Newfoundland, sponsored by Petro-Canada, the federally owned oil company active in the Lubicon area. The company was spending $5.5 million to get a torch bearing an Olympic flame to McMahon Stadium in Calgary, where it would ignite a cauldron under the giant tepee. The band called for protests along the route.

"It is hoped that 88 days of protest, night after night on the evening news, in full view of people across the country and around the world, will demonstrate the breadth and depth of concern to Canadian politicians," Lennarson told the mailing list.

Over the next eighty-eight days, knots of protestors met the flame in every province and territory except Prince Edward Island. Ominayak attended demonstrations in Ottawa, Regina, Saskatoon, Edmonton and Calgary. "Petro-Can't Hide Native Genocide," placards said. "Thou Shell Not Kill." In Thunder Bay, Ontario, an Ojibway artist named Rebecca Belmore sat immobile in the snow for two hours as the torch passed through town. She sat behind a large wooden frame and a sign saying, "The Spirit Sings, sponsored by Shell Canada." A smaller sign identified her as "Artifact #671B 1988."

But the protestors had difficulty getting noticed. Night after night, the evening news showed emotionally charged people "sharing the flame," as a Petro-Canada slogan put it. Only occasionally could placards be glimpsed in the background. Petro-Canada personnel were shooting most of the videotape themselves, feeding segments daily to television stations across the country via satellite. Even the national networks were using the company's tapes between major cities.

When the torch arrived for the opening of the games in Calgary, civic pride swept the city. Suddenly the organizers were heroes. All was forgiven. Spectators lining the final leg of the relay route threw snowballs and ice pellets at three hundred pro-Lubicon demonstrators. A city policeman told a *Calgary Herald* reporter to be sure to report "the public's reaction to those fucking Indians."

For Lubicon supporters, the high point of the Olympic boycott came a few weeks earlier with the official opening of the Glenbow exhibition. The final tallies were in. Duncan Cameron said that out of 110 museums and private collectors approached, 12 were boycotting. Nobody would miss them, he said. Lennarson said that 23 museums were boycotting, badly diminishing sections of the show. The Norwegians had withheld their important Roald Amundsen collection from the Northwest Passage. The Danes had withheld their comprehensive Fifth Thule Expedition collection. In New York, James Smith said that his museum had refused to send "many pieces that were considered critical to the exhibit because there is nothing else like them in the world." Ted Brasser, one of the show's curators, said that a painted Blackfoot skin held by a boycotting Swedish museum was to have played "a most essential role in my exposé of Plains Indian symbolism." Christian Feest, the European coordinator of the show, said he found the Plains section weak. Refusals to lend coupled with an uninspired installation made the Plains section "the most difficult portion of the show," he wrote in the *European Review of Native American Studies.* Canadian editorial reaction was sharp from some quarters. "Pinning dead butterflies under glass," wrote Keith Spicer as editor of the *Ottawa Citizen.* "It is as though," wrote *Edmonton Journal* editor Steve Hume, "the Berlin Olympics had put on a display of Jewish religious objects to celebrate the diversity and pluralism of German culture."

At the opening, reporters all but ignored External Affairs Minister Joe Clark, concentrating instead on the two hundred demonstrators outside the Glenbow—including former Olympic runner Bruce

Kidd—and a packed news conference next door with more than a dozen native leaders from across the country.

"I say if we share the flame, we should share the blame, and we should share the shame," said Matthew Coon-Come, grand chief of the Quebec Cree, in the most memorable speech of the day. "It's a national shame for the Canadian people to allow the government of Alberta and Canada to continue this bureaucratic warfare."

14 THE PREMIER TAKES CHARGE

IT IS HARD TO IMAGINE an Indian band better prepared for land talks with Ottawa than the Lubicon Lake band of early 1988. By the time the Olympic Games opened in Calgary, the Lubicon people were enjoying a kind of zenith. They commanded international support and the means to convert such support into political power. They had prevailed in disputes with Union Oil and all the dozens of other oil companies that had gone from posting "No Trespassing" signs to asking the band's permission to work in Lubicon territory. Catskinners had stopped burying traplines, and oil-company trucks had stopped running Lubicon drivers off the road. Band members controlled the ninety square miles they had identified as a future reserve. Plans for a new community were ready for tender. With the buffalo herd and brush-clearing company, the transition to a new way of life had begun. Social and health problems were on the rise, but residents were still coming to meetings and holding together. Essentially, the Lubicon Lake Cree remained the cohesive Indian society that Schmidt and L'Heureux had met in 1939, led by purposeful elders and a gifted chief. But it is equally hard to imagine an Indian Affairs administration less prepared to deal with native land rights than the one headed by Bill McKnight, the former grain farmer who had replaced David Crombie.

"At this time of year, Mr. McKnight gets almost physically twitchy, wanting to get back to the farm and get the machinery ready to seed," a *Globe and Mail* reporter wrote of the minister two years into his new job. As labour minister after 1984, McKnight had been "solid" and "straightforward," the story said. At Indian Affairs, he was "plodding ahead with the thankless job of reducing the Government's commitments to native people."

Reducing commitments and lowering expectations formed the essence of McKnight's Indian policy. He returned Indian Affairs to its old Malcolm McCrimmon pursuits of cutting expenses and promoting assimilation. His guide was the report of a task force on government spending conducted by Erik Nielsen, then deputy prime minister, soon after the Tories came to power. Native peoples are "in a state of socioeconomic deprivation," the study found, but native programs go "far beyond the government's legal responsibilities." Nielsen recommended that many programs be cut. Virtually point for point, he resurrected the infamous White Paper of 1969, proposing that Indian Affairs be disbanded, that the provinces take over Indian programs and that funding to native political organizations end.

Officially, the recommendations never became policy, but McKnight was farmer enough to know which way the wind was blowing. In late 1986, he broke provisions of the James Bay Agreement to withhold $190 million in programs. When criticism erupted from some quarters, McKnight held his ground. A confidential report to the department suggested that anti-Indian sentiment in the country was on the rise, a factor which the report said might work to the government's advantage.

"Non-native Canadians are becoming somewhat tired with the image of native peoples with their hands out," said the report, prepared in 1987 by Continental/Golin/Harris Communications Inc. of Ottawa. "Currently, these sentiments are strongest in the West and are significant enough to sway the national balance. This may be indicative of a growing groundswell against the native position . . . and negotiations [on James Bay] must take these changes into account." The same study urged that a news-management team be created to orchestrate the coverage of talks with the James Bay people. The S.W.A.T. team, it would be called—Special Words and Tactics. "To ensure a primary media position for its pronouncements, the government must at all times control the dialogue."

Other documents leaked during McKnight's tenure further signalled fidelity to Nielsen's line. "We should carefully avoid expanding the scope of our responsibilities for aboriginal people," said one policy development paper, recommending that a national day-care program not necessarily be extended to reserves. Fewer schools for native children should be built, another paper said, with the reduction justified as an effort to improve quality. One sentence stood out as an exception: "As we prepare for the next election, we may want to consider selected program extensions."

Nielsen's talk of strict "legal responsibilities" became a McKnight refrain. He wrote to Ominayak saying he wished "a successful, fair and just resolution of your claim within the bounds of Canada's legal obligation to you." O'Reilly reminded the minister that Canada's obligations to the Lubicon people were the subject of proceedings in federal and provincial courts, and of a complaint before the United Nations Human Rights Committee.

≈

As the Olympic boycott gathered momentum through the fall of 1987, McKnight cast around for a means to respond. Roger Tassé had resigned as negotiator over what officials called a "potential conflict of interest"—while representing the department in dealings with Lubicon, he had been representing five Manitoba bands in dealings with the department. To fill the vacancy, McKnight named Brian Malone, a Calgary lawyer, as federal negotiator. Malone promptly told the band to "stop the nonsense" and let provincial representatives come to the table. "It's provincial land the band is claiming," he said.

Malone later apologized for depicting the land as provincial property, saying he hadn't appreciated the complexities of the case right away. But he continued to be impatient and jumpy. "Why don't you talk to the band!" he shouted into the phone early in his mandate. "They'll give you an interview! They love talking to the press!"

Malone was under pressure to secure an agreement with the band before the games, or at least to get talks started by then, and McKnight had given him little to work with. Malone was saddled with the old Tassé mandate of starting with status Indians and negotiating from there. To the band the position remained a non-starter, but Ominayak kept channels open. He had O'Reilly call Malone occasionally, and the calls led to several lawyer-to-lawyer meetings.

The band's strategy was to avoid entering negotiations staged only to assuage international concern aroused by the UN complaint and the Olympic boycott. The band was ready to negotiate if Ottawa was serious, however. The whole point of applying public pressure was to get talks moving. To test McKnight's intentions, Ominayak asked that E. Davie Fulton be reinvolved as an independent mediator in talks between the band and Ottawa.

"Fulton's too busy," McKnight replied.

"I'm ready," Fulton told a reporter, "to do anything to help, whether as negotiator, arbitrator or mediator." And he had written McKnight to say so.

Malone said he would use Fulton's discussion paper as the basis for negotiations and made the paper public. But when Ominayak again pressed for Fulton's reinvolvement, Malone said no. Fulton "had taken a position in favour of the band," he said.

With talks going nowhere and the games approaching, Malone secretly opened discussions with Alberta. The two governments would settle the land dispute themselves, he announced two months before the Winter Olympics. Discussions were going "swimmingly." Agreement on reserve size was expected before Christmas, he said.

But Christmas came and went without result. Progress was at a standstill. Three weeks before the games, O'Reilly arranged a top-level meeting in Ottawa to try to get something going. On January 28, 1988, he arrived on Parliament Hill with Ominayak and Lennarson to meet Bill McKnight and External Affairs Minister Joe Clark, in Clark's office. It was the first time since 1984 that major players in the dispute had come together. Malone and justice department lawyer Ivan Whitehall also attended. A photo of E. Davie Fulton wearing a Clark button hung on the wall.

Ominayak proposed that bilateral talks begin at once, with Fulton as mediator. McKnight dismissed the idea and issued an ultimatum: the band must accept Alberta as a full participant in negotiations and must release to the province, within eight days, genealogy records of everybody the band considered to be a Lubicon member. If the band refused, McKnight would call a federal inquiry on membership, with the power to subpoena records. If the band challenged the inquiry's findings, McKnight would send the case to court.

It was Ottawa's toughest stand yet. Five years earlier, federal and band researchers had agreed that genealogy records would be used only to establish whether the Lubicon people formed a separate aboriginal society, not to establish membership. They also agreed that the records would be kept confidential. The band had insisted on confidentiality for two reasons: all other bands in northern Alberta had determined their own membership when they settled with Canada, and the release of sixteen volumes of genealogies could delay a settlement indefinitely. Scrip records alone could keep lawyers arguing for years.

McKnight said the inquiry would take ten days—finishing in time to announce a settlement before the games. In his view, the records would prove that, with a few exceptions, only recognized status Indians were legitimate Lubicon members. The rest would be shown to be Metis, he said, or members of other bands.

"We couldn't agree to anything," Ominayak told waiting reporters after ninety minutes with McKnight.

"Where do you go from here?" a reporter asked.

"Well, we can't make any headway this way," Ominayak replied. "Until the federal government is serious and wants to negotiate, they're going to come up with a million excuses as to why we can't proceed. We've been trying for the past forty, fifty years to get a settlement and what I'm not prepared to do is fool around with the membership question, because then I'm deleting some of my own people, leaving them out in the cold. As long as the federal government is asking me to do that, I don't see any progress being made."

McKnight emerged a few minutes later. "Alberta has the right to see band membership and the genealogy," he said. "Alberta owns the land."

For a few weeks, nothing further seemed to happen. McKnight did not call his inquiry. The Olympic Games came and went. Two days after the games ended, however, Alberta Premier Don Getty made an unexpected move.

His attorney general, Jim Horsman, was briefing the entire cabinet on Lubicon talks with Ottawa. All was well, Horsman said. He and McKnight had just agreed that Alberta would set aside the promised 25.4 square miles for a reserve. Horsman called the agreement "an interim step which will be of great significance." Getty walked out in disgust. "I'm going to meet with the chief," he said, according to people who were there, and he walked straight to his office to phone Ominayak.

Two days later, Getty and Ominayak met alone in the premier's office for ninety minutes. "It's a meeting I enjoyed," Getty said afterwards. "I should have done it sooner. I'm kind of kicking myself that I left it in the hands of lawyers."

Suddenly Getty became a major player in Lubicon events, a participant who was to influence greatly developments in the coming year. The move surprised everybody—partly because Getty seemed to have almost no grasp of native issues, and partly because Getty was not known as a take-charge premier. After more than two years on the job, he was still viewed as a lumbering ex–football player. "Lougheed on Valium," people called him.

As quarterback for the Edmonton Eskimos, Getty had been a genuine football hero, achieving one of his crowning moments in a decisive 50-27 victory over Montreal at the 1956 Grey Cup. He entered politics in 1967 at Lougheed's urging, and when Lougheed swept to power four years later, Getty became minister of intergovernmental affairs, then of energy. He left in 1979 to become chairman and chief executive officer of Nortek Energy Corporation, answering a leadership call in 1985 when Lougheed retired.

As premier, Getty appeared unenthusiastic, even lazy. Lougheed had been tough, articulate and hardworking; Getty became known for his holidays. He took six or seven weeks off a year, mostly to golf in Palm Springs or to hunt ducks in northern Alberta. He also liked to spend time at the track. His favourite reading, he once said, was the Bible, the racing form and the *Thoroughbred Record*.

When Getty was off, he was off. Once when reporters went to his house, his wife, Margaret, emerged to say, "My husband doesn't comment on weekends." And while she was trying to fend off questions, Getty got up to shut the door, leaving her on the steps alone. When the $1.2-billion financial conglomerate Principal Group Ltd. of Edmonton collapsed in August 1987, creating the biggest political and financial crisis of his term, reporters found him on the golf course. Getty continued to see himself as a quarterback passing the ball to others. "All you can do is call the plays and rely on the other people to let it happen," he said shortly after assuming office. "If it doesn't, then maybe the playbook needs changing. So change it."

On native rights, Getty displayed an ignorance that bordered on contempt. After the 1987 first ministers' conference, he said Alberta might have separated from Canada if aboriginal rights had been entrenched in the constitution. "We would have gone home and talked about maybe having to pull out of the bloody country," he said.

His sole statement on Lubicon prior to the Winter Olympics had been equally aggressive. "We only give up your land when it seems the right thing to do," he told a news conference in Lethbridge during the 1986 provincial election. "I don't think we have the right to give up something that belongs to you just because someone else asks for it. It has to be proven that it should go, because it's part of your province." When Ominayak said that he was an Albertan, too, and that the land would not leave the province, Getty responded by passing the matter to Jim Horsman, who had been one of Lougheed's most powerful ministers and shared Lougheed's view on Lubicon. Getty named Horsman minister for federal-provincial relations, deputy leader of the legislature and attorney general with responsibility for native affairs.

Throughout the boycott campaign, Horsman was in charge of Lubicon for Alberta. "After the Olympics, we'll never hear of Lubicon again," provincial officials often told reporters then, taking a cocky attitude, and perhaps Horsman was telling Getty the same thing. But five days before the games provincial officials became overaggressive. Forestry Minister LeRoy Fjordbotten announced the sale of logging rights over the entire traditional Lubicon territory to Daishowa Paper Manufacturing Co. Ltd. of Japan. The company planned to build the largest hardwood pulp mill in Canada near Peace River, he announced. It would cost $500 million and would consume four million trees a year, taken from 11,000 square miles of forest between the Peace and Athabasca rivers. Two thousand jobs would be created. The province would spend an additional $65 million on roads, rail access and other services, and the federal government would contribute $9.5 million through a newly created Western Diversification Fund. Horsman's role in events wasn't clear, but the deputy minister of the federal fund was Bruce Rawson, who had moved from Indian Affairs. The minister responsible for the fund was Bill McKnight, who also remained Indian Affairs minister.

"They're coming in for the kill," Ominayak said of both governments. "They know what they're doing to our people and yet they go ahead and do something like this."

Whether the announcement was timed to spite the boycott is uncertain, but reaction was instant. "Japanese get land claimed by Lubicons," the *Edmonton Sun* announced across page one. Editorials, commentaries and letters to the editor in Alberta ran overwhelmingly against the government. Even people unsympathetic to the boycott expressed shock at the official arrogance. Native-rights supporters, environmentalists and nationalists against foreign ownership of natural resources expressed fierce opposition. Demonstrations took place in front of the company's Vancouver offices. Daishowa executives became nervous.

"We had assurances that this problem would be resolved," the vice-president of Daishowa Canada Ltd., Koichi Kitagawa, complained. Upset over the publicity, he called Getty for guarantees that the project could "proceed in an orderly manner." When he got no firm answers, he went to Edmonton, and was there the day Getty walked out of the cabinet meeting. Two days later, the premier and the chief met for the first time, in Getty's office with nobody else present. Getty offered to transfer the 25.4 square miles if doing so would be helpful.

"Doing so would not be helpful," Ominayak said.

"Then what can I do to help?" asked the premier.

Ominayak urged Getty to encourage Ottawa to enter bilateral talks with the band, having E. Davie Fulton sit as mediator.

Getty agreed to push Ottawa to get talks started with the band, but said he could never sell Fulton as sole mediator. The premier suggested a mediation tribunal. He proposed that Fulton be one member, that Ottawa name a second member and that the two members choose a third. The tribunal would mediate issues that the two parties could not resolve themselves. Getty also proposed to take the idea straight to the prime minister, bypassing McKnight. Ominayak said he liked the idea; he would present it to the band for discussion. As the meeting ended, Getty wrote his home phone number on the back of a business card, adding, "Call me anytime—Don."

The next day, band members gathered at a new aluminum Quonset hut that doubled as a work shed and community hall. They raised questions about Getty. He seemed sincere about wanting progress, but would he follow through? The tribunal idea proved popular. The band's dealings with Fulton had been tense at times but people trusted him. The federal appointee would be a risk, but Fulton would help select the third. In the end, the band endorsed the tribunal idea and, in appreciation to Getty, voted to open talks with the province on non-land issues such as wildlife management and environmental protection. Ominayak walked to the band office to call Getty at home. It was Saturday night, but he took the call.

For the premier, entente with the band brought overwhelming praise. "Getty emerging from the shadows," one newspaper headline read. "Getty calls play," read another. No longer was he bumbling old Don. He was a leader. "The premier, too often perceived as indecisive and inept, has in this instance shown firm leadership and refreshing common sense," a *Calgary Herald* editorial said.

For the band, the entente signified crucial progress. The premier of Alberta, so long a synonym for "enemy," had become a sort of ally. "What can I do to help?" had sounded a lot like Crombie saying, "I think it's time to make a deal." The question was whether Getty would follow through. His short work days, his frequent breaks, his other pressing responsibilities all raised concerns that he might lose his resolve, as Crombie had, and get outmanoeuvred by Horsman and McKnight.

Asked about the tribunal idea, McKnight pretended that it had nothing to do with him. "If Alberta wishes to be bound by a tribunal in providing Alberta land to the Lubicons, that is Alberta's right," he said. "Alberta has the land." Asked about Getty's intention to deal directly with the prime minister, McKnight said: "That's not going to accomplish anything." In an address to the standing committee on aboriginal affairs, McKnight said he expected a settlement soon. He had asked Horsman to turn over forty-five square miles as the full Lubicon entitlement, he said. If Horsman refused, Ottawa would sue the province for the land.

Horsman did refuse. "We can't just give out land without having legal and constitutional justification for doing so," he told reporters, reiterating the Lougheed position.

On March 30, 1988, four weeks after their first meeting, Getty and Ominayak met for the second time. They confirmed their commitment to the tribunal idea and talked briefly about horses. An odd rapport was developing. Getty suggested that they go moose hunting together after the issue was resolved. "If there's anything left," Ominayak said, smiling.

In another room, a possibly odder alliance was being forged.

Lennarson and the premier's executive assistant, Gordon Young, were discussing specifics of the tribunal. For nearly a year, Lennarson and Young had awkwardly avoided each other, finding themselves on opposite sides of the Lubicon issue while one of Lennarson's daughters dated Young's son. Now they were exchanging private numbers and working out ways to stay in touch. Each side wanted a means of reaching the other in an emergency.

Weeks passed. Alberta opposition members asked about Ottawa's response to the tribunal proposal. Horsman told the legislature that he had outlined the idea to McKnight, but McKnight told reporters: "I have not received any information on the make-up of the tribunal, its actions, or its supposed goals except from what I have seen in the media." He then pronounced the idea "unworkable."

On May 17, 1988, McKnight made good his threat to go to court. He filed a suit against both Alberta and the band to determine Lubicon membership and reserve size. Going to court served McKnight in three ways: he could refuse further questions on Lubicon, saying that the case was before the courts; court action rendered moot the tribunal idea; and the suit reduced the Lubicon matter to a simple reserve issue, ignoring questions of aboriginal title and compensation.

"Court is the wrong way to go," said Getty.

The suit "will just exacerbate things," said E. Davie Fulton.

"We're back to square one," said Ominayak. He and other band members began to contemplate an action of last resort: if Canada didn't want to negotiate the band's formal entry into Canada, maybe the band should keep its aboriginal lands. Already the band controlled ninety square miles. Maybe members should extend their control to the oil fields. "I think it's time that we say, 'If you don't want to deal with us, we'll take back our lands,' " Ominayak began to tell audiences.

Asserting a physical presence over a large oil field is no easy undertaking. A sustained occupation would take hundreds of people and substantial amounts of money, and it would pose risks the Lubicon people had previously not been prepared to take. But McKnight's lawsuit pushed band members to a new militancy. In the previous eighteen months, they had buried twenty-two people at Little Buffalo. All had died violently: in fires, car crashes, accidents and, in the one case, by suicide.

"We don't have any option," Ominayak said. "Our people are dying left and right and the government seems to like it."

At the end of May 1988—three months after the games—Ominayak and Lennarson flew to Sweden for the fourth annual congress of the European Support Groups for North American Indians. To rousing applause, they announced plans to "assert jurisdiction on the ground."

"Having been effectively denied all hope of achieving recognition of their aboriginal land rights through normal Canadian legal and political channels, the Lubicon people are preparing to assert their jurisdiction over unceded Lubicon lands and to defend themselves on the ground as best they can," Lennarson wrote supporters afterwards. Passport control points would be established on all major routes into Lubicon territory. Lubicon laws regulating wildlife management, environmental protection and development work would be enacted and enforced. No date was specified, but Lennarson said that McKnight ran "the very real risk of precipitating a major confrontation in northern Alberta."

The prospect of direct action appeared to unnerve the minister. He wrote to Ominayak in a conciliatory, almost maudlin tone about the need "to build bridges, not blockades."

"I have followed your recent statements with reference to blockades and possible violence with considerable sadness," the minister began.

"I have made my position as clear as I can. I want the Band to have a reserve! I want the Band to have modern facilities! I want the Band to have self-government and economic prosperity!"

McKnight then reiterated his preconditions for talks: full Alberta participation, no role for Fulton and immediate transfer of the original 25.4 square miles. But for the first time McKnight also offered to appoint an independent mediator.

Ominayak accepted the single-mediator idea, prompting discussions about a suitable candidate. "Somebody as high profile as possible," Brian Malone said. He suggested Emmett Hall, the former Supreme Court of Canada justice who as Crombie's envoy had settled the Grassy Narrows compensation dispute. Malone also suggested Stephen Lewis, who was soon to retire as Canada's ambassador to the United Nations. When Ominayak endorsed both suggestions, Malone withdrew them, citing objections from "federal colleagues."

The band put forward three other possibilities: Joyce Fairbairn, a senator from Alberta, Andrew Thompson, chairman of the native justice committee of the Canadian Bar Association, and Tim Christian, dean of the University of Alberta law school. Malone rejected the first two and asked for time to think about the third. He also suggested Gordon Henderson, an Ottawa lawyer. When the band accepted Henderson, Malone said the federal government no longer considered him acceptable.

Eventually, Ominayak concluded that McKnight wasn't serious about a mediator. He decided to make his move. On October 6, 1988, O'Reilly appeared in the Alberta Court of Appeal at Calgary, scheduled to address a procedural issue that had blocked the band's parallel aboriginal-rights suits. Instead, he stood to tell three grim-faced judges that his clients were pulling out of the courts altogether.

"This effort has been in vain," O'Reilly said, his hand trembling as he read a prepared statement. "From this day, [the band] will no longer participate in any court proceedings in which the Lubicons are presently a party, whether in this court, the Court of Queen's Bench of Alberta, the Federal Court of Appeal or the Federal Court of Canada."

On October 15, he said, "the Lubicon Nation intends to assert and enforce its aboriginal rights and its sovereign jurisdiction as an independent Nation, with its own law-enforcement and court systems." "We don't have any choice," Ominayak told reporters on the courthouse steps. "It's time we tried to protect what is ours. As of 1:00 P.M. on October 15, anybody who wants to come on our land will have to deal with us and recognize this land as ours."

15 LUBICON LAKE NATION

THE PLAN WAS to erect checkpoints on the four main oil roads into Lubicon territory. As of October 15, 1988, band members would stop all vehicles. Anybody wishing to work in the area would have to buy permits from the band office at the same rates as those paid to the Alberta government. All payments would be due in advance. Companies would have to submit copies of existing provincial authorizations to the band and post copies of approved Lubicon permits at all work sites. Five days prior to the start of a project, a company would have to notify affected registered trapline owners and pay $550 for every kilometre of seismic line, pipeline or access road to be built through a trapper's territory. "If the oil companies pay the fees and work at last year's level," Plodzein said, "the band will take in $400,000."

Oil-company employees refusing to acknowledge the band's authority would be turned back at the checkpoints. Officially, band members would be unarmed. But they had prepared spiked boards to throw across the road in an emergency, and some members hinted broadly that guns would also be near at hand. "In case we see a moose," they said.

The risks for the band were substantial. A truck could try to run a checkpoint. The police could be called in, or the army. "If we go down, we go down fighting," Ominayak said. But the idea was to bring issues to a head peacefully. Band members were not erecting a blockade, Ominayak emphasized. They were erecting checkpoints. Lubicon territory remained open to oil development as long as Indian people reaped some of the benefits. In practice, oil companies would have to buy licences from both the Alberta government and the band if they wished to keep operating, but they could still make a profit. Only if the band levied royalties on oil would the companies lose money, and Ominayak said the band had no immediate plans to do so.

Company reaction was restrained.

"We're certainly not going to provoke or engage in any confrontation in the area," said Basil Skodyn, speaking for Shell Canada.

"We do not want to inflame the situation by confronting the blockades," said Arnie Amundrud, speaking for Husky Oil of Calgary.

Even Getty had options other than confrontation. Normally, the premier could not allow Alberta citizens to take power into their own hands. But he had come to know Ominayak and to understand the band's desperate circumstances. Ultimately, Lubicon complaints were with Ottawa, anyway. The band was challenging provincial jurisdiction not to do battle with the province but as a way to push the province to force Ottawa to settle. Getty didn't have to push back. Instead of calling in the Mounties, he conceivably could fly to one of the checkpoints and stand with the Indians. Such a move would be bold, but he could afford to be bold. Being bold on Lubicon had served him well so far.

≈

Four days before the deadline, supporters began to arrive from Europe and elsewhere. Ominayak had asked organizations to send only a few delegates who could be replaced later by others should the occupation last a long time. Four representatives of the European Support Groups arrived from Sweden, Vienna and West Germany. Three Quakers arrived from Vancouver, Toronto and Halifax. James O'Reilly landed, adrenalin pumping.

"The Lubicons are now desperate," he told a waiting television camera at Edmonton airport. "After fifty years of trying to get their own home recognized as their home, and their own land, and a fair deal, and being thrown around from federal broken promise to federal broken promise and nothing happening, and nothing on the horizon, and their way of life having been destroyed, and the United Nations having reproached Canada to do something about it and Canada saying basically, 'We don't care what you say,' and flouting international law—enough is enough! The Lubicons intend to make this literally their last stand. And it may be the last stand for some of them and for myself."

Radio talk shows focussed on the issue. "Do you recognize the Lubicon nation as sovereign?" asked the moderator of CBC Edmonton's "Phone Forum." Responses ran 80 per cent in the band's favour.

"It's a desperate move, but I don't blame them," said one caller.

"I'm black from South Africa and I know how they feel," said another.

The RCMP issued a public warning to stay clear of the Lubicon area after October 15. "We're just acting in a peace-keeping role right now," said Sgt. Darryl Derouin of the Peace River detachment. "We have our contingency plans in place."

Bill McKnight was nowhere to be found. A federal election had been called for November 21, and McKnight was said to be in Saskatchewan campaigning as events moved towards the biggest crisis of his term at Indian Affairs.

Getty made the crisis a priority. Four days before the deadline, he told a morning news conference that he was available to help resolve the dispute—all the band had to do was ask. When no request came by midday, Getty phoned Ominayak. Getty said he didn't agree with what the band was doing, or maybe didn't understand it, but he was willing to hear the band's view. Ominayak suggested that the premier come to Little Buffalo. His schedule wouldn't allow him to get away, Getty said, but he would send a plane to bring the chief to Edmonton. Ominayak demurred. A community meeting was scheduled for the following evening to review plans. Ominayak said he would call the premier afterwards with an answer.

On Wednesday—three days before the deadline—Little Buffalo was alive with purposeful activity. Outside the band office, a dozen men hammered latrines together for use at checkpoints. Teenagers painted placards nearby: "Lubicon Land." "Justice for the Lubicon." Families doubled up to make entire homes available to visiting supporters.

That evening the community assembled at the Quonset hut, filling all the chairs and every space on the stacks of lumber stored along the walls. John Felix Laboucan and his cousins Edward, Albert and Summer Joe took positions near the front. By coincidence, New York anthropologist James Smith was in the crowd. He had recovered enough from his apartment fire to return to Little Buffalo for more research.

Most of the discussion was in Cree, the atmosphere upbeat and businesslike. Steve Noskey led the group clause by clause through a document entitled "Law of the Lubicon Lake Indian Nation." In it, band members defined themselves as a nation under international law and declared all lands, mines, minerals, forests and other natural resources within traditional Lubicon territory to be under their ownership and control. No lands or resources would be disposed of or settled upon except under the authority of Lubicon law. The paper made provisions for licensing restrictions, the erection of checkpoints and the establishment of a police and judicial system. No hunting, no firearms and no alcoholic beverages were to be permitted to oil-company personnel within Lubicon lands. Alleged violations of any rule would be heard by a tribunal of band judges taking into account "traditional law, customs and practices of the Lubicon Lake Nation."

At one point, people in the crowd appeared to stiffen as Mary Sawan—the wife of Peter Sawan, who had sided for years with the L'Hirondelles—stood to ask if Peter would qualify for a share of any fees paid by an oil company for permits on his trapline. Peter had been rethinking his position, she said. He might seek to be counted as an official band member. After an awkward silence, Ominayak said that Peter Sawan had the same rights as everybody else in the community. The Lubicon Lake Cree were one people.

Three hours into the meeting, Ominayak slipped out to call Getty. He moved slowly and deliberately, the way he often does under pressure, crossing the open ground between the Quonset hut and the band office to dial Getty's home number. No answer. He tried five minutes later. No answer.

Lennarson reached the premier's executive assistant, who tracked Getty down at an Edmonton Oilers game. Getty called back from Northlands Coliseum.

"How are you doing?" Ominayak said in a tone at once polite and cordial. In a brief exchange, the leaders agreed to meet at nine o'clock the next morning at the lieutenant governor's residence in west Edmonton. Getty again offered to send a plane, but Ominayak said he would charter his own.

On Thursday morning before dawn—two days before the deadline—Ominayak headed south with a small entourage. He and Plodzein dozed lightly. Lennarson and O'Reilly were wide awake.

"This is high drama!" Lennarson said. "Two political leaders meeting in a summit conference on the eve of a confrontation!"

"God save the Chief!" said O'Reilly.

The sun peeked over the horizon as the plane flew over the west end of Lesser Slave Lake, suffusing the clouds with autumnal reds and golds. Below lay the site of the first Treaty Eight signing in 1899.

"What we're seeking now is a government-to-government agreement regarding coexistence on traditional Lubicon lands," Lennarson said. "We're seeking an agreement where some of the lands [a reserve] would be the exclusive jurisdiction of the Lubicon people, and the rest would be shared jurisdiction [under a wildlife-management regime]. We are also seeking compensation to be a source of income for the Lubicon people independent of the federal government."

O'Reilly rifled through historical documents looking for references to Indian "nations," finding one in the first line of the Royal Proclamation of 1763. He read it aloud in a swirl of pipe smoke: "And whereas it is just and reasonable, and essential to our Interest, and the security of our Colonies, that the several Nations or Tribes of Indians with whom We are connected . . ."

≈

Getty was angry. In a tense one-on-one meeting at Government House, he asked Ominayak to suspend the takeover of the oil fields for thirty days and use the time to find an agreement with the province on all major issues. Once agreement was reached, the two men could take it jointly to Ottawa.

Ominayak said no. The band had not spent months bringing the issue to a head just to have the premier offer to talk.

"Twenty days," Getty said.

Without a signed agreement by 1:00 P.M. Saturday the checkpoints go up, Ominayak said.

Getty said he wouldn't talk with "blockades" up.

"Let's talk now then," said Ominayak. "We have two days."

At that point, Ominayak recalled later, Getty rose from his chair and paced the room, incensed at the idea of provincial roads being blocked. He told Ominayak to call the thing off. They could trust each other. Ominayak replied that he trusted Getty, but the players could change. One Alberta premier had passed retroactive legislation, he said.

After almost two hours, the leaders emerged to face a wall of reporters standing in the harsh October sunlight on the flagstone drive. The premier spoke first, sounding simultaneously tough and conciliatory.

"The very important thing I wanted to stress with the chief is how firmly I believe in law and order in this province and that the laws of Alberta must be upheld, and that the laws of Alberta will be upheld," he said. "Putting that to one side for a moment, we have come to agreement on a certain course of action at least over the short term. For the first time, the band and the Alberta representatives will meet directly, immediately, in negotiations. That has never happened before."

The representatives would try to reach an agreement on major issues, Getty said, then present it to Ottawa. If problems developed at the talks, he would intervene personally. The chief and federal representatives might also suddenly be asked to take part.

"As I pointed out to the premier," said Ominayak, taking his turn at the microphone, "we've got to have everything in place. We are proceeding with the checkpoints as of Saturday at 1:00 P.M. if we haven't really arrived at any kind of solution." The premier was concerned about Alberta law, Ominayak said. The band was concerned about Lubicon law. "We can't afford to wait and wait and wait for another forty-eight years. We are going to protect our traditional lands."

Before heading home, Ominayak assembled a negotiating team in Edmonton consisting of Lennarson, O'Reilly, Larry Ominayak, Steve Noskey and an Edmonton criminal lawyer, Bob Sachs, who had represented several Lubicon members in connection with the band's increasing social problems.

The talks began that afternoon. The head of the provincial delegation, a Calgary lawyer named John McCarthy, asked if the band had a map of the proposed ninety-square-mile reserve. The band provided one. As McCarthy and his colleagues pored over it, they lopped off the entire east end where Sonics had tried to explore, made a few other border changes, and cut a swath through the northeast corner saying the province needed access to the lake. They left fifty-five to sixty square miles of reserve land. McCarthy called the offer "generous." Band negotiators called it "unacceptable." The Lubicon people should be allowed to retain 128 acres per person, they said, the same as other bands in northern Alberta.

"You're not prepared to negotiate?" McCarthy asked.

"Not over land," said Lennarson. "Either the band has a right to land or it doesn't. You can't talk about having 60 per cent of a right, or 25 per cent. We're not haggling over a used car."

"Are you saying you want ninety square miles, period?" McCarthy asked again.

"Ninety-five," said Lennarson.

"Ninety-five! That's more!"

Lennarson explained. "A year and a half ago the Lubicon population was 457. Now it's 477. If ten people die, the land entitlement is less. If ten people are born, it's more. Until we establish a cutoff date, the numbers will continue to fluctuate."

"Are you prepared to go below ninety or not?" McCarthy asked hotly.

"No," said Steve Noskey, ending the exchange.

Talks on compensation went no better. Lennarson suggested that the province table the value of all resources extracted from the area so that both sides could discuss a dollar figure on compensation. The province refused, asking the band what figure it had in mind. Lennarson suggested 2 per cent of total revenues; the government's cut had been about 20 per cent of the total, so the band was asking 10 per cent of that. In dollar terms, the band was asking for thirty-four cents on every seventeen-dollar barrel of oil. McCarthy said the demand was unreasonable. Almost no discussion took place on wildlife management and self-government.

All afternoon and the next day, Friday, oil workers pulled out of Lubicon territory. "We're out of here," said Lorne Bekevich, a contractor in charge of a road crew north of Little Buffalo. Workers capped wells, closed their camps, packed equipment and headed down the highway to Peace River, kicking up clouds of dust. Pipelines closed. Pump jacks nodded to a stop. Representatives of every oil company in the area announced that they were suspending operations to avoid the looming confrontation.

At Little Buffalo itself, supporters and journalists arrived in steady dribs and drabs. The two national television networks erected a transmission dish next to the band office. A reporter-photographer team from the *Calgary Herald* hauled in a camper. The band office became increasingly congested. Plodzein claimed one of the four tiny rooms as a licensing/administration centre. The Quakers staffed the telephones and photocopy machine. O'Reilly returned from Edmonton with bleak news.

"It's a clash of cultures," he said of the talks. "Both parties start from principles which are almost at opposite ends. It's obvious that it's going to be pretty, pretty difficult to close the gap."

McKnight continued to refuse all comment, but Getty spoke to reporters regularly of developments. He tried to sound positive.

"Our government supports the band and is trying to help them in every way possible," he told Ruth Anderson in a live interview with CBC Radio, Edmonton.

"What's the stumbling block?" Anderson asked.

"Well, I guess the number-one issue is how many acres of land, or square miles if you like, would make up the band's reserve," Getty said. "Unfortunately, over the years the federal government and the band have been unable to agree on the number of members—whether they have added people from other bands, whether they have just added people who have come up and moved into their community—and should Canadian people give land to all the members of the community up there, or should the Lubicons have to prove that they really are members of their band?"

"What are you going to do, Mr. Premier, when they put a roadblock up on the highway up there?"

"We cannot have the laws broken," Getty said, his voice grave. "They must be enforced and upheld. Now, the reason that's important to emphasize, Ruth, is because sometimes when you're talking to people and you like them, and you're helping them, you have to make sure that they don't misread that like and help into any kind of a weakness or an indecision about laws."

"Is a blockade an illegal action?" asked Anderson.

"The only thing I will say, Ruth, is that the laws of Alberta will be upheld, must be upheld."

By Friday night—the eve of the deadline—the talks were going nowhere. McCarthy and the other provincial negotiators left the meeting room to talk to Getty, and Getty, frustrated by what he was hearing, phoned Ominayak.

It was a tense conversation. Getty offered seventy-five square miles. Ominayak repeated the principle of equity: other bands in northern Alberta had retained one square mile for every five people; the Lubicon band was entitled to the same amount.

Getty raised the offer to seventy-nine, saying he would have to twist arms in cabinet to get it. Ominayak said no, all band members must be counted.

Getty said he felt cheated. He had expected the band to compromise at about eighty. Ominayak said he felt cheated, too. He had thought the premier was seeking a fair settlement.

"You have my phone number," Getty said. When the band was prepared to accept seventy-nine, Ominayak was welcome to call.

"You've got my number, too," Ominayak replied. When the premier was prepared to include all band members, he was welcome to call, too.

McCarthy hustled outside to speak to reporters. The province had boosted its offer to sixty square miles and had been prepared to go higher, he said. "Unfortunately, there has been no reciprocation and the band has refused to reduce the 95.4-square-miles amount in the same spirit of compromise and generosity."

Lennarson emerged minutes later, his voice nearly breaking with emotion and fatigue. "If the provincial government thinks that invading the traditional lands of the Lubicon people, destroying the traditional economy, forcing 95 per cent of the population onto welfare, creating circumstances where a third of the population comes down with tuberculosis, creating situations where babies are born dead with regularity, where others are born premature with a variety of medical problems, where families are breaking down, where horrendous social problems exist—that's a different definition of generosity than I would use."

Shortly before noon on Saturday, three hundred band members and supporters gathered at the Quonset hut. They parked helter-skelter around the satellite dish and milled around in the sharp autumn sunlight as though at an impromptu country fair. Faces in the crowd brought to mind earlier periods of the struggle. William Beaver of the Isolated Communities Advisory Board stood out tall and beefy next to Walter Whitehead, the Lubicon chief who had signed the caveat application. Joe T. Laboucan, who had helped in Whitehead's election, chatted in a clump with the key elders—Edward, John Felix, Albert and Summer Joe Laboucan. "I'm so happy I feel like crying," Edward said. "The chief and I have travelled around the world. We have tried the best we could to have the government keep its promise." Eugene Steinhauer of Saddle Lake, a former president of the Indian Association and one of Alberta's best-known Indian leaders, had left a hospital bed to be there. Chiefs from other bands around Alberta could be seen, including Lawrence Courtoreille, vice-president for Alberta of the Assembly of First Nations, and leaders such as Mohawk Chief Billy Two Rivers of Kahnawake near Montreal. Members of the Committee Against Racism from Calgary held placards saying "Support the Lubicon." News reporters and photographers were out in force, representing the national television networks, the radio networks, the Southam and Canadian Press news services, an Italian wire service and dozens of Alberta print and broadcast outlets. As one o'clock approached, everyone jammed into the meeting hall around Ominayak.

"I want to welcome you and thank you for coming," he told the crowd evenly. "It's very important that native people start showing a united front. The provincial and federal governments could have saved themselves a lot of trouble but now it's time for us to stand up to these guys and say, 'Hey, this is ours, and we're going to treat it as such.' We're going ahead with our checkpoints and we're going to continue for however many years it will require to get recognition of our rights. With your help, I'm sure we can pull this off."

The crowd dispersed into a dusty convoy heading out of town, some of the vehicles branching off in different directions. Steve Noskey took a crew south to the Slave oil-and-gas field. Larry Ominayak took a crew northeast to the road from the Red Earth oil fields at Trout and Peerless lakes. Walter Whitehead took a crew northwest past the Norcen battery in the Golden oil field. Almost everybody else headed west along the highway towards Peace River to establish the main checkpoint near Marten River. Terry Laboucan, a twenty-two-year-old Lubicon member dressed in camouflage clothes, was in charge. As an infant, he had been bundled into John Halcrow's wagon for the move from Marten River, and he was among the recent TB victims. At one o'clock, he strung a yellow rope across the highway between two upright logs planted in the road. Others in his crew erected signs saying "Stop" and "No access or work without permit."

The checkpoints were up. Now everyone waited. A couple of hundred people mingled on the highway behind the rope. In the distance, seven officers from a number of RCMP detachments maintained their own checkpoint, ostensibly to inform motorists of events. Periodically, a Twin Otter with police markings circled overhead, and a police cruiser charged the yellow rope once, turning back at a hundred metres. "If they cross this line we'll arrest them," Terry Laboucan said. But the police did not cross the line. The only vehicle to challenge the checkpoint all day was a gasoline truck serving the L'Hirondelles. Ominayak let it pass.

In midafternoon more supporters arrived. A group of clergy led by Peter Hamel of the Anglican Church of Canada joined the ranks. A Dutch member of the European Parliament, Herman Verbeek, arrived separately, telling reporters, "It is important that Canadians be aware that people in Europe and all over the world know what is happening here."

In Edmonton, Getty gave a news conference, his first public remarks since the breakdown of talks. "There was no negotiation and that's sad," the premier said. "It's sad because I felt there was a chance to build on the good will between myself and Chief Ominayak. Without any negotiations there was nothing else for us to do and therefore the talks were terminated. I'm sorry about that because I think I'm the biggest ally that they have."

On land and membership, Getty said, the province had raised its offer from 25.4 square miles to 60. The band had raised its demand from 90 to 95.4.

On compensation, he said, the band had asked 10 per cent of provincial oil revenues from the territory. That meant the band was asking for "in excess of $100 million," he said, revealing for the first time that total oil-and-gas revenues from Lubicon territory had exceeded $5 billion so far.

"I'm prepared to start negotiations whenever the chief requests," the premier said. "But I won't negotiate with people who are breaking the law."

Late in the afternoon, protestors at the main checkpoint drifted into smaller groups on the grassy rights-of-way next to the road. Campfires were lit. At the Quonset hut, Ominayak called a meeting of fifteen visiting chiefs to discuss how to maintain the occupation at its current level. Senior members of labour unions, churches and political parties were scheduled to arrive over an extended period; Ominayak wanted a continual flow of native people through the area as well. "Indian people are on the move," said Eugene Steinhauer of Saddle Lake. One by one, chiefs pledged to phone bands in their area, seeking support in the way of food, money and volunteers to help staff the checkpoints. Lawrence Courtoreille said he would arrange for all Treaty Eight chiefs to meet in Peace River in four days. "We need them nearby," he said.

By nightfall, the grassy areas next to the main checkpoint had become a tent encampment speckled with cooking fires and dominated by a giant tepee from Saskatchewan.

Lennarson got in his truck to check the other camps. He drove north through the Golden oil field past the silent Norcen installations and an extinguished flare pit. The stars stood out. He drove fast and expertly, agonizing aloud over the direction events were taking.

"We're heading into a major pushing match with somebody who clearly is not an evil person, and that's sad," he said, hammering lightly on the steering wheel and sounding oddly like Getty himself. "Lougheed was clearly an enemy but Getty simply never understood our position. He still doesn't. In his view, the province was offering twenty-five square miles and the band was asking ninety. He went up to sixty, he expected the band to come down to eighty, and the band went up to ninety-five—that's his view. We tried to explain it to his dummy negotiators but it was like talking to a tree stump. And to be fair, we didn't understand what they were doing either—me included. Now Getty's feeling that the band jumped up the numbers. And Bernard is thinking that Getty's a liar, that he went from talking about fairness for all band members to talking about sixty square miles. 'What we got here is a failure to communicate'—Paul Newman says that in *Cool Hand Luke* just before the cops shoot him through the chest and kill him."

Lennarson seemed to pick up energy as he drove. He'd been sleeping less than anybody all week, except possibly O'Reilly, but he kept turning over ideas, searching for a way to bring the two worlds together.

"We have immense power now," he said. "We've got roadblocks, we've got people from all over, we've got the Treaty Eight chiefs coming, we've got the oil companies shut down, we've got the whole thing before the United Nations—Getty is under horrendous pressure. We've got power and important things to accomplish, but if we can possibly accomplish them by breaking as few bones as possible, that has so many advantages."

He fell silent as he sped over the rough road, blackness on either side, then laid out a happy ending.

"Getty could just say, 'It doesn't make any sense for me to impose a settlement that the Lubicon people will never be happy with, so as a leader, as a statesman, as someone who needs to have these questions settled, I'm going to sign off at ninety-five square miles. I don't agree with them, but if they believe this is an essential principle of equity and if that's the only way they're going to think they've been treated fairly, then I'm going to do it.' The problem with saying that now is that his political opponents will be calling him a pushover. So he's saying the only way talks are going to start again is if Bernard pulls down the barricades and calls. I want to talk to Bernard about that. Calling might assuage Getty's feelings."

The next morning—Day Two of the occupation—Lennarson, O'Reilly and Bob Sachs crammed in around Ominayak, who sat hunched over his desk at the band office, smoking a cigarette. His face was lowered almost to his desk blotter, the peak of his cap obscuring his expression.

"Getty's feelings are hurt," Lennarson was saying. "He's called you twice. I think he genuinely wants to settle. I think it's very important to him that you call him this time."

Ominayak shook his head slowly back and forth.

"I don't have the whole answer," said Lennarson. "I don't know when to call or under what circumstances, but my job is to give you my analysis and that's my analysis."

Later in the day, word reached Little Buffalo that Getty was saying he might have settled at ninety square miles.

"Maybe I would have gone to ninety," he told a CBC Edmonton reporter in a segment to be aired on television that night. "But I wanted to know, 'Was ninety going to do it?' And it wasn't. They were moving away. It has to be based on some facts, so as you explore these things, you explore them to determine if the other side wants to make a deal. And they don't."

"Ninety" was almost certainly a slip of the tongue, reporters speculated privately. He must have meant "sixty" or maybe "eighty." But Getty's press secretary stuck to the ninety figure all day. Asked about the remark that afternoon, Ominayak responded sharply: "If Getty is serious about ninety square miles, he'd better give us a phone call quick."

≈

Plodzein spent the afternoon of Day Two driving south from Little Buffalo to an oil camp. Licence sales had fallen short of expectations. A few oil people had inquired about permits but none had bought one, and when one company asked to leave two employees to monitor idle equipment, Ominayak granted permission free of charge. With little else going on, Plodzein decided to pay the employees a visit.

They worked for Unocal, formerly Union Oil, the company that had proposed to run a pipeline across the 25.4 square miles during the Fulton inquiry. Unocal operated thirty-five wells south of Little Buffalo, employing ten full-time workers and a number of part-time staff at a camp complete with recreation hall, satellite television and flush toilets. A maintenance foreman and a supervisor named Bill Pearson currently had the camp to themselves.

"A lot of people, including my wife, are worried about me being here, but I don't have any qualms," Pearson said over coffee in the dining area. "I've met face to face with Bernard at least half a dozen times. I know the purpose of the roadblock is to get the parties together."

Pearson was canny and personable, the ideal trouble-shooter.

"When we wanted to extend the pipeline, the band was cooperative," he said, glossing over tensions of the period. "They let us run our lines to the edge of the 25.4 square miles, which really got us out of a bind. Otherwise, we would have had to limit production to 40 per cent of capacity. Since then, we've run a few pipelines in this area, drilled a few wells, built a gas plant. I haven't had a problem with the band and I hope the band hasn't had a problem with what we've done."

"If everyone was as conscientious as you, we wouldn't have a problem," said Plodzein, equally effusive.

Then they got down to business. Pearson was the senior man for Unocal in northern Alberta, based at Slave Lake, and although he said he had been sent "for safety and environmental reasons," he was also the eyes and ears at that moment for all oil companies with operations in the territory. He had attended a meeting of executives from eight oil companies in Calgary a few days earlier, where the decision was taken for everybody to pull out. Now he delicately fished for details on what the band had in mind.

"The big fear in Calgary is a double whammy on royalties," Pearson told Plodzein. "With the drop in oil prices, we're down to making fifty cents to two dollars a barrel profit. The provincial royalty is between $2.50 and $4.00 a barrel, so paying again to the band is a money-losing proposition. If the band were clear about not charging royalties, most operations would go back to work."

Plodzein said no royalties would be charged in the short term, but the band was leaving the royalty option open. Then he went fishing, too, for details on what the royalties might be worth.

Pearson gave a rundown on royalty structures. He talked about "old oil" and "new oil," about different rate structures and percentages that applied depending on when a well came into production, and how under some incentive programs a well might not be taxed on its first million-dollars' worth of oil. Changing the subject, he asked what Unocal might be expected to pay the band in licensing fees should the company restart operations. Plodzein floated a figure: $77,000.

Keeping a poker face, Pearson said having the oil field idle was already costing the companies plenty. "Oil production out of the Lubicon area is maybe 20,000 barrels per day," he said. "Times $12 or $13 a barrel, that's about $260,000 a day."

"More," said Plodzein on the drive back to Little Buffalo. "Much more. The government people who monitor these things in Calgary estimate a loss of $430,000 a day. This is costing them a bundle."

≈

All night Ominayak pondered Getty's "ninety" remark. On Monday morning—Day Three—he gave a news conference in the Quonset hut to make the band's position clear.

"Our position on land and membership is not a negotiating position," he said into a nest of microphones. To be a Lubicon member, a person must be of aboriginal ancestry linked by historic and family ties to the traditional Lubicon area, he said. In a census three months earlier, 477 people met the criteria. On the day the checkpoints went up, the number rose by one when his cousin had a baby, Charmaine Amber Ominayak. At 128 acres per person, the band's reserve entitlement for 478 people stood at 95.6 square miles. "We don't believe that Premier Getty would ask us to compromise the heritage and rights of the new baby girl if he fully understood the significance of our position," Ominayak said. On the other hand, a proposal of ninety square miles would be taken seriously. He challenged Getty to make the offer directly.

In Calgary, where he was spending the day, Getty backtracked on the "ninety" figure. "That wasn't an offer," he said. "That was a comment I made to illustrate that they were running away from our offers. The offer that's on the table is sixty square miles, more than double the original."

On radio newscasts all day, the two leaders carried on a kind of dialogue of sound bites.

"I'm prepared to meet with Mr. Getty one on one," said the chief.

"There's no discussions while the barricades are up," said the premier.

"I'm prepared to meet the premier between our barricades and the RCMP barricades."

"As soon as the barricades are down, I will phone the chief and invite him into new negotiations."

"We're not prepared to dismantle barricades just to get a phone call from Premier Getty."

For the third straight day, in the middle of a federal election campaign, Lubicon events were at the top of the national news. The prime minister refused to comment, but his opponents spoke out.

"Prime Minister Mulroney should intervene immediately," said Liberal Leader John Turner.

"The federal government hasn't been negotiating in good faith," said New Democratic Party Leader Ed Broadbent. "They must do so and do so quickly."

The protest spread to other parts of the country. In Montreal, the Mohawks of Kahnawake slowed traffic on the Mercier Bridge for the second straight day to distribute 10,000 Lubicon support flyers. In Brantford, Ontario, fifteen members of the Six Nations Mohawk reserve blocked highway traffic briefly in a similar show of solidarity. In Labrador, partly emboldened by the Lubicon move, a community of Innu Indians camped at the end of a military runway in Goose Bay to protest low-level military flights over their caribou lands. More than 150 people were arrested, then released.

At Little Buffalo, a routine began to develop as the standoff settled into a test of wills. Community members and volunteers took turns at the checkpoints. Lennarson and O'Reilly separately patrolled most of the night, rolling in at five or six in the morning to Albert Laboucan's place to doze briefly in sleeping bags on the floor. Ominayak patrolled most of the night, too, boosting morale. He moved deliberately, his face hardened into an aspect of perpetual determination. He would roll out of bed after two or three hours sleep, wash his face at an enamel basin in a closet next to his bedroom, walk outside to the outhouse and drive to the band office for another twenty-hour work day.

At sunrise on Tuesday—Day Four—a helicopter landed 200 metres from the main checkpoint as band members and supporters cooked breakfast at a fire. Two RCMP officers jumped out with video-tape equipment. They panned the campsites, the placards, the two posts in the ground with the yellow rope stretched between them, and Terry Laboucan in his military fatigues standing defiantly on the road. The police repeated the manoeuvre at the three other checkpoints. In Edmonton, the Alberta cabinet met in emergency session to discuss the next step.

On Wednesday—Day Five—the weather changed. Light snow and a dull sky ended the series of clear fall days. Vigilance slackened, and for a while that morning Plodzein found himself standing alone at the main checkpoint. The drama of a few days earlier was waning. Both television networks pulled out, taking the satellite dish.

After lunch, Ominayak took a long drive north through the bush. Snow that would otherwise have signalled a new drilling season lay undisturbed on the road ahead, heightening the sense that his truck was the only thing on the move in the whole of Lubicon territory. Pump jacks stood motionless in their clearings like statues. Ominayak said nothing. He fixed his gaze steadily on the road, as though working through something. The key decisions were his now. If he made a mistake, people could get killed. Ten years of struggle could be lost. Pressure was on him to call Getty.

"Getty's all over the place with his numbers," he said half an hour into the ride. "When we talked at Government House, he never went below eighty square miles. McCarthy and them were talking forty-five in negotiations. They went to sixty. Then Getty phones and says he'll go to seventy-five, maybe seventy-nine. On TV he says ninety. Now he's saying sixty again. I can't help feeling he's just toying with me."

Ominayak fell silent for a few minutes, then resumed.

"At Government House, we talked about a wildlife advisory board, and he said if I sat on it, he would too. I told him, 'It doesn't matter who sits on it, the important thing is that it not be just advisory. Why don't we just call it a board for now instead of advisory board?' I had him talked into that. And then he said, 'Maybe I should be writing some of these things down.' So he made a list, and at the end of the meeting Rostad [Ken Rostad, the attorney general] came in and looked at the list, and he told Getty to change 'wildlife board' to 'wildlife advisory board.' And Getty did."

Ominayak again fell silent, as though replaying the conversations in his mind. He drove all the way to the northeast checkpoint on the Red Earth road, stopping for a cup of tea with his brother Larry. When Ominayak started back he was still tense, saying little. Ten minutes later, he slowed down.

"What's wrong?"

"I thought I saw a moose," he said.

"Where?"

"Up the last road."

He turned back. A dark mound stuck out of the scrub a long way off, between the left side of the road and the woods. It looked like a stump, but as Ominayak continued slowly towards it, the stump suddenly rose. We were within range. Ominayak stopped, opened the door, and in one seamless motion took a rifle from behind the driver's seat, crouched and fired. The moose slumped to its knees. Ominayak fired again. It fell over.

Ominayak approached on foot to see a young bull lying sad-eyed in the scrub with holes in its shoulder and side, heaving final breaths. A kind of age-old exchange seemed to take place. As life ebbed out of the animal, Ominayak appeared subtly revitalized, his face reassuming a sense of deep calm.

≈

Mounties raided before dawn the next morning. In a military-style operation, half a dozen uniformed officers approached the yellow rope while camouflaged troops with loose dogs and automatic weapons fanned into the darkness on either side. A helicopter whipped low overhead.

"This road must be cleared," said the commanding officer, Sgt.

John Oman of the Peace River detachment. He waved a court order to dismantle the barricade.

"We don't recognize your authority," said Terry Laboucan, standing with a cluster of band members and supporters in the morning chill.

"It's noisy here!" cried CBC radio's Byron Christopher, pulling up to the checkpoint while reporting live to the Edmonton morning show. "There's a police helicopter just over my car. The barricade has been taken down. I heard a chain saw as a large pole on either side of the road has been cut. There's all kinds of police here. There's police cars in front of me and behind me. There's police cars all over the place."

Oman read the order aloud as another officer held a flashlight for him. *Calgary Herald* photographer Tom Walker took pictures, his electronic flash lighting the area in bursts.

"You have five minutes to disperse," Oman said.

"This is Lubicon territory!" cried O'Reilly, jumping from a truck as he arrived on the scene. "You have no jurisdiction."

"You know we do," said Oman, letting O'Reilly read the injunction himself.

Two officers stepped towards Terry Laboucan. "Time's up," Oman said. The officers took Laboucan's arms. He planted his feet apart, poised to resist, then glanced at Lennarson, who had just arrived. "Better go," Lennarson said. One by one officers began to escort protestors into waiting vans.

Ominayak raced towards the scene as the first daylight touched the sky. In the distance, he could see the helicopter hovering over the road to the right. He saw abandoned vehicles on either shoulder of the road, some with their headlights illuminating the area, and he could make out some of the people being arrested. They waved and shouted at him to go back, so he slowed and turned around. A minute later he turned again.

As he rushed towards the line the second time, Ominayak studied the scene carefully. Precise details appeared to him in a kind of slow motion, he later recalled: the helicopter, the arresting officers, the tactical troops in a flank position to the left. (The view to the right was blocked by trucks.) He thought of his own arsenal of shotguns and hunting rifles stashed behind his seat. If he drove close enough, stopped and got out smoothly without arousing suspicion, he could pick off the helicopter before anybody could react, then swing left to fire at officers near the sawed-off posts. The officers wore bulletproof vests, Ominayak noticed. He would aim at the armholes. He could hit a couple before anybody blasted him.

But he decided against it. The helicopter could crash anywhere, and the tactical troops were poised to shoot. One move could start a massacre. There had to be another way, he decided, and turned for the last time towards the band office.

The instant he entered the building, the phone rang. It was Getty. Now that the barricades are down we can talk, Getty said.

"There was no need to storm the place," Ominayak replied coldly. "If we are to talk, our people must be released right away."

Fine, Getty said. The prisoners would be arraigned for breach of a court order and released. Talks could then begin—not in Little Buffalo but perhaps somewhere in northern Alberta.

Putting together various pieces of information reaching the band office, Ominayak established that fifty Mounties had moved simultaneously against the checkpoint on the Peace River highway and the one northwest of the Norcen battery, arresting twenty-seven people altogether. Twenty-one people were taken at the main checkpoint, six at the other. The two other checkpoints were later dismantled unopposed. The prisoners included eleven Lubicon people, four of them minors; the youngest was fourteen years old. Among them were Terry Laboucan, Walter Whitehead and four of Whitehead's sons. "We're all stubborn, I guess," he said later. Among the supporters arrested were Lennarson, O'Reilly, Plodzein, the two Germans and two Quaker women. At the Quonset hut, the twenty-seven were listed under the heading "POWs."

Within an hour, the Mounties erected a trailer camp outside Little Buffalo and began patrolling the community in police vans. Oil workers and equipment began trickling back into the territory.

"I'm a friend of the Lubicons," Getty said on the radio. "I'm going to work with them to get that reserve."

"I feel fortunate that we don't have many friends like the premier," Ominayak replied.

At midmorning, he called a meeting at the Quonset hut. Two new faces were at the table. Miles Richardson, president of the Haida Nation in the Queen Charlotte Islands, had arrived by truck the night before with Jim Fulton, the Indian Affairs critic for the federal New Democratic Party.

"What I would like to do," Ominayak said, "is start discussions with the premier and at the same time get organized here, so that we have people present at all the checkpoints—not to interfere with the traffic or anything, just to be there, so that if talks break off those barricades go back up immediately. What I'm thinking right now is we'll just keep sending more people in as they arrest us. We can't let them push us around. They've pushed us around long enough. We've taken a stand, we've moved to this stage, we've got to follow through."

Lawrence Courtoreille reported that the Treaty Eight chiefs had vowed to replace people at the checkpoints "body for body" as arrests continued. Plans were being made for all Alberta chiefs to assemble near Edmonton in one week.

"People are on their way from Edson, Marlboro and Valleyview," one chief said.

"They're coming in from Fort St. John."

"And Saskatchewan."

"We cannot be afraid now," Edward Laboucan told the gathering, with Ominayak translating. "Never mind about people getting picked up, there are lots of other people coming behind. I am ready to be arrested, too."

"There's a lot of support out there," said Miles Richardson, who had led the blockade of a logging road three years earlier, a protest that ended in seventy-two arrests and an eventual end to logging in the South Moresby wilderness. "The issues that we've put before this country have been around for a long time. It's been too long since they've been dealt with. The Lubicon Nation is showing leadership now and we support it. I have confidence in Bernard's leadership, and in the strategies he's laid out. Let's everybody focus on our objective. Let's get people out here. Let's escalate this action and force McKnight to deal with us."

McKnight still wasn't returning calls. His sole response to events had been to send his lawyers back to court in Calgary to reactivate his lawsuit.

≈

The arraignment of the twenty-seven began at ten o'clock that night in Peace River, the defendants looking worn and drawn. All were released on condition that they appear in court at a later date and not erect more checkpoints.

All the next day, momentum continued to build. Newspapers across the country carried Tom Walker's pictures of police wielding chain saws and hauling away demonstrators. The TV crews returned to Little Buffalo with their satellite dish. A busload of supporters arrived from Edson, 200 kilometres west of Edmonton. Several carloads pulled in from Loon Lake. A church delegation arrived from Grande Prairie. The World Council of Churches donated $5,000. The Alberta Federation of Labour announced support. Indian groups from Saskatchewan and British Columbia phoned to say they were on their way. In Edmonton, 200 demonstrators erected a mock checkpoint in front of the Alberta legislature. With pressure mounting, Getty announced that he would meet Ominayak the following morning in Grimshaw, a few kilometres west of Peace River.

≈

"The Grimshaw summit," it came to be called. On Saturday, October 22—one week after the checkpoints went up—the chief and the premier met in Room 122 of the Mile Zero Hotel at the southern start of the Mackenzie Highway. Getty's support people waited in a room next door. Ominayak's team, including Lennarson and O'Reilly, took another room. Reporters, photographers and camera crews sat in the dimly lit corridor.

The morning session went poorly. Getty left to eat lunch in his room, while the band delegation conferred grimly over sandwiches in the coffee shop.

The afternoon seemed to go better. Getty stepped outside at one point to walk around the building for air. "The chief smokes," he said. He wore cowboy boots, jeans and a pullover sweater pushed to the elbows. The day was cold but sunny. Getty raised an imaginary shotgun to his eye, panned and blasted an imaginary goose from the sky.

For the rest of the afternoon, support staff were constantly summoned and dismissed from the negotiating room. Hours passed. Finally, Lennarson came out to make a phone call. "I think we got a deal," he said quietly. "There've been about sixteen drafts of an agreement. Bernard's been throwing things at Getty that Getty has never heard of. Getty's technical people have been saying, 'You can't do that,' and Getty's been going ahead and doing them anyway."

Half an hour later, Getty and Ominayak walked to the ballroom together. A crowd of native people arriving from Saskatchewan stood by as the news contingent set up their tripods and microphones. Hotel personnel crowded the doorways.

"I'm pleased to say that we have an agreement," Getty said. "I wanted to help the band within the constraints that I face as premier, and the chief of course represents the needs of his people."

Under the agreement, the Lubicon people would get ninety-five square miles of reserve land, Getty said. There were two conditions. The first was that the ninety-five was to be considered a negotiated settlement not tied explicitly to membership: the Alberta government did not suddenly have to admit to 478 members after years of presenting the figure as 9. The second was that only seventy-nine square miles—Getty's offer of a week earlier—would come with full subsurface rights. The remaining sixteen square miles were to be purchased from Alberta by Ottawa for the band's use, with Alberta retaining subsurface rights. A further stipulation gave the band veto power over how the province might exercise subsurface rights. In effect, the deal gave the band control over the entire ninety-five square miles while allowing Getty to present the agreement to cabinet as a seventy-nine-square-mile reserve. At Ominayak's request, the land would be selected in three locations: one square mile at a Bison Lake burial ground, one square mile at Haig Lake and the balance at Lubicon Lake. Getty said that he and Ominayak would soon take the agreement to Ottawa for ratification. Meanwhile, talks would start on Monday between the province and the band on environmental and wildlife-management issues.

"I want to thank the chief," Getty said, turning to Ominayak. "I've enjoyed negotiating with him and working with him. He has coop-erated and he has really negotiated in a spirit of good will. I thank him for that. I'm looking forward to working with him in the future and we have agreed to stay in close communication on all matters that might be important to him, and I certainly give him my commitment to always being available. Thank you very much. I'm sure the chief would like to say something."

"We understand that we still have a ways to go in dealing with the federal government," Ominayak said, "but I want to thank the premier for taking this effort and coming to an agreement with us. I think this man has great courage for doing what he has done. He deserves a lot of credit."

Getty looked down at the floor and blinked several times. A

reporter asked if he was feeling "a bit emotional."

"The emotion I feel is from the comments of the chief," Getty replied. "He caught me by surprise with those comments and I want to publicly thank him very much for them."

The spectators from Saskatchewan burst into applause. Getty gripped Ominayak's sleeve and held his arm aloft.

That night in Little Buffalo, the Quonset hut filled to capacity. Almost everybody was standing. For more than an hour Lubicon members and visitors took turns speaking. Finally, Ominayak stepped forward.

"We've done something today that could have been done years ago in a very short time compared with the forty-eight years we've been waiting," he said, sounding tired and oddly bitter. "All we're asking for is to be respected like everybody else, and as the first people of this country we are subjected to all sorts of problems and racism. I hope we have shown today that if we put up a united front, there is not too much that they can do to stop us .... And with that, I thank all the community members, and say, 'Federal government—the Lubicons are coming at you.' "

Wearing his trademark black cap,
Chief Ominayak flashes a smile.
TOM WALKER, *CALGARY HERALD*

"I don't feel right that these guys come in and take over," says band elder Albert Laboucan. "Those big trucks go by until way past midnight and start again early in the morning, shaking us in our beds." TOM WALKER, *CALGARY HERALD*

A telephone pole in formerly rich hunting and trapping territory becomes an impromptu signpost to the oil fields. TOM WALKER, *CALGARY HERALD*

At dinner in Vienna, Bernard Ominayak (*centre*) checks the afternoon newspapers for coverage of the third annual congress of the European Support Groups for North American Indians. With him are delegates Elisabet Fastesson from Sweden and John van Tilborg from Holland. JOHN GODDARD

Singing star Buffy Sainte-Marie meets Chief Ominayak backstage after an emotional benefit concert at Jubilee Auditorium in Calgary, not long before the 1988 Winter Olympic Games. "Some museums are only concerned with dead Indians," she said in reference to the Glenbow Museum's The Spirit Sings exhibition. JOHN GODDARD

Steve Noskey (*right*), with help from band lawyer James O'Reilly, leads a discussion at the community meeting where the Lubicon Lake people declare themselves to be a nation. The initiative opened the way for the band's assertion of jurisdiction over their traditional lands. JOHN GODDARD

Bottom: Lubicon members and supporters led by Terry Laboucan (*in camouflage*) stand their ground as RCMP Sgt. John Oman reads a court order to dismantle the main checkpoint near Marten River. Troops with loose dogs and automatic weapons fanned through the darkness on either side. TOM WALKER, *CALGARY HERALD*

In a moment of shared triumph, Alberta Premier Don Getty hoists Chief Ominayak's arm aloft after a grueling day of negotiations at Grimshaw. Everything the band had been working towards seemed close at hand. TOM WALKER, *CALGARY HERALD*

A bit of Grimshaw spirit returns to Little Buffalo as band members raise their arms to elect a council of elders to serve with the re-elected chief, Bernard Ominayak, ending a federally backed leadership challenge. Among the people not voting are local teachers, the elders themselves and band consultant Fred Lennarson. JOHN GODDARD

Facing page, top: On the eve of confrontation in October 1988, Fred Lennarson kisses his wife, Avis, goodbye as he leaves Edmonton for Little Buffalo. Looking on is the pilot (*left*), a German representative of the European Support Groups, Dionys Zink (*second from right*), and the youngest of the six Lennarson children, Nels (*far right*). JOHN GODDARD

With elder Edward Laboucan nearby, Chief Ominayak accepts an award for "valiant, effective and creative" leadership in New York City, one of many honours conferred on him over the years. The occasion was the twentieth anniversary of the Interreligious Foundation for Community Organization. JEFF JACOBSEN

Experience honed in Ominayak a harder edge. By 1989, with the gold lettering on his cap changed to read "Lubicon Lake Nation," and with the federal initiative underway to create a competing band in Lubicon territory, the hardness had begun to show in his face. CANAPRESS PHOTO SERVICE—RAY GIGUERE

16 TAKE IT
OR
LEAVE IT

WHAT AN ENORMOUS VICTORY the Grimshaw Agreement was. More had been accomplished in a week of confrontation than in a decade of official meetings and court appearances. Everything the band had been working towards seemed close at hand. Getty had hung in there. He had developed an appreciation of how badly the Lubicon people had been treated over the years, telling Ominayak privately that he felt "ashamed" to have been part of the earlier government that had introduced the land-tenure program. For band members, the agreement vindicated a long-term strategy to build power and use it. The victory seemed to show that even the smallest and most remote of Canadian native societies, by holding together and working hard, could develop enough muscle to prevail over legal and political inequities. In a way, the agreement showed that "the system" worked after all. Tough negotiations lay ahead on economic development and compensation. But the Alberta government, once such a ruthless adversary, was now an ally, and with the band so clearly holding the political initiative, final resolution with Ottawa appeared imminent.

McKnight's response was characteristically churlish, but his opinion seemed to carry less weight than before. At a news conference in Edmonton, he congratulated Getty and Ominayak for agreeing to seventy-nine square miles, raising problems about the other sixteen. He also said that only status Indians would be entitled to federal programs. "Bands have the opportunity to place anyone on their membership list," he said. "But we do not provide services to people who are not Indian." Four times he insisted that no compensation was owing. "Since 1945, the band has received all the benefits accorded to treaty Indians," he said obscurely. "What they have lacked was land. What they have lacked was a reserve. That now has been addressed and we're prepared to establish a community with federal funds."

The prime minister was more gracious. The federal election campaign was still on, and Mulroney was slipping badly in the polls. Less than two weeks after the Grimshaw meeting, he was scheduled to address an Edmonton rally, which Lubicon supporters from all over western Canada planned to attend. Campaign handlers arranged for Mulroney to see Ominayak beforehand.

Sequestered with the chief in a hotel room, Mulroney proposed to appoint his chief of staff, Derek Burney, to oversee negotiations between the band and Ottawa after the election. Ominayak agreed. "I think the prime minister understands the problems that we face in trying to deal with the federal government," Ominayak told reporters. "At least [the Burney appointment] will be a way to communicate with him." Beyond that, Ominayak wasn't sure what he had. Burney was known as a problem-solver who moved with dispatch, but on New Year's Day he was to become ambassador to Washington. Perhaps the deadline would hasten a deal. Or perhaps Mulroney only wanted to get through the election.

≈

On voting day, Brian Mulroney and the Progressive Conservative Party swept to a renewed majority. One week later, on November 29, 1988, formal negotiations to reach a settlement of Lubicon land rights began at the National Conference Centre in Ottawa. Negotiators for the band included Fred Lennarson, James O'Reilly, Walter Whitehead, Steve Noskey and Edward Laboucan's son Michael. Larry Ominayak was to join the group later. Richard Plodzein would participate in technical discussions.

Leading the federal delegation was Brian Malone, reporting daily to Burney and to McKnight, returned as a member of parliament and as Indian Affairs minister. Also to be briefed regularly was a newly formed cabinet committee on Lubicon, which included McKnight, Deputy Prime Minister Don Mazankowski, External Affairs Minister Joe Clark and Finance Minister Michael Wilson. Sitting with Malone at the table were Ivan Whitehall, the justice department lawyer who had been setting Ottawa's legal strategy on Lubicon since

1976; Bob Coulter, a functionary responsible for monitoring Lubicon for Indian Affairs in Ottawa; Fred Jobin, a senior official at Indian Affairs in Edmonton; and a Calgary media consultant named Ken Colby. (Lennarson had objected to Colby being included, saying the use of a PR person conformed to the Special Words and Tactics strategy submitted earlier to Bill McKnight. But Burney had brushed aside the complaint, saying essentially: "We'll choose our people, you choose yours.")

The talks began well. Under the agenda set by Burney and Ominayak, band membership was to be dealt with first, followed by reserve size, community construction, economic development and compensation—all the key discussion items agreed to by David Crombie four years earlier.

Almost immediately, the parties reached a breakthrough on membership. Whitehall proposed to register as status Lubicon Indians virtually everybody on the band membership list—Fulton's position of three years earlier. Whitehall raised questions about 34 members, rejecting only 5 people outright. The next day he accepted the 34, and both sides agreed to a membership list of 506 people, up from the Grimshaw number because of natural increase and updated research.

The parties also agreed on land, adopting the Grimshaw formula. Ninety-five square miles would be set aside as a Lubicon reserve, seventy-nine square miles of which was to include full subsurface rights.

On reserve establishment, steady progress was made. Plodzein's original estimates totalled $52 million for infrastructure, housing and public buildings. Indian Affairs could contribute only $20 million, said the department's specialist, Bill Van Iterson, leaving a gap of $32 million. For two weeks, each side worked on its numbers. Plodzein shaved the band's requirements to items totalling $41 million. Iterson calculated ways to squeeze a total of $34 million from existing guidelines. They reduced the gap to $7 million.

As Christmas loomed, the two sides appeared to have settled land and membership, and to have narrowed their differences on construction costs. Two major items remained: economic-development and compensation. At Burney's request, Ominayak flew to Ottawa for top-level discussions. Then came the crunch. To meet economic-development needs, Burney offered a trust fund of $5 million, from which the band could draw interest annually as "seed capital" to lever grants from existing federal programs. As for compensation, nothing was owed, Burney said. If the band wished to pursue compensation, the band would have to sue the federal government through regular channels. Ominayak said no—compensation must be part of a negotiated settlement. Ominayak also reported a problem with membership. The acting Indian registrar, Jim Allen, was going through the band list asking for documents on dozens of Lubicon members, refusing to register them in the meantime as status Indians.

Talks resumed in the New Year under a cloud. Burney was gone, the acting registrar was still refusing to respect the membership agreement, and Malone would not confirm whether compensation was still on the agenda. Discussions began with economic development. Lennarson said the Lubicon people had not come to Ottawa after ten years of struggle just to be told that they could apply for regular programs. They had come to negotiate a land-rights agreement. He explained that the Lubicon economy had been destroyed during the extraction of billions of dollars' worth of oil from Lubicon territory and that measures must now be taken to create a new local economy. Such measures must include jobs, training and business development, he said. The band's economic plan called for a combined educational and community-maintenance centre, the development of reserve lands for agriculture, and a combination of commercial enterprises, facilities and services geared to community self- sufficiency.

The longer the talks continued, the more strained they became. "One guy from Indian Affairs said to me, 'We have 400 development projects across the country,' " Lennarson later recalled. "I said, 'Yeah—and every single one of them a total failure.' "

On the morning of January 24, 1989, Malone surprised band negotiators with a formal written offer. "I want to emphasize that this is a final, take-it-or-leave-it settlement offer," Lennarson's notes record Malone as saying. Compensation was not part of the offer, Malone said, but to guarantee fairness the band would be allowed to sue. He suggested that band negotiators study the offer and return that afternoon with a response.

≈

The "final" offer was close to the minimum the federal government could possibly have put forward. Provisions for economic development were negligible. Compensation, considered by E. Davie Fulton as essential to a settlement, was entirely missing. There would be no mediator, no independent tribunal, no direct reference to the Supreme Court of Canada on the aboriginal-rights question, no avenue of redress except regular legal channels that Fulton had predicted would be "very lengthy and exceedingly costly."

One of the most striking features of the offer is how loosely it is written. Almost none of the terms is definite, and the formal text often contradicts assurances that Malone gave orally to band negotiators— a discrepancy reminiscent of early treaty negotiations.

Membership is left unclear. One clause provides for "100 houses for those 506 Indian individuals whose names are on the Lubicon Lake Band membership list as of December 12, 1988." But housing would be available to registered Indians only, the document states elsewhere. Nowhere does the offer address the problem of an acting registrar refusing status to more than one third of the band.

The land provision is clear enough. As in the Grimshaw Agreement, the band would get ninety-five square miles of land, seventy-nine of which would include full subsurface rights.

In the section on community construction, some of the items are firm, others are not. Roads, water, sewers, electrification, houses, a small firehall, a school and accommodation for teachers are all covered for a cost of nearly $30 million. A further $500,000 is recommended for a combined band office and community hall, "based on a revised policy currently under consideration." No recreation centre is included, no combination old people's home and day-care centre, and no health unit, although the offer says that "preliminary information indicates that National Health and Welfare may fund $350,000." No police lockup would be provided, no garbage incinerator; only partial funding would be available for a storage shed and heating utility.

As for economic development, annual interest on a $5-million trust fund is provided as "ongoing seed capital to lever project funding from public and private sources." No other economic provision is firm. Responding to the band's forty-page agricultural plan detailing projects valued at $16 million—including the cattle herd, grain operation, saskatoon-berry orchard and wild-rice project—the offer provides "up to $100,000" to examine the proposal, and suggests that any approved enterprises "be eligible for consideration for funding." The offer also rejects plans for a $2.6-million vocational centre and maintenance shop, providing instead a maximum grant of $100,000 "to fund a variety of training opportunities." And while Colby later said that enterprises such as a coin laundry, a guest accommodation, a gravel-crushing operation and a concrete batch plant would be funded at a cost of $4 million, the actual text prevaricates: "The Department of Industry, Science and Technology will seek ministerial approval in principle for funding from the Native Economic Development Program up to a maximum of $4 million .. . provided that [the projects] meet normal program requirements." Colby put the dollar value of the entire offer at $45 million, or what he called "$450,000 per family." (The band's push for a better deal was based on "greed, not need," he also said.) Ominayak and Lennarson estimated the value at between $30 and $35 million.

Nothing in the written offer suggests that the band is free to sue the federal government for compensation. The current wording obliges the band to "cede, release and surrender" all aboriginal claims and all rights to current and future legal actions related to aboriginal rights. Under the provisions, the band must also agree to withdraw its complaints from the United Nations Human Rights Committee, "to acknowledge settlement of its grievance against Canada," before the compensation issue was settled.

Ultimately, nothing in the offer is binding, unlike the original treaties, which are guaranteed in the Canadian constitution. "Any agreement arising out of this offer . . . will be subject to parliamentary appropriations during the applicable fiscal year," the text of the Lubicon offer states. If Parliament failed for any reason to advance enough money to fulfill the agreement from year to year, implementation would be suspended.

Ominayak, studying a faxed copy of the offer the day it was tabled, faced a terrible decision. More than three months had passed since the October confrontation, and Lubicon had faded from public attention. Band members were anxious to have matters resolved. If nothing were to come of the Grimshaw Agreement and the Ottawa talks, there was a danger that some members would lose hope. Yet Ominayak found the offer unacceptable. Reserve size appeared to be settled to the band's satisfaction, and perhaps a basic community could be built. Maybe even membership could be sorted out. But Ominayak could see no realistic means of building a new local economy, no prospect at all for the Lubicon people to carry on as a viable aboriginal society. He ordered his negotiators to reject the offer, and band members ratified the decision unanimously a week later.

"What do you need?" a radio reporter asked Ominayak at the time. "How much?"

"Well, basically what we're looking at is to try and build a community that is going to be viable, both economically and as a community," Ominayak replied in his steady way. "We've got people whose livelihood has been destroyed by the oil development. We don't want to just build a community where people are going to have nice houses but remain on welfare. We want to get out of that system. We don't want to get into it deeper."

"Well, where do you go now that talks have broken off?"

"We're going to be looking at all the options," Ominayak said. "We tried to negotiate with the federal government. We put the best effort we could into the talks, and they're not prepared to settle at this point in time. So we're going to be looking at all the possibilities. But we're not going to go begging to anybody. These guys have taken billions of dollars in resources from our lands. They keep saying that we're trying to take the taxpayers' dollars. That isn't the case."

17 THE WOODLAND CREE

REJECTION OF the final offer provoked a vicious response from federal authorities. Almost immediately, they began work on a new kind of master strategy designed to end, once and for all, the band's ability to carry its aboriginal- rights case forward. Compared to Lougheed's advisors, the federal people behaved like amateurs. They seemed to make up their program as they went along. But the community at Little Buffalo was weaker than before, and the new effort was to have devastating consequences.

A central feature of the new strategy was an element common to almost all previous government dealings with the Lubicon people: the arbitrary rule of law. When the treaty commissioners failed to penetrate the interior, aboriginal title was declared extinguished there anyway. When federal authorities no longer wished a reserve at Lubicon Lake, they reclassified the site from "well suited" to "barren." Rules were changed to strip people of Indian status, quitclaims were signed to allow Marten River to be destroyed, and retroactive legislation was passed to win the caveat case. All through history a show had been made of correct legal procedure, while laws were twisted to serve vested interests. And when the Lubicon people rejected the final settlement offer, federal negotiators moved to implement it against the band's will.

" 'Get a settlement,' " Ken Colby later said of the instructions Burney had issued before the talks. " 'Get a settlement without trampling over policy too much and without setting precedents we're not willing to live with. And if you can't get a settlement, find a mechanism that will make it possible to deliver social and economic relief to people on the ground.' " Pressed later on what he meant by "a mechanism," Colby defined it as "a partial settlement of some sort which would allow the government to address the living conditions of band members."

Shortly after the band rejected the offer, federal players looked for a "mechanism" with which to impose it. Malone remained on contract as federal negotiator, in charge of the operation. Other members of the negotiating unit also remained in place, including Colby, Jobin and Coulter, with Whitehall continuing to offer legal advice. To what extent the prime minister's office and the special cabinet committee continued to be involved is uncertain, but officially the unit operated directly under Pierre Cadieux, who after the breakdown of negotiations replaced Bill McKnight at Indian Affairs.

Over the next several months, the federal people grew unusually circumspect with reporters. Colby became increasingly testy, blowing up occasionally and sometimes refusing to answer questions altogether. Malone would agree to be interviewed, set elaborate preconditions about the location and who would be present, then cancel. He never did grant an interview, insisting instead on receiving questions in writing, to which he responded in writing, always two or three months later. Sometimes his answers proved revealing, however; and when pressed for evidence to back up his version of events, he occasionally released documents that in the context of other information provided insight into what was happening.

Sometimes the moves were hard to follow. First, the federal unit tried to identify a dissident faction within Lubicon ranks that might be used to overthrow Ominayak. When such a faction proved nonexistent, federal players tried to create one, aiming to overthrow Ominayak or, alternatively, split the band. When that attempt also failed, federal players recruited native people from all over northern Alberta to create a new band designed to lay claim to Lubicon territory and accept the federal offer. The idea was cynical and brutal, but it provided the mechanism with which federal authorities could impose a settlement, ward off the United Nations Human Rights Committee, scotch the Grimshaw Agreement, and divide native people in the interior against each other so that the Lubicon people could never again mount an effective aboriginal-rights challenge.

The federal unit's first move was to contact Henry Laboucan, a resident of Grouard on Lesser Slave Lake. By blood, Laboucan was a Lubicon Indian. He had spent part of his childhood in the Lubicon area, and he was registered in Ottawa as a status Indian belonging to the band. To retain Lubicon membership after a settlement, however, he knew he would have to move to the Lubicon area, and he didn't want to.

During the Ottawa talks, Laboucan had tried to call Malone several times to request "land in severalty," an obscure provision of Treaties Eight and Ten. It allowed an individual or family to take land apart from the rest of a band to establish a kind of miniature reserve calculated at 160 acres per person. Nobody in the Treaty Ten area of northern Saskatchewan had exercised the option, but a few people in Treaty Eight had, including people at Grouard. Laboucan also claimed to be "able to produce a majority of native people who are not really excited about the 'Ominayak deal,' " according to a message taken by Malone's secretary. During the talks, Malone ignored Laboucan entirely and, according to Lennarson's notes, Whitehall told Lubicon negotiators: "There will be no land in severalty." If the band pursued severalty for any member, Whitehall said, "We'll tie you up in court forever." His position conformed to established policy. Ottawa opposed the creation of family reserves and was currently fighting a number of severalty claims in court, including one from Harold Cardinal, the former Indian Association president. Lubicon negotiators raised no objections. Henry Laboucan was welcome to live on a reserve at Lubicon Lake, but the band had no interest in pursuing severalty. Any band members applying for severalty, band representatives said, would be on their own.

Immediately after talks ended in Ottawa, Malone returned Henry Laboucan's phone calls; and two weeks later—on February 10, 1989—Malone and Jobin flew north to speak to Laboucan in person. The meeting took place at a hotel near Grouard, in High Prairie. Laboucan arrived with seven other native people, all members of the group he had described as "not really excited about the 'Ominayak deal.' " When Malone questioned the seven, however, he found that none was on the Lubicon band list of 506 people that Malone, Whitehall and the Lubicon negotiators had agreed to in Ottawa. Only two of the seven were registered status Indians.

Malone plowed on. In a report to superiors, he said he gave the group information about "the registration process to become a status Indian." He also talked about "membership in the Lubicon Lake Band and the rights of qualified individuals to become band members." Jobin gave out registration forms and said the government might fund a test case taking "the issue of band membership" to court.

Malone has been careful to say that he did not define "land in severalty" for the group, and he has refused to define the term since. Treaty Eight is clear: "160 acres to each Indian, the land to be conveyed with a proviso as to non-alienation." It was like a reserve. Colby gave a different definition, however. "You get the land in fee simple," he said in an interview. "It's no different from you owning your house." By Colby's definition, severalty would be like scrip, or land tenure, which might explain why federal authorities were offering it to the Henry Laboucan group while fighting other severalty claims in court. A day after he gave the definition, Colby retracted it, saying that federal lawyer Ivan Whitehall was furious with him for saying anything. "There is no severalty policy, no box entitled 'severalty' that we can take off the shelf," Colby paraphrased Whitehall as saying.

Whatever Malone meant by "severalty," he made one additional point clear at the meeting: only after the Lubicon band signed the federal offer would severalty claims be considered. Put another way, the "severalty" group had a direct interest in having Ominayak sign the federal offer. To what extent Malone spoke overtly about organizing dissent within the band is not publicly known. But after the meeting Malone sounded optimistic about moving federal objectives forward. "It was obvious," he reported, "that there may be a large number of individuals living at Little Buffalo or elsewhere that would want to take land in severalty and that Henry Laboucan would most probably be acting as a focal point in coordinating these dissenting interests."

Two weeks later, two members of the High Prairie group wrote to Indian Affairs Minister Pierre Cadieux. They said they represented 182 people who were unhappy with Ominayak and wanted "severalty from the Lubicon band." They used the word "severalty" as though it meant "severance" or "separation." The letter was signed by Melvin Laboucan and Roy Letendre, both residents of Little Buffalo who were not on the approved Lubicon band list. Attached was a list of names that they referred to as signatures, but all of which later turned out to be in Melvin Laboucan's handwriting. "So if the government allows us to . . . start a new council," the letter said, "we are more than willing to settle for what the government thinks is fair."

No copy of the petition surfaced publicly for weeks, but Colby gave dozens of interviews about it, fudging details. Never did he clarify that all the names were signed by one person. Rather, Colby said the petition bore 182 names, 30 of which belonged to Metis people and 152 of which belonged to people describing themselves either as status Indians or as native people eligible for Indian status. He also said another 60 to 70 names "are familiar to those who know the [Lubicon] band list," suggesting that the group included 60 to 70 Lubicon band members. He then referred to the group as a "faction" within the Lubicon band who wished Ominayak to accept the federal offer.

"There appears to be a faction in the community saying, 'We want to get on with our lives here, we think the offer is reasonable and fair, we think the band ought to be pursuing it, and if they're not, can we pursue it?' " Colby said. Hinting at a possible overthrow, Colby also said: "The Lubicon election is scheduled for the fall, and if these guys follow through they could have a tremendous impact on this community." Colby was beginning to present the severalty group as a dissident faction of the Lubicon Lake band that could prevail in the next band election or deal with Ottawa independently.

Indian Affairs Minister Cadieux replied promptly to the petition with two major initiatives. First, he offered to pay for a lawyer to help the group with what he called "severalty claims," which would include helping people register as Lubicon Indians. Second, he poked holes in the Grimshaw Agreement, the high point of the Lubicon struggle and the document that united the band and the province.

"In my review of the Grimshaw Agreement of October 22, it appears that both Chief Ominayak and Premier Getty failed to address the question of land in severalty," the minister wrote.

In the same vein, he wrote to his Alberta counterpart, Ken Rostad, to suggest that honouring the Grimshaw Agreement could cost the province extra land. "A number of members of the Lubicon Lake Band have advised me that they may elect to choose land in severalty pursuant to Treaty 8," Cadieux wrote. "Could you please advise me as to your views on an appropriate mechanism for providing land . . . . I would be particularly interested in knowing if such land is to be deducted from the 95 square miles provided for in the accord, or if it is to be additional to that received by the Band."

Alert to the federal manoeuvres, Premier Don Getty invited Ominayak to Edmonton. "The chief and I should meet with the prime minister," Getty said after another long consultation. "We think that if we can come to some meeting of minds on the principles then our negotiators will follow. We can get the momentum going again." But when Getty phoned Ottawa, the prime minister refused to take the call. Indian matters, Getty was told, were Pierre Cadieux's responsibility.

On April 17, less than three months after the breakdown of negotiations, Cadieux again sent Malone and Jobin to High Prairie. Again they met a group of eight native people led by Henry Laboucan. This time, however, Malone cut Laboucan loose.

"Suddenly, I was pushed aside," Laboucan said later.

"It is evident," Malone wrote to Ottawa, "that Henry wants severalty land near Grouard while others wanted land at Cadotte Lake . . . . Response that federal government will pay only one lawyer for the group."

During the second meeting, Malone's attention shifted to three other people present, all of them residents of Little Buffalo: Melvin Laboucan and Roy Letendre, who had sent the petition, and Archie Cardinal. All three were saying that Ominayak had struck them from the Lubicon band list before the Ottawa talks. A new theme emerged. Malone dubbed the three men "disenfranchised Lubicons." After years of accusing Ominayak of "jacking up" membership figures to get more land, federal authorities were now accusing him of cutting members out.

Melvin Laboucan indeed has blood ties to the Lubicon area, but in 1957 his family transferred to Whitefish Lake as part of Malcolm McCrimmon's final drive to make the Lubicon band disappear. When he was older, Melvin returned to Little Buffalo, moving in with a woman who had had a child with Ominayak before he was married. Melvin's relations with Ominayak were never comfortable. Melvin was accepted as a Lubicon member but after the Grimshaw Agreement he refused to confirm his Lubicon status. He chose instead to remain a Whitefish Lake member, and was counted in negotiations to settle a land shortfall at the Whitefish Lake reserve.

Roy Letendre's story is a sad one. His mother was from Lubicon Lake and his father was from Whitefish Lake, but he was abandoned as a baby and raised by white people in a series of foster homes. In the mid-1970s, he moved to Little Buffalo. He established a family with a Lubicon woman and was accepted as a Lubicon member, but the woman later left him for his half-brother, who was a close friend of Ominayak's. Letendre blamed Ominayak for the breakup. One night, when Ominayak was away, Letendre appeared outside Ominayak's house with a gun, threatening to shoot Ominayak's wife and children. By the time of the Grimshaw Agreement, he had moved to Edmonton.

Archie Cardinal is a former Lubicon member who excluded himself from the band by taking land tenure. The others at the meeting lived at Cadotte and had never been Lubicon members. Essentially, Malone was dealing with a rag-tag group of unhappy people who in many cases had never had their legitimate aboriginal rights addressed, and who were united in their desire finally to get something from the government, but who were not Lubicon Lake Indians.

When the meeting ended, Malone invited Melvin Laboucan and Joe P. Whitehead of Cadotte to board a chartered plane with him to Edmonton. By prearrangement, a Calgary lawyer named Bob Young was waiting for them. Young agreed to help the group register as Lubicon Indians, and Indian Affairs arranged to have Ottawa cover Young's fees and expenses.

Ominayak responded by calling an election for the end of May, challenging rivals to show themselves. For the next six weeks federal authorities scrambled to get the "dissidents" registered. Bob Young flew to Peace River two or three times a week. From Ottawa, Bob Coulter twice flew to Peace River with an entourage from the registrar's office. But as voting day at Little Buffalo approached, it became clear that the group was in no position to oust Ominayak. Asked how many group members could be considered Lubicon Indians, Coulter replied, "Substantially more than twenty." Of the others, some belonged to the Bigstone band, some to Whitefish Lake, and there were "a lot who were just native people living in the area," Coulter said.

On election night, a bit of Grimshaw spirit returned to Little Buffalo. Community members packed the Quonset hut to overflowing, everyone raising their arms in unison to reelect Ominayak to another five-year term. Nobody ran against him, and nobody known to be meeting with federal authorities made an appearance.

Indians willing to do the government's bidding are the kind of Indians that Ottawa is looking for, Ominayak told the crowd after the vote. "Any time you ask for justice or for some halfways fair treatment then you're the bad guy, and I think we found that out ourselves through these years. I would like to do my best in trying to get whatever I can for you people. I'm not promising anything but I will continue to do my best for you."

Federal authorities switched tactics. Two days after the election, Bob Young flew to Ottawa with Melvin Laboucan and Roy Letendre. They met Don Goodwin, the assistant deputy minister of lands, reserves and trusts. Bob Coulter and Ken Colby were also present as Young formally asked that his clients be granted status as a separate band with its own reserve. The new band, Malone paraphrased Young as saying, "would provide a mechanism to deliver social and economic relief to former Lubicon Lake Band members and other members of the Isolated Communities who wish to 'get on with their lives.' "

On August 28, 1989—eight months after the Ottawa talks—Pierre Cadieux constituted the newly registered Indians as an official band. The Woodland Cree band, he called it, using a generic term for the Cree of the northern woodlands. Not since the early treaty days had a band been formalized so quickly—within twelve weeks of Young's application, and ahead of about seventy aboriginal societies across the country who had been waiting for up to fifty years for band status, including six of the isolated communities in the Lesser Slave interior. Woodland members registering as status Indians had also jumped queue on thousands of native people waiting to regain status lost through marriage. Registration can often take years; some of Young's clients were processed in a week.

Asked how the government could legally bring the new band into existence, Colby cited an obscure clause of the Indian Act—Section 17—which gives Ottawa power to divide or amalgamate bands virtually at will. "The Minister may, whenever he considers it desirable, constitute new Bands and establish new Band Lists with respect thereto from existing Band Lists, or from the Indian Register, if requested to do so by persons proposing to form the new Bands," the section says, and "no protest can be made."

Who the Woodland members were, exactly, remained a mystery. The band list was kept secret. Even the number of members was secret. "In excess of 300," said Colby. "Three hundred and fifty," said Young. A so-called "initial" list approved by the minister included only 110 people, however. Sixty-three of them were said to be former Lubicon Indians. The others were said to be former members of five other northern Alberta bands. And now all of them were members of the Woodland Cree: an amalgam sharing few family ties, holding few common traditions and occupying no single common hunting-and-trapping territory. The group's sole common denominator appeared to be a Calgary lawyer introduced and paid for by federal representatives originally hired to negotiate land rights with the Lubicon Lake Cree. For the next several months, no Woodland member came forward to speak on the group's behalf. Nor could members agree immediately on a chief, although they did manage to choose four representatives to accompany Bob Young to land-rights talks with Brian Malone.

Four days after the creation of the Woodland Cree, a Canadian representative lied outright to the United Nations Human Rights Committee. Rather than say that Henry Laboucan tried to reach Malone during the Ottawa negotiations to request land in severalty, an anonymous official stated that 350 native people came forward during the talks to request separate band status. "In December 1988," the submission reads, "Canada was made aware of a new group within the community, who sought to resolve the rights of its members under Treaty 8, independent of the Lubicon Lake Band. This group, comprised of approximately 350 native people, sought recognition from the Government as a new band. The group consists of Lubicon Lake Band members who have formally stated their intention of joining the new band, former Lubicon members who were removed by the Band in January 1989, and other native people living within the community."

Several months later, the committee issued its ruling. "Historical inequities ... and certain more recent developments threaten the way of life and culture of the Lubicon Lake Band," it said on one hand. "The State party proposes to rectify the situation by a remedy that the Committee deems appropriate," it said on the other. After considering the Lubicon case for six years, the committee had rendered a decision that was all but meaningless.

Soon, Woodland negotiators accepted a settlement offer from Ottawa that showed just how badly the new group was being used.

By then, federal officials were saying that approximately 700 people belonged to the band, of whom 570 were registered treaty Indians. In the federal offer, about half the members, or 355 people, were counted for land purposes, which meant a reserve of seventy-one square miles. Of that area, sixteen square miles would be sold to the federal government for $512,000, or $50 an acre, leaving an actual reserve of fifty-five square miles. In theory, subsurface rights would be included, but the agreement specified that ownership of the two known oil deposits in the area—all of which has been extensively surveyed—was to remain exclusively with the oil companies. Also under the agreement, housing and infrastructure would be provided at a cost of $29 million for 450 people. How the other 250 people were supposed to be housed and serviced was not stated. Trust funds from both the federal and Alberta governments totalling $19 million would be established for "economic development," although no specific projects were planned. In a joint news release, federal and provincial authorities padded figures to portray the agreement as a $58-million package. The new Indian Affairs minister, Tom Siddon, called the deal a "clear indication of the federal government's commitment to honour its obligations."

Ominayak, recognizing similarities to the earlier federal offer, called the Woodland deal a formula to put welfare Indians into nicer houses. "It's a great deal for the federal government," he told a live television audience in Edmonton. "The Woodland Cree recruited 700 members and yet they are getting land for maybe 275 people which they have to share. If people are looking towards the future and their younger generations, then it's not so good for native people. But if you're looking from the government's point of view then it's an awfully good deal, because you've probably 400 people or better giving up their rights for absolutely nothing."

Woodland members were invited to vote on the offer in a plebiscite scheduled for July 5 and 6, 1991—an event that was to boldly exemplify the pattern of arbitrary law. A list of 268 eligible voters was posted in public places around northern Alberta as required under the Indian Act. Four polling booths were established to accommodate the widely dispersed membership: one at Canada Place in Edmonton, the federal building that houses the Indian Affairs administration for Alberta; one in the community of Slave Lake; one in Peace River; and one in Cadotte, one of the original isolated communities, which had evolved into a local Woodland headquarters and was the site of the proposed reserve. Jobin organized the event, Malone oversaw it, and Coulter acted as media liaison. (Ken Colby had resigned his post several months earlier.)

On July 5 in a trailer at Cadotte, the first voter approached a table presided over by Roger Cardinal, an Indian Affairs employee from Edmonton acting as chief polling officer. Another Indian Affairs official and two Woodland members were also at the table. The voter gave his name, took a ballot, walked behind a cardboard screen to mark the ballot secretly, and dropped the marked ballot into an aluminium box of the type used in federal elections. Then, under the nose of the federal polling officer, the band secretary made out a cheque to the voter for $50.

At all four polling stations, eligible Woodland members were paid $50 each to vote. They had also been promised beforehand that every member would be paid $1,000 if the agreement passed. There were other irregularities. The number of eligible voters steadily rose during the plebiscite, from 268 to 295 by the end of the first day, to 309 by the end of the second; and polls were kept open more than thirty minutes past the official closing time. When the ballots were counted, the chief polling officer announced that 87 per cent of eligible voters had participated, ratifying the federal offer by a whopping 98.5 per cent. In Ottawa, Bob Coulter said he was "not an expert on the administration of referendums" but was satisfied the vote had been conducted properly.

A few days later, band members received word that the $50 and $1,000 payments they thought they were getting as part of their aboriginal birthright would be deducted from their welfare payments. An estimated 90 per cent of band members would be affected. Slowly, the significance of the arrangement began to sink in. The payments totalled $713,400. They were to come from the $512,000 fund created by the sale of the sixteen square miles of otherwise inalienable Indian land, plus $201,400 in economic-development money. But almost all the money was going back to the federal government in the form of welfare savings. "The fairness lies in that [the Woodland members] are being treated the same as everybody else in Canada," said Susan Williams, director general of social development for Indian Affairs in Ottawa. "If you come into cash through earnings or whatever, you don't qualify for the same level of social assistance."

Two days after the vote, Brian Malone spoke in Cambridge, England, at a symposium organized by the Canadian Institute for Advanced Legal Studies. He made a startling announcement. "Talks have just begun with representatives of another isolated community at Loon Lake, located about forty miles northeast of Lubicon Lake," he said. It turned out that for the previous six months, Malone had been meeting people at Loon Lake to discuss a Woodland-type land settlement. As federal negotiator for Loon Lake, he had travelled north at least five times for meetings, out of which had come a petition to the minister. It was said to represent 172 people, from a community of 250, asking to be recognized individually as status Indians and collectively as a band. Ward Mallabone, a lawyer who had worked on Woodland with Bob Young, had been hired to represent the group. He was being paid from a special fund established by Indian Affairs.

With the Woodland agreement to the west and an impending Loon Lake agreement to the northeast, Lubicon society was slowly being pulled apart. Exactly how many Lubicon members had defected was not certain. Malone told his Cambridge audience that 180 had gone to Woodland and 80 to Loon Lake, although representatives for the two groups put the numbers at "about 100" and "fewer than 25" respectively. Whatever the figures, the damage was enormous. People signing their names to the new band lists were following a course logical to anybody living in a world where the law is arbitrary, and where rewards and punishments are distributed at random; but almost everybody seemed to be paying a price. In some Lubicon families, one spouse had joined the Woodland group, the other had not. In some families, several children had joined the Woodland group, the rest had not. A sense of awe at the government's power again swept through Little Buffalo, and residents questioned whether Lubicon objectives could still be achieved. More and more, people were channelling their frustration into drinking, or fighting, or joining evangelical congregations.

By the time of the Woodland vote Ominayak, too, had become a victim of the general social malaise. His wife, Louise, had moved to Cadotte a few months earlier, taking the children with her. Relations between the couple remained cordial, but the stresses of thirteen years of political struggle appeared to have made irreparable divisions in the marriage. After the Woodland deal was ratified, band leaders ordered Louise out of Cadotte because she refused to join, and she faced moving out of the interior altogether, to Peace River.

Somehow Ominayak kept travelling and making speeches, but he began to spend more and more time at a cabin he had built at Fish Lake. There, out of telephone range, he took part in healing ceremonies led by a medicine man from Fort Vermilion who was now camped more or less permanently nearby. Outwardly, Ominayak still looked steady and determined, but he was spending much of his energy trying to keep body and soul together, and tending to ever-increasing problems in the community. His office sometimes went unstaffed for days. Band business began to fall desperately behind.

From almost every point of view, prospects for the Lubicon people looked grim, with little sign that they would improve over the short term. Getty appeared to have abandoned the Grimshaw Agreement; his people were participating in the Woodland and Loon Lake deals. The Japanese conglomerate, Daishowa, had completed its $500-million pulp mill north of Peace River and was preparing to move into Lubicon territory at freeze-up, beginning immediately north of the ninety-five square miles. Lennarson grew increasingly alarmed. He expressed concern that the start of logging might signal the end of the struggle to assert Lubicon land rights, and fear that the Lubicon people now lacked the strength to fend off the latest territorial challenge. He announced another letter-writing campaign, asking supporters to make clear to elected representatives that the latest actions against the Lubicon Cree were unacceptable. He also encouraged supporters to take matters into their own hands. "People should be thinking about taking action in their own name and on their own behalf," he wrote, "since it's not at all clear that the Lubicon people are up to once again leading the charge."

Not long after the polls closed in the Woodland plebiscite, more than two hundred Lubicon band members gathered at Fish Lake for a tea dance. Preparations had been underway for days. Young men had trimmed saplings into poles for the lodge and thrown tarpaulins over the skeleton for walls. Working collectively, several older hunters had shot a moose, which a crew of women had spent all day stewing in large black pots over open fires.

The weather was perfect. At the height of summer, the sun sets late in northern Alberta, and as people assembled, the light angled off the water in a way that seemed particularly radiant and pure. Inside the lodge, families moved clockwise, settling on blankets spread over spruce boughs around the periphery. Four fires burned in a row down the middle. Prayers were said, drums were beaten, food was sacrificed; and as people danced that night together in an unbroken chain around the fires, they called on the spirits of their ancestors to bring direction and strength to the living.

SOURCES
AND
ACKNOWLEDGMENTS

THIS IS THE FIRST BOOK to deal in any depth with the Lesser Slave interior of northern Alberta. Major events such as the McCrimmon removals, the destruction of Marten River, and the Lougheed government's "master strategy" to subvert native land rights are being documented here for the first time.

Much of the historical material comes from Indian Affairs archives and other government and church sources, and was compiled in the 1970s by researchers in the Treaty and Aboriginal Rights Research unit of the Indian Association of Alberta. The documents number in the hundreds. They include reports and correspondence on the Lubicon reserve promise, the land-survey plans and the McCrimmon removals—including the reports of Judges McKeen and Macdonald, which remained secret at the time. Dennis Madill at the Treaties and Historical Research Centre of the Indian Affairs department provided additional material on the western treaties, the Indian Act and the isolated communities.

While crosschecking historical material, I conducted a number of interviews. In 1988, I met Malcolm McCrimmon at a retirement home in Ottawa, about a year before he died at the age of ninety-four. He was guarded about his work in the Lesser Slave Lake Agency, but unremorseful. On Judges McKeen and Macdonald, he said: "All they had was the Indian point of view." On L'Heureux, he said: "Nice lad to talk to but not a bloody clue what he was doing." On native people generally, he said: "They would lie like hell if they knew they were going to be thrown out." Others I interviewed about the early days included Yvonnette Comeau, daughter of Napoleon L'Heureux; Rose L'Hirondelle, who grew up in Harold Laird's household and later married the Metis farmer Fleuri L'Hirondelle at Lubicon Lake; Nicolas Roué, the Oblate priest who witnessed McCrimmon's first visit to Lubicon Lake in 1942; and Robert Walker, expelled by McCrimmon from the Driftpile band.

Rev. Jean Marsan, at the Archbishop's Residence in McLennan, provided me with documentation concerning events at Marten River, including correspondence between Bishop Henri Routhier and Public Works Minister F. C. Colborne. Librarians at the Energy Resources Conservation Board in Calgary sent me details on oil exploration and drilling in the Marten River area. Barb Deters, speaking for the Alberta attorney general, said government files on Marten River were sealed from the public because of "litigation," but she did release a copy of the quitclaim that John Ed Laboucan was asked to sign, and authorized a telephone interview with Murray Doherty, the forest ranger involved. The interview was supervised by Carl Leary, the forest superintendent in Peace River. Other people interviewed on Marten River but not named in the text include Johnny Johnson, who attended meetings at Marten River for the Alberta forestry department; Jock Fyfe, who attended some of the same meetings for the social services department; Oblate Brother Donat Leblanc, who helped relocate people at Cadotte; Joyce Lambert, Harry Lambert's widow; and Jim Peacock, community-affairs coordinator for Shell Canada Ltd., Peace River.

Documents from the caveat period were collected by Fred Lennarson when he was a consultant to Harold Cardinal. They include correspondence, internal memos, minutes of meetings, legal advice, court decisions and the caveat itself. Back issues of an Edmonton weekly newspaper, *The Native People*, were also helpful on some aspects of the case.

James O'Reilly and his assistant, Manon Blanchet, gave me full access to the library at the Montreal law offices of O'Reilly Mainville. The library contains all the key documents on Lubicon court challenges, including affidavits quoted in the text, and a thirty-one-volume transcript of the hearings before Mr. Justice Gregory Forsyth.

During the Alberta government's attempt to implement the land-tenure program at Little Buffalo, Lennarson built a large file, which he made available to me in its entirety. I also interviewed many people on the subject. Among those not mentioned in the text were Hiske Gerding, director of the land-tenure secretariat when the program was introduced at Little Buffalo; Chuck Curr, regional director for municipal affairs in Peace River; Murray McKnight, director of land programs for municipal affairs in Edmonton; Cliff Supernault, head of the native services unit for municipal affairs in Edmonton; and Roy Piepenburg, a social-development strategist and first director of the land-tenure secretariat, who quit the Alberta government in 1977 because of the direction the program was taking.

In 1984, I began to witness events first-hand, beginning with the Crombie-Ominayak meeting at Sturgeon Lake. I travelled through Austria, Germany and Switzerland with Ominayak and Lennarson in 1987, and made a number of trips to Little Buffalo over the years, usually staying one or two weeks at a time. I was there for the showdown between the band and Premier Getty, and later witnessed the Woodland Cree plebiscite at Cadotte. I have been receiving the band's mailings since 1984, and since 1987 Terri Kelly has sent me almost weekly packages of raw material—every conceivable printed reference to the Lubicon issue, from Daishowa logging plans to proceedings of the United Nations Human Rights Committee.

Federal authorities were generally uncooperative about inquiries, sometimes to a fanatical degree. Bruce Rawson, the deputy minister of Indian Affairs under David Crombie, denied me access even to a press release about himself, a document I later obtained from the *Edmonton Journal*. On another occasion, Bob Coulter blocked my request for the Woodland Cree agreement-in-principle. When I applied under access to information rules, the request was blocked a second time by Margaret Bloodworth, the assistant secretary to the federal cabinet in the privy council office, a sign that the Lubicon case was still being monitored from lofty government levels. On appeal, the privy council again blocked the application, citing a rule that said the document could not be released for twenty years. I finally got it over the counter by asking at the Indian Affairs office in Edmonton.

Most of the people who contributed in some way to this project appear in the text; but some do not, and they deserve special mention. Ronald Blumer gave generously of his time and talent, particularly in the early stages of the work when his help was especially valuable. Dianna Symonds at *Saturday Night* has been a constant source of support and motivation. I owe her a great debt. I am also grateful to John Fraser for his encouragement and many kindnesses.

For vouching for me on grant applications, I thank Mark Abley, Susan Aihoshi, Sheila McLeod Arnopoulos, Barbara Carey, Jean Murray Cole, Doris Cowan, Bruce G. Trigger and Graham Trotter. Funding was provided by the Explorations Program of the Canada Council, the Arts Awards Service of the Canada Council and the Writers' Reserve of the Ontario Arts Council. I particularly thank Richard Holden and Robert Richard at the Canada Council for facilitating my applications. For various other forms of help, I also thank Mike and Carol Green, Chris and Margaret Greenshields, Bennett Lee, Avis Lennarson, Norman and Susan Levine, Bennett McCardle, Wandzia Muszynski, Susan Phillips, Elaine Shatenstein, Ken Staroszik and Margaret Whitehead.

My agent, Lucinda Vardey, was the first person to express enthusiasm to me about the book idea, and she has been an invaluable ally to me throughout the research and writing process. I am also indebted to Linda Turchin at the agency, and to Anne Gilbert. I thank Denise Schon for motivating me to find a good publisher. Rob Sanders at Douglas & McIntyre was a constant source of enthusiasm. Barbara Pulling gave the manuscript detailed editing; the grinding demands of a busy fall season did not deter her from lavishing on this book her time, energy and exacting skill.

BIBLIOGRAPHY

Alberta Municipal Affairs Department. *Report on the Land Tenure Project, 1975-1983*. Edmonton: Government of Alberta, 1983.

Alinsky, Saul D. *Reveille for Radicals*. New York: Vintage Books, 1969.

Bankes, Nigel. "Judicial Attitudes to Aboriginal Resource Rights and Title." *Resources*, No. 13, December 1985.

Berger, Thomas R. *Fragile Freedoms: Human Rights and Dissent in Canada*. Toronto/Vancouver: Clarke, Irwin & Company Limited, 1981.

Biegert, Claus, and R. Wittenborn. *A River Drowned by Water*. Montreal: The Montreal Museum of Fine Arts, 1981.

Brown, George, and Ron Maguire. *Indian Treaties in Historical Perspective*. Ottawa: Research Branch, Indian and Northern Affairs Canada, 1979.

Cardinal, Harold. *The Unjust Society: The Tragedy of Canada's Indians*. Edmonton: M. G. Hurtig Ltd., 1969.

Chalmers, John W. *Laird of the West*. Calgary: Detselig Enterprises Ltd., 1981.

Continental Golin/Harris. *Strategic Communications Overview*. Ottawa: For Indian and Northern Affairs Canada, 1987.

Daniel, Richard. *Land Rights of the Isolated Communities of Northern Alberta*. Edmonton: Isolated Communities Advisory Board, 1975.

Finks, David P. *The Radical Vision of Saul Alinsky*. New York: Paulist Press, 1984.

Foster, Peter. *The Blue-Eyed Sheiks: The Canadian Oil Establishment*. Toronto: Totem Books, 1980.

Fulton, E. Davie. *Lubicon Lake Indian Band Inquiry: Discussion Paper*. Ottawa: Government of Canada, 1986.

Fumoleau, René, OMI. *As Long as This Land Shall Last*. Toronto: McClelland and Stewart Limited, 1975.

Hammond, M.O. *Confederation and Its Leaders*. Toronto: McClelland, Goodchild and Stewart, 1917.

Human Resources Development Authority. *An Analysis of People and Resources of the Little Buffalo Lake Area*. Edmonton: Government of Alberta, 1969.

Indian Affairs Canada. *Contemporary Indian Legislation, 1951-1978*. Ottawa: Research Branch, Indian and Northern Affairs Canada, 1981.

Indian Affairs Canada. *Indian Acts and Amendments, 1868-1950*. Ottawa: Research Branch, Indian and Northern Affairs Canada, 1981.

Indian Chiefs of Alberta. *Citizens Plus*. Edmonton: Indian Association of Alberta, 1970.

Indian Association of Alberta. *Statement on the Indian Title to Lands Surveyed "In Severalty" Under Treaty Number Eight*. Ottawa: Treaty and Aboriginal Rights Research, 1980.

Ivany, Randall. *Special Report of the Ombudsman for Alberta Regarding Complaints of the Lubicon Lake Indian Band*. Edmonton: Government of Alberta, 1984.

Jappsen & Associates Consulting Ltd. *Little Buffalo Land Use Plan and Plan of Subdivision*. Edmonton: Alberta Municipal Affairs Department, 1981.

Joussard Homesteaders. *Lakeside Pioneer: Local History of Joussard and Biographies of the Pioneers*. 1986.

Laird, David. *Our Indian Treaties*. Winnipeg: Manitoba Free Press Company, 1905.

Leslie, John, and Ron Maguire, eds. *The Historical Development of the Indian Act*. Ottawa: Treaties and Historical Research Centre, Indian and Northern Affairs Canada, 1979.

MacGregor, Roy. *Chief: The Fearless Vision of Billy Diamond*. Markham: Viking, 1989.

Mair, Charles. *Through the MacKenzie Basin: A Narrative of the Athabaska and Peace River Treaty Expedition of 1899*. Toronto: William Briggs, 1908.

Madill, Dennis F. K. *Treaty Research Report: Treaty Eight*. Ottawa: Treaties and Historical Research Centre, Indian and Northern Affairs Canada, 1986.

Morris, Alexander. *The Treaties of Canada with the Indians of Manitoba and the North-West Territories*. Toronto: Belfords, Clarke & Co., 1880. Reprint, Toronto: Coles Publishing Co., 1971.

Morse, Bradford W., ed. *Aboriginal Peoples and the Law: Indian, Metis and Inuit Rights in Canada*. Ottawa: Carleton University Press, 1985.

O'Reilly, James. *Whither the Indian?* Montreal: Prepared for the Civil Liberties Section of the Canadian Bar Association, 1969.

Price, Richard, ed. *The Spirit of the Alberta Indian Treaties*. Montreal: Institute for Research on Public Policy, 1980.

Richardson, Boyce. *Strangers Devour the Land*. Toronto: Macmillan of Canada, 1975.

Sissons, Jack. *Judge of the Far North*. Toronto: McClelland and Stewart Limited, 1973.

Smith, James G. E. "Western Woods Cree." In *Handbook of North American Indians*, Volume Six, Subarctic. Washington: Smithsonian Institution, 1981.

Stanley, George F. G. *The Birth of Western Canada*. Toronto: University of Toronto Press, 1975.

Titley, E. Brian. *A Narrow Vision: Duncan Campbell Scott and the Administration of Indian Affairs in Canada*. Vancouver: University of British Columbia Press, 1986.

Tobias, John L. "Canada's Subjugation of the Plains Cree, 1879-1885." In *Sweet Promises*, edited by J. R. Miller. Toronto: University of Toronto Press, 1991.

Weaver, Sally M. *Making Canadian Indian Policy: The Hidden Agenda 1968-1970*. Toronto: University of Toronto Press, 1981.

INDEX

AP